Preservation and Social Inclusion

Preservation and Social Inclusion

Edited by Erica Avrami

TABLE OF CONTENTS

— Introduction

Erica Avrami

1
David Crouch
and Gavin Parker,
"'Digging-up' Utopia?
Space, Practice
and Land Use
Heritage," *Geoforum*
34, no. 3 (August
2003): 395–408.

2
Merriam-Webster,
s.v. "heritage" (n.),
https://www.
merriam-webster.
com/dictionary/
heritage.

3
See appendices for
a literature review
examining this and
other developments
in heritage research
related to inclusion.

Spatial encounters within the built environment have power; the narratives such encounters represent shape our understanding of who we are and who we can be. The decisive use of space has power: it determines which publics and stories can stake a claim in the landscape and be encountered. No matter how much historical narratives are challenged or reinterpreted in prose or imagery, spatial encounters bear repeated witness to particular ideas of self and community that are profoundly experiential. Landscape, as a representation of history, is "not only observed, read or understood," it is "practiced." 1 For those working in the realms of historic preservation, planning, and urban policy, there is as much to learn from the pathologies of this power as there is from its judicious use.

Historic preservation, as a form of public policy, seeks to enable such spatial encounters through heritage designation and management. The preservation enterprise helps fashion the physical contours of memory in public space, and thus has the power to curate a multidimensional and inclusive representation of societal values and narratives. This is an awesome responsibility. Yet all too often, preservation is characterized as a reaction—to change, to deterioration, to encroaching development, to impending loss, to forces beyond its control. Its affirmative role in spatializing history is cast as one of stewardship, suggesting that decisions about what to preserve, what represents our diverse stories, are largely driven by the actions of those who came before. Even the word "heritage," defined as "something transmitted by or acquired from a predecessor," suggests that the past, through such bequeathals, has a certain authority over how we in the present see ourselves. 2

Scholarship over the past quarter century has challenged this passive concept of heritage by asserting that heritage does not possess some sort of inherent value, imbued by our forebears and later discerned by architectural historians, archaeologists, and other experts. There is a growing body of knowledge examining the socially constructed nature of heritage, whereby multiple publics ascribe value to places and such values change over time. 3 There is likewise an increasing awareness within the preservation field of the ways in which narratives are reinforced by spatial encounters with the past, and thus there is greater scrutiny of whose narratives are represented—or not—in the built environment. Beyond whose stories are told and whose are excluded, there is also mounting concern for how multiple publics actually participate in the political processes of preservation. How diverse communities value and experience particular places and memories may not necessarily conform to expert norms or dominant worldviews, and the field of preservation is now recognizing the need for platforms and practices that allow for discursive decision-making and shared agency among a multiplicity of stakeholders. Heritage and its preservation are also increasingly mobilized as vehicles for positive change, to give voice and spatial recognition to the underrepresented and the disempowered, and to challenge hegemonic narratives.

While more inclusive storytelling and decision-making are gaining traction and prompting innovation at the project level and among some practitioners, shifts in preservation governance structures and the policy toolbox have been slower to develop, with exploration of inclusive practices happening in more ad hoc ways. How government policy will evolve to better ensure just representation and processes may hinge, in part, on the question of government's role in just outcomes. Advocacy-driven research has quantified the positive economic effects of preservation on communities, but recent scholarship suggests that preservation benefits—economic and otherwise—may not be equitably distributed.

As a form of public policy, preservation is compelled to reconcile disparate outcomes with its purpose of serving society writ large. Thinking about systemic shifts toward inclusion at the policy level requires the field to also reflect on its own actions in both perpetuating and combating patterns and practices of exclusion. For example, the geographic distribution of recognized heritage in the urban landscape can often be uneven. In the case of New York City, as of 2014, less than 4 percent of lots across the city's five boroughs were regulated by the Landmarks Preservation Commission (LPC), though 27 percent of lots in Manhattan were LPC-regulated. [4] Residents of historic districts across New York City tend to be wealthier, more educated, and more likely to be white, as are those who support designation of historic districts in New York, suggesting that some narratives and publics may be more privileged in the preservation process. [5]

The built environment itself can serve as a conduit for inequality. The persistence of certain structures or sites and the effects of decisions over time can perpetuate patterns of segregation and exacerbate injustice. There are long histories of spatially marginalizing populations—especially people of color, the foreign-born, and/or the poor—through decisions about land use, zoning and restrictive covenants, building codes, transportation, affordable housing, and financial lending. Redlining and urban renewal, for example, have had disproportionate impacts on vulnerable communities that continue to resonate today. Despite the seemingly endless churn of creative destruction in cities, urban landscapes still signal "the cumulative buildup of investment and planning decisions inherited from previous eras" [6] and what Dolores Hayden characterizes as the "architectural legacies of wealth and power." [7] Such legacies of exclusion are entrenched within the built environment and contribute to inequitable decision-making about what constitutes "historic."

The lack of minority histories on heritage lists from the municipal to the national level helped spur the establishment of the National Trust's African American Cultural Heritage Action Fund, Asian and Pacific Islander Americans in Historic Preservation, Latinos in Heritage Conservation, the New York City LGBT Historic Sites Project, and other advocacy and funding entities. But simply adding more diverse sites to heritage lists is not enough to redress social and spatial disparities. Racial, ethnic, and religious minorities, enslaved and indigenous people, the

4
Ingrid Gould Ellen, Brian McCabe, and Eric Stern, Policy Brief: Fifty Years of Historic Preservation in New York City (New York: Furman Center, New York University, 2016).

5
Ellen, McCabe, and Stern, Policy Brief; Erica Avrami, Cherie-Nicole Leo, and Alberto Sanchez Sanchez, "Confronting Exclusion: Redefining the Intended Outcomes of Historic Preservation," Change Over Time 8, no. 1 (Spring 2018): 102–120.

6
Rachel Weber, From Boom to Bubble: How Finance Built the New Chicago (Chicago: University of Chicago Press, 2015), 18.

7
Dolores Hayden, The Power of Place: Urban Landscapes as Public History (Cambridge, MA: MIT Press, 1995), 8.

8
Erica Avrami,
"Heritage Data and
the Next Generation of
Preservation Policy," in
*Preservation and the
New Data Landscape*,
ed. Erica Avrami (New
York: Columbia Books
on Architecture and the
City, 2019), 9–17.

economically disadvantaged, women, and those identifying as LGBTQ could not historically claim or occupy space freely or equally. Spaces representing their narratives have been underinvested in and undervalued, and were often made invisible or systematically destroyed. Accordingly, preservation must grapple with how its norms and standards, which privilege architectural value and material integrity, can perpetuate injustice.

The importance of the historic built environment in shaping sociospatial relationships through time precludes a simple reinterpretation of the past to acknowledge more narratives. Promoting inclusion means embracing the affirmative role heritage and its preservation can play in reconciliation and restorative justice. It likewise involves tackling difficult questions about preservation's own past and future with reflection and intentionality.

Urban Heritage, Sustainability, and Social Inclusion is a collaboration of the Columbia University Graduate School of Architecture, Planning, and Preservation, the Earth Institute–Center for Sustainable Urban Development, and the American Assembly, with the support of the New York Community Trust. The collaboration seeks to explore the horizon of preservation policy by examining the social, environmental, and technological factors that shape and challenge its evolution. Through invitational symposia and the publication series Issues in Preservation Policy, this initiative seeks to forge stronger connections among researchers, decision-makers, and practitioners in the field and to spur a dialogue about the systemic shifts needed to reform preservation policy so it can better foster equitable and resilient communities.

This volume evolved from a symposium in February 2019 that centered on questions of preservation and social inclusion. The symposium examined how multiple publics are—or are not—represented in heritage decision-making, geographies, and policy structures. It follows a previous symposium and publication, *Preservation and the New Data Landscape*, which examined how the preservation enterprise is engaging, shaping, learning from, and capitalizing on the new landscape of urban data to forge evidence-based research, co-produce knowledge with communities, and inform policy agendas. A key theme of this previous inquiry was the need for preservation to ask better questions in order to tell better stories, "stories that represent the diversity of our communities, stories that redress spatial and social inequities, and stories that reflect our collective agency in promoting a sustainable environment." [8]

To prompt this subsequent inquiry, we asked participants to consider the following questions:
- How are diverse narratives and communities being represented or excluded through preservation?
- Who is participating in preservation processes, and how can preservation decision-making better engage multiple publics?
- What are the effects of preservation policies and processes on communities?

Attempts to answer these questions are what form this hybrid volume—comprising research texts, interviews, and commentaries—and constitute a burgeoning dialogue among scholars and practitioners seeking to challenge the status quo. Several themes emerged that can inform efforts to shift preservation policy toward greater social inclusion.

9
Lila Asher, Joe Curnow, and Amil Davis, "The Limits of Settlers' Territorial Acknowledgments," *Curriculum Inquiry*, 48, no. 3 (2018), 316–334; Stephen Marche, "Canada's Impossible Acknowledgment," *New Yorker* (September 7, 2017), https://www. newyorker.com/ culture/culture-desk/ canadas-impossible-acknowledgment.

— ACKNOWLEDGING THE PAST

Seated in a conference room in the Empire State Building, surrounded by privileged views of the ever-rising New York skyline, we began our exploration of preservation and social inclusion with a land acknowledgment, recognizing that the symposium was taking place on Lenape lands. This practice has been both praised and criticized, but one might argue that it is a persuasive, though inadequate, vehicle for helping us to be accountable for our part in history. 9 The past is complicated, and the preservation enterprise—as a means of constructing collective identity through perceptions of the past—is highly political in that it confronts decisions about whose narratives should occupy space and be encountered. Such acknowledgments help to restore a sense of historical context and may enable us to broach difficult and uncomfortable questions about both the past and the present with greater awareness and sensitivity.

The need to acknowledge the past echoes throughout this volume. Understanding historical processes and their influence on present conditions is at the heart of the preservation toolbox, and applying these methods to the social dynamics and political contexts of heritage decision-making is a critical first step in healing rifts and redressing inequalities. Janet Hansen and Sara Delgadillo Cruz illustrate this poignantly and in very practical terms with the case of the Kinney-Tabor house in Venice, California. The site was rejected for heritage designation in 1968 because the house had been relocated and altered, thereby compromising its historic integrity per preservation standards. Abbot Kinney was the founder of Venice, and after his death the house was gifted to his longtime employee and confidante, Irving Tabor, who was Black. In 1925 racial covenants and neighbor objections thwarted Tabor's attempt to occupy the home, so he moved the house to Oakwood, an African American enclave of Venice. In 2008 the house was reconsidered and formally designated as a result of this complex history, which tells an important story of marginalization both in terms of the right to occupy space and preservation's complicity in perpetuating injustice.

Exclusion is not limited to particular sites but can also be endemic in the chronicles of preservation activism. Fallon Samuels Aidoo dives deeply into the history of preservation efforts in West Mount Airy, Philadelphia, which is regarded as an early success in neighborhood racial integration. Community members embarked on grassroots efforts to preserve their railroad station houses in the face of economic and environmental challenges. Archival research into the organizational actors who advocated for, implemented, and funded projects reveals how philanthropic investment created new dynamics and distrust between citizen efforts and "professional" preservation, which at times discounted and undermined community-based preservation and the bonds of cooperation upon which it relied. In studying preservation in the Buckeye neighborhood of

Cleveland, Ohio, dating from the 1970s, Stephanie Ryberg-Webster found that biases toward architectural significance and origin stories continue to undermine African American residents and their heritage more than forty years later: "Without direct efforts to value the complexity of stories and meaning, preservationists will also be implicated in the othering and dismissal of marginalized people."

Maria Rosario Jackson observes that "one of the markers of an unjust society is that the ability to transmit heritage has been hampered, as is the case with a lot of marginalized communities." She cautions that planning, community development, creative place-making, and even preservation are not ahistorical and should include analyses of socioeconomic conditions, root causes, and power dynamics. Donna Graves drives this point home by noting that this "through line between an ongoing legacy of historic discrimination and contemporary injustice" serves as a powerful impulse toward recognizing new stories and forms of heritage. It likewise serves as a cautionary reminder of the need for preservation to interrogate its own history to make inclusion meaningful.

Such reflection on preservation's past is not limited to decisions about what to preserve and how. As a form of public policy that exercises sociospatial control, how preservation has historically positioned itself within a societal agenda and in relation to other policy arenas teaches valuable lessons for advancing inclusion. In charting the intersecting histories of preservation and community development in New York City (both of which emerged as citizen-led movements), Vicki Weiner finds important synergies and shared aims between the two but also a reluctance on the part of preservationists to directly engage social justice. By defaulting to the ways that market forces affect *buildings*, with limited focus on *people*, preservation evades important sociospatial dynamics and forgoes opportunities to systematically instrumentalize its work to achieve economic equity and inclusion. In examining the historical and discursive connections between preservation and affordable housing, Caroline S. Cheong likewise finds that the intersectional history is rife with conflicting narratives and research. Preservation asserts its positive role in simultaneously improving property values and protecting affordability, with evidence often tailored in response to particular criticisms of and challenges to the status quo. Greater accountability on the part of preservation and more unbiased research into the politics of the field's past is needed to identify the barriers to and opportunities for such shared agendas and policy reform.

— BUILDING AGENCY

Forging agendas that instrumentalize heritage work toward more just and inclusive ends means not only incorporating more voices but also sharing decision-making and ceding some of preservation's normative power. Emma Osore asserts that a key to more inclusive preservation lies in co-creating opportunities with the communities who contend with legacies of marginalization every day. In her work with BlackSpace, in the New York neighborhood of Brownsville, Osore notes that those involved in the project "became heritage conservationists according to

our own definition. As Black urbanists, we sought to save and understand cultural touchstones unique to Black people." Brent Leggs, Jenna
Dublin, and Michael Powe explain how the National Trust, working in
historically African American neighborhoods, brought on emerging
scholars and practitioners as fellows to engage with communities as
part of their efforts to diversify *who* is ascribing value to older places. By
empowering both a younger generation of preservationists as well as
underrepresented publics, the National Trust acknowledges a role for
preservation in promoting social justice and civic agency.

10
Ned Kaufman,
"Historic Places
and the Diversity
Deficit in Heritage
Conservation," *CRM:
The Journal of Heritage
Stewardship* 1, no. 2
(2004): 68–85.

A critical observation emerging from the symposium was that the
burden of inclusion cannot be borne solely by the excluded. Aidoo reflects
that a greater understanding of past and present alliances is warranted
to inform new kinds of allyship in preservation. The National Trust's
establishment of the African American Cultural Heritage Action Fund,
which supported the aforementioned research, serves as a case in point
for how preservation institutions can—and should—support the agency
of others. Michelle G. Magalong recounts how in 2011, in an effort to
address the "diversity deficit" in heritage conservation, the National
Park Service (NPS) embarked on an initiative to enhance representation
of Asian Americans, Native Hawaiians, and Pacific Islanders, as well as
Latino Americans, Native Americans, African Americans, women, and
LGBTQ communities in the National Historic Landmarks Program and
other areas of the NPS. [10] This, along with support from the National
Trust, helped to spur the creation of the organization Asian and Pacific
Islander Americans in Historic Preservation, which leverages the efforts
of local groups across the country to a national platform.

Several contributors speak to questions of agency through the lens of
community engagement. Jackson emphasizes the need for *ethical* engagement through a deep understanding of the complexity of community
stories and desires. Ciere Boatright, in discussing the work of Chicago
Neighborhood Initiatives (CNI) in the historic Pullman neighborhood,
describes their emphasis on *authentic* engagement. Through iterative
processes of listening and responding, CNI shares decision-making about
multimillion-dollar investment and development with the community,
and leverages the interests of local residents as part of community benefits
agreements with incoming businesses. By integrating preservation within
broader strategies for job creation, affordable housing, and neighborhood
revitalization, Boatright and CNI build trust and position preservation
as a vehicle for broader benefits. Likewise, Sangita Chari, with the NPS
Office of Relevancy, Diversity, and Inclusion, underscores the need for
communities to see preservation in relation to more commonly understood
public benefits, like good schools and health care, in order to more fully
realize their agency. Claudia Guerra, as cultural historian with the Office
of Historic Preservation in San Antonio, Texas, characterizes her role as
that of a translator between communities and policy-makers, interpreting
values and interests as well as building trust in both directions to achieve
mutually beneficial goals.

Both Ryberg-Webster and Guerra observe that professional preservationists are not always well equipped to navigate these complex processes
of engaging and sharing decision-making with diverse publics. Andrea

11
"Five Views: An Ethnic Historic Site Survey for California," California Department of Parks and Recreation, Office of Historic Preservation, December 1988, https://www.nps.gov/parkhistory/online_books/5views/5views.htm.

12
Brian J. McCabe and Ingrid Gould Ellen, "Does Preservation Accelerate Neighborhood Change? Examining the Impact of Historic Preservation in New York City," *Journal of the American Planning Association* 82, no. 2 (2016): 134–146.

Roberts's work with the Texas Historical Commission demonstrates how such processes often involve the delicate work of decentering dominant narratives with long-vested stakeholders. Chari contends that "telling the more accurate story—the one that's more inclusive, the one that is potentially less happy—takes a great deal of skill… it takes resilience, and it takes the ability to weather pushback when the public is challenged to rethink its assumptions." While calls for community engagement resonate throughout the heritage field, professionals and institutions still must build their own capacities to undertake such processes with integrity, sensitivity, and intentionality.

— CONFRONTING CONSEQUENCES

Taking inclusion seriously obliges preservation to look at how it identifies and designates heritage with respect to underrepresented or marginalized communities, and also to examine the effects of designation. Graves harks back to the seminal study "Five Views: An Ethnic Historic Site Survey for California" as both a moment of insight and a missed opportunity. The study was conducted in the 1980s expressly "to broaden the spectrum of ethnic community participation in historic preservation activities and to provide better information on ethnic history and associated sites," and it positioned itself as a starting point for additional research and engagement. [11] While Graves sees more awareness and change within policy infrastructure today, it has taken a long time to understand how these issues complicate the way we think about and manage heritage.

One such example of shifts in the policy landscape is SurveyLA. Hansen and Delgadillo Cruz explain the use of historic contexts to reflect and integrate ethnic and cultural histories in Los Angeles, but they also acknowledge the complexity of addressing intersectionality as well as immigration, settlement, and migration patterns across the urban landscape. With more than 140 nationalities represented in the city, they speak to the factors that shaped priorities in creating the historic contexts and caution that "contexts themselves can be exclusionary when not all groups are recognized."

Beyond informing designation, there is a need to better understand how landmark and district designation impact neighborhoods. Ingrid Gould Ellen, Brian J. McCabe, and Gerard Torrats-Espinosa note the limited attention "paid to the types of neighborhoods that are actually designated or the impact of the designation process on neighborhoods and the people living in them." Building on previous research that suggests that the designation of historic districts may accelerate the process of demographic change, they examine New York City neighborhoods before historic district designation and after in an effort to describe economic characteristics and effects. [12] Predesignation, they find that these neighborhoods housed more economically advantaged residents compared to other neighborhoods with housing stocks from a similar era. Postdesignation, residents grew even more advantaged. Similarly, in the National Trust's analysis of African American neighborhoods in cities across the United

States, Leggs, Dublin, and Powe explore economic exclusion alongside race. They find that while historically African American neighborhoods are underrepresented in local and national heritage designation programs, some traditional preservation tools—like designation—may exacerbate issues of affordability and displacement. Such findings compel preservation advocates and policy-makers to invest resources in such research, so as to better align their work with agendas promoting affordability and economic inclusivity alongside other forms of inclusion.

Indeed, another critical aspect of inclusion within the preservation enterprise is understanding the many dimensions of and means of characterizing exclusion, including race, ethnicity, class, religion, gender, sexual orientation, and more. Mark J. Stern analyzes the varying lenses on and perceptions of exclusion as a backdrop for asking questions about the role and effects of historic and cultural resources within communities. Through his work on the Social Impact of the Arts Project, Stern finds that the presence of cultural assets in low- and moderate-income neighborhoods in New York City is associated with significantly better social well-being (though still below the citywide average), suggesting that "although the presence of cultural assets corresponds with a reduction in the impact of structural social exclusion, it does not erase the process and practice of exclusion." Such evidence likewise suggests important points for policy-makers as they decide where and how to invest in heritage preservation.

— CLAIMING SPACE

To confront the geographies and structural legacies of exclusion through and within preservation, space is a critical and complicating factor. The physical vestiges of marginalized groups are more than just underrepresented within heritage rosters; many have been systematically devalued, destroyed, or made invisible due to long-standing histories of bias. Hansen and Delgadillo Cruz, in discussing SurveyLA's historic context on women's rights in Los Angeles, observe the challenges of identifying significant places associated with women when their stories are underrecorded and underrepresentative of women of color. Andrew S. Dolkart, through his work on the NYC LGBT Historic Sites Project, explains how space becomes a vehicle for reconstructing incomplete or false histories. Popular narratives, for example, wrongly demarcate Stonewall as the moment that initiated gay history in part because the events and places where LGBT people interacted in the past were intentionally hidden or transient.

Mapping and digital platforms serve as additional tools for staking spatial claims and reconstructing histories and countermemories. The NYC LGBT Historic Sites Project, for example, interprets places through an interactive map. 13 Magalong references the crowdsourced online map East at Main Street, which "documents and tells the stories of people, places, and events associated with Asian Americans and Pacific Islanders."14 And Andrea Roberts explains how the Texas Freedom Colonies Atlas, another online mapping tool, serves as a platform for collaborators to

13
NYC LGBT Historic Sites Project, https://www.nyclgbtsites.org.

14
East at Main Street: APIA Mapping Project, Asian and Pacific Islander Americans in Historic Preservation, https://www.apiahip.org/apia-mapping.

15
Texas Freedom
Colonies Atlas,
https://tamu.maps.
arcgis.com/apps/
MapSeries/index.
html?appid=48f89e
0f870c4400a990682
a09cf919f.

collect and store data about Black settlements. 15

But as Roberts asserts, rendering such places visible and geographic requires spaces for cocreation with those whose stories have been omitted, annulled, or deliberately forgotten. Her work with East Texas freedom colony descendants to record the origin stories of Black communities critically illustrates how dominant white constructions of place and public history obscure past and present Black agency in place-keeping and preservation. While the archival void of Black histories and places complicates this disremembering, Roberts explores new ways of listening for and documenting the "null value." She describes place-based activities of storytelling, stewardship, and annual commemorative events, which at once reproduce cultural knowledge about freedom colonies and create spaces of counternarrative.

Settlements like the freedom colonies are becoming increasingly invisible with the loss of populations and buildings, especially as access to traditional preservation tools—like designation of historic districts— has been limited due to structural barriers and bias. But the persistent relationship between people and place, even if largely dependent on oral traditions rather than historic buildings, speaks to the power of space and spatial encounters for memory, recognition, and the decentering of dominant narratives.

But claims to space can be complicated, particularly in dynamic urban areas with diverse populations. To counter the displacement of marginalized communities and their living traditions, San Francisco has pioneered a new form of cultural district, several of which have been created in association with LGBTQ communities. As Graves comments, "foregrounding queer identity and sexual practices as legitimate aspects of culture really pushes the boundaries of preservation and what heritage means." Encouraging such claims to space as part of the preservation toolbox is groundbreaking, but Graves cautions that such policy tools are still being tested: recognizing and creating spatial boundaries for a particular community can exclude others who may inhabit the same neighborhood. How multiple narratives occupy and stake claim to the same spaces remains a significant challenge.

— CHALLENGING MATERIALITY

Closely tied to questions of spatial claims are those of materiality. Ryberg-Webster observes, "Architecture and integrity are often the gateways to preservation protections and benefits, but, in marginalized communities, they are an excuse for exclusion"—as is evidenced by efforts in Cleveland to survey African American historic resources. Dolkart and Graves contend that architectural historians, while crucial to the preservation enterprise, are overrepresented in the field. This contributes to an underrepresentation of diverse social histories and values and an emphasis on the material, formal, and aesthetic dimensions of heritage. These factors, in turn, further exclude already disadvantaged communities who often did not have the means or freedom to invest in design, construction, and maintenance, or whose historic spaces were transient,

17

hidden, or demolished. Roberts extends this assessment of exclusion to the documentation standards established for National Register listing, which privilege text-based archives and photographic records, thereby discounting other, less material forms of knowledge keeping and contributing to a "preservation apartheid."

Such material barriers are not limited to designation. Cheong and Weiner argue that the prioritization of original form and fabric precludes stronger alignment with affordable housing and community development agendas, respectively, and thus further distances preservation from potential policy allies. Osore found that in their heritage work in Brownsville, BlackSpace members "had to unlearn the habits of our professions, which treat disinvested spaces as a blank slate ripe for urban development and new design ideas."

Public outcry after the demolition of the building in San Antonio that housed Univision, the first Spanish-language broadcasting station in the country, compelled the city's Office of Historic Preservation to reconsider its architecturally focused criteria for designation to better incorporate cultural significance. Guerra likewise underscores preservation's material focus and its limitations in recognizing "how the intangible is manifested in the tangible." However, she describes new efforts to better recognize social and use values, as in the case of the planned replacement of the historic Almaguer studio, where the intangible heritage associated with its use as a dance studio trumped its material significance. Such issues surrounding materiality and the tensions between intangible and tangible heritage will continue to challenge the preservation enterprise as it works toward more inclusive policies and practices. An important test will be whether the field can productively step back from and reflect upon long-standing norms to envision alternative futures.

— INTERNALIZING CHANGE

An important indicator of the need for more inclusion in preservation lies in the operational structures and demographics of its institutions. While change may be slow, there are positive shifts on the horizon. Chari, in noting that the NPS workforce is over 80 percent white, questions how such a reality influences the organization's ability to adequately and sensitively represent diverse narratives, such as the story of civil rights. But in establishing its Office of Relevancy, Diversity, and Inclusion, the NPS asserted its affirmative obligation to represent all Americans and to create a space for the agency "to have critically important, if uncomfortable, conversations." The training Roberts provided through the Texas Historical Commission's Certified Local Government Program to address implicit bias and include more freedom colonies in survey processes is one important intervention on the part of the state to promote inclusive preservation. In Los Angeles, collaboration across city agencies has led to the incorporation of heritage resources in the city's thirty-five community plans. As Hansen and Delgadillo Cruz observe, "Understanding that heritage resources need not be exemplary architectural specimens—or buildings, for that matter—challenges planners

16
Lisa Kersavage,
"Preservation in a
Diverse City: Recent
Initiatives of the
NYC Landmarks
Preservation
Commission"
(PowerPoint
presentation,
Preservation and
Social Inclusion
Symposium, New York,
NY, February 7, 2019).

to craft policies that sustain and celebrate community heritage in ways that serve the growth and well-being of neighborhoods." The New York City Landmarks Preservation Commission is recognizing more sites for cultural, not just architectural, significance and is proactively engaging in neighborhoods that are underrepresented in current designations. 16 Both San Francisco and San Antonio have instituted legacy business programs to recognize more diverse forms of heritage as part of the social and commercial fabric of the city.

While few and dispersed, such policy shifts within governance structures indicate some momentum toward systemic change. But there is still much work to be done. As Chari concludes, "Diversity and inclusion are really about dismantling the specific ways in which we have operated that are detrimental to everybody... What it becomes about is our capacity to create the change needed to break down silos, to create deliberate connections, and to solve problems that may have felt entrenched but really just needed a new perspective and a willingness to change." The field of preservation is confronting thorny challenges both within and beyond its core institutions. But a thorough reckoning of its role in inclusion and exclusion presents opportunities for positive social change and a new horizon for the field. As a critical medium of shared identities, values, and stories, heritage practice and policy are uniquely positioned to promote more equitable and inclusive communities through hope, justice, and healing.

— Examining Questions of Exclusion
— Shifting Policy Toward Inclusion
— Challenging and Redefining Narratives
— Connecting to Community Development

Toward an Inclusive Preservation: Lessons from Cleveland

Stephanie Ryberg-Webster

Examining Questions of Exclusion

Within the field of historic preservation, concerns about diversity, equity, and inclusion are increasingly in the foreground. But ideals about fully representing the diverse narratives of American history and preserving cultural heritage for a wide range of communities often clash with the profession's standardized methods, policies, and regulations. For instance, windshield surveys, wherein preservationists primarily identify historic buildings by their architecture and aesthetic qualities, are still common practice. Preservation policies, such as those guiding the National Register of Historic Places, emphasize the need for material integrity. In low-income communities, meeting the test of material integrity is particularly challenging given the decades of structural disinvestment in these neighborhoods. Heritage preservation in Cleveland's Buckeye neighborhood is exemplary of the ongoing difficulties and recent progress in preserving African American urban neighborhoods. For communities with primarily social, cultural, or other nonarchitectural significance, preservationists lack robust strategies.

1
Stephanie Ryberg-Webster and J. Rosie Tighe, "The Landscape and Future of Legacy Cities," in *Legacy Cities: Continuity and Change amid Decline and Revival* (Pittsburgh: University of Pittsburgh Press, forthcoming).

— CLEVELAND'S RACIAL GEOGRAPHY

Cleveland is racially segregated, predominantly along an east-west divide. The city's African American neighborhoods are mostly east of the Cuyahoga River and downtown. In the nineteenth and early twentieth centuries, the Central neighborhood, just southeast of downtown, was the center of the city's African American community. As Cleveland developed into an industrial powerhouse in the early 1900s, economic opportunities drew African Americans and immigrants, particularly from Central and Eastern Europe, to the city. Facing severe segregation and discrimination, African Americans settled in Central, establishing residences, businesses, religious institutions such as St. John's AME Church (est. 1830) and Shiloh Baptist Church (est. 1849), and social service organizations such as the Phillis Wheatley Association (est. 1911), which provided housing for single African American women.

Despite widespread narratives that characterize urban population decline and white flight as late twentieth-century phenomena, many of Cleveland's core urban neighborhoods began losing population as early as the 1920s and 1930s, a trend that continues today. Beyond Central, the city's east-side neighborhoods were home to Eastern European immigrants, including one of the nation's largest Jewish communities. As these residents migrated outward, African American residents followed suit, moving east to neighborhoods formerly inaccessible to them. In many instances, African Americans became the second generation of residents in already built-out neighborhoods such as Hough, Glenville, Fairfax, Buckeye, and Mount Pleasant. In other instances, African Americans were first-generation residents in areas including Lee-Miles and Lee-Harvard, two neighborhoods built after World War II primarily for middle-class Blacks. Today, many of Cleveland's predominantly African American neighborhoods are more than 80 to 90 percent African American, and Cleveland is one of the most segregated cities in the nation. 1

2
The Cleveland
City Planning
Commission divides
the neighborhood into
two planning areas:
Buckeye-Shaker (also
known as Buckeye-
Shaker Square) to the
east and Buckeye-
Woodhill to the west.
Buckeye is also split
between two wards:
Ward 6 to the north and
Ward 4 to the south.

3
Cleveland's poverty
rate is around 35
percent.

4
James M. Naughton,
"Quit-City, Join-Shaker
Plan Eyed by Civic
Group," Plain Dealer,
May 2, 1967; Paul
Wilkes, "It's Not So
Much Fun to Go Home
Again," New York
Times, January 24,
1971; "Buckeye Group
Cancels Parade," Plain
Dealer, August 19,
1976.

Buckeye is located on the city's east side and shares an eastern border with Shaker Heights, a prominent inner-ring suburb. 2 In the early twentieth century, the area was a thriving immigrant enclave, at one point home to the nation's largest Hungarian American population. It was also home to a large Slovak population, along with smaller groups of other European immigrants. Buckeye's development spread from west to east (outward from the core) in the early 1900s, and by 1950 it was home to nearly twenty-one thousand residents.

During the 1950s, the area's white ethnic residents began migrating to newly available housing in the suburbs. At the same time, African Americans began moving eastward out of more central neighborhoods, often driven by forced relocation stemming from urban renewal demolition and freeway construction. During the 1960s, western Buckeye became predominantly African American; similar racial turnover occurred in eastern Buckeye during the 1970s.

After peaking in 1950, the neighborhood's population has decreased by about 40 percent; today, fewer than fourteen thousand residents call Buckeye home. As a result of that population decline, Buckeye faced increases in the rates of vacant and abandoned housing and the deterioration of its local business district. Racist lending and real estate practices exacerbated this decline because African American residents lacked access to capital to reinvest in housing or to open businesses. Public investment was increasingly constrained as the city's tax base eroded. Since 1980 more than 6 percent of Buckeye's housing has been demolished. During that same period, the housing vacancy rate skyrocketed from 6 percent in 1980 to 19 percent in 2010. The poverty rate in eastern Buckeye is 29 percent, and it is an astounding 51 percent in the western part of the neighborhood. 3

Preserving Buckeye in the 1970s

Preservation efforts in Buckeye first emerged during the 1970s but had little lasting impact. In the late 1960s, the Buckeye Neighborhood Nationalities Civic Association (BNNCA), a community organization representing the interests of the remaining Hungarian and other white ethnic residents, vociferously opposed the rapid racial change in the neighborhood. The association threatened that the neighborhood would secede from Cleveland, and members formed their own vigilante-style police force. From the point of view of the white residents, Buckeye needed to be protected from property deterioration, rising instability, escalating crime, and urban crisis. The BNNCA leaders were inspired by efforts elsewhere that grounded urban revitalization in ethnic identity, particularly the example of the Columbus, Ohio, neighborhood of German Village. In 1970 they formed a Hungarian Village Committee that organized cultural festivals, held ethnic parades, and promoted Hungarian businesses. These efforts continued through 1975, but by 1976 the annual Hungarian parade was canceled due to low participation and lack of interest. 4

The Buckeye Area Development Corporation (BADC) and Buckeye-Woodland Community Congress (BWCC) formed in the early 1970s.

The former was a local development corporation focused on Buckeye's mixed-use business district along Buckeye Road and the surrounding residential areas; it turned to preservation as one strategy within a broad revitalization agenda. FIG. 1 The latter was more of an organizing and advocacy group that emphasized anti-redlining strategies, community coalition building, and housing improvements. The BWCC advocated for both demolition and rehabilitation, depending on conditions. For instance, to advocate for housing rehabilitation, it helped establish low-interest loan programs in the area. At the same time, it lobbied the city for more aggressive demolition of blighted properties, even demolishing buildings on its own when the city failed to act. 5

5
Kent State University, School of Architecture and Environmental Design (KSU-AED), *A Community Design Study for the Buckeye Area Community* (Cleveland: City of Cleveland Departments of Community Development and Economic Development and the Buckeye Area Development Corporation, July 1975); Marcus Gleisser, "Buckeye Rd. Showcase of Urban Revitalization," *Plain Dealer*, October 30, 1977; Caren Goldman, "Buckeye," *Plain Dealer Sunday Magazine*, September 5, 1976; William F. Miller, "Residents Won't Wait for the Wrecker," *Plain Dealer*, June 19, 1975.

6
Cleveland Landmarks Commission, meeting minutes, July 12, 1974, and September 13, 1974, Robert C. Gaede Papers, box 4, Cleveland Landmarks Commission, 1964–1974, Cleveland Public Library; Cleveland Landmarks Commission, *1975 Annual Report* (Cleveland: Cleveland Landmarks Commission, 1975), 3; John D. Cimperman, "Neighborhood Revival—The Buckeye Plan," *Façade* 1 (October 1976), 5.

7
KSU-AED, *Architectural Character Study: Buckeye Road Community, Cleveland, Ohio* (Cleveland: Cleveland Landmarks Commission, 1975), 33.

8
KSU-SAED, *Architectural Character Study.*

9
KSU-SAED, *A Community Design Study for the Buckeye Area Community* (Cleveland: City of Cleveland Departments of Community Development and Economic Development and Buckeye Area Development Corporation, July 1975), 8.

FIG. 1: *Buckeye Road. Photograph courtesy of the author.*

In the early 1970s, the Cleveland Landmarks Commission (CLC) also turned its attention to Buckeye. From 1974 to 1975, it led an architectural survey of the neighborhood in collaboration with Kent State University. 6 The report focused on Buckeye Road and concluded that the "architectural character of the Buckeye Community is a strong and potent element." 7 The study highlighted about a dozen landmark buildings and significant architectural characteristics in three categories: religious, residential, and commercial. Overall, the CLC focused on the area's architecture and materials more than its cultural or social heritage. 8

Simultaneous with the CLC study, the BADC partnered with Kent State on a planning study for Buckeye Road. That these two studies occurred in the same year but were not coordinated reveals the lack of collaboration between preservationists and community developers. The BADC study noted Buckeye Road's architectural uniqueness and the diverse mix of businesses along the corridor. While the number of Hungarian-owned businesses had declined significantly, they still retained a presence alongside a growing number of African American-owned enterprises. 9

The idea of establishing a neighborhood conservation district in Buckeye emerged out of these studies. The CLC, working with the ward

10
John D. Cimperman, letter to Councilman David Strand, May 25, 1975, Robert C. Gaede Papers, box 5, Cleveland Landmarks Commission, 1975–1976, Cleveland Public Library; Cleveland Landmarks Commission, meeting minutes, June 11, 1976.

11
The boundaries of the proposed conservation zone were East 90th Street to the west, South Moreland Boulevard to the east, Forest Avenue to the south, and Shaker Boulevard to the north. William F. Miller, "City Called Bad for Cable TV," Plain Dealer, June 19, 1976; Cleveland Landmarks Commission meeting minutes, September 10, 1975, and July 9, 1976; Buckeye Historic Conservation Zone Committee, meeting minutes, September 28, 1976.

12
Malcolm C. Douglas, "Neighborhood Conservation Zoning," unpublished memo, November 29, 1976, Robert C. Gaede Papers, box 7, Cleveland Landmarks Commission, 1977–1979, Cleveland Public Library; Cleveland Landmarks Commission, meeting minutes, March 11, 1977, 2–3.

13
City of Cleveland, Department of Community Development, Buckeye Neighborhood Commercial Preservation Project (Cleveland: City of Cleveland, Department of Community Development, 1976), n.p.

14
Caren Goldman, "Buckeye," Plain Dealer Sunday Magazine, September 5, 1976, 12.

15
Buckeye Area Development Corporation, "A Report to the People of Buckeye," Thomas Campbell Papers, box 8, folder 5, 1976, Western Reserve Historical Society.

council member, proposed the Buckeye Historic Conservation Zone, wherein the CLC would serve in an advisory role without the binding authority that came with traditional landmark designations. 10 By the summer of 1976, the CLC, the planning commission, the BWCC, the BADC, and the city council supported the idea. 11 The CLC produced a draft ordinance and design manual, but the proposal hit a roadblock in 1977 when the city's legal department concluded that conservation zones were not permissible under the existing landmarks ordinance and that either new legislation or an ordinance amendment was necessary. 12 No such changes were ever implemented.

Even without preservation protections, the BADC ramped up revitalization along Buckeye Road. In July 1976 it received a $241,800 grant from the US Department of Housing and Urban Development to support improvements, including city-funded beautification efforts (e.g., streetscaping) and BADC-driven reinvestment (e.g., building rehabilitations). 13 The BADC marketed the area's Hungarian roots; for instance, it planned a small park designed with an "ethnic motif" as a "visible statement of Hungarian renewal in the community." 14 In reports to the community, the BADC promoted the area's Hungarian and Slovak heritage while downplaying its current "cosmopolitan" character. 15

In the early 1980s, the BADC launched another short-lived effort to secure historic district designation for an area with boundaries nearly identical to those of the earlier conservation zone. BADC leaders believed that a historic district would protect against incompatible development, including fast-food restaurants and convenience retail. The Hungarian narrative still dominated these efforts, with BADC leaders arguing that Buckeye was "the center of Hungarian culture and heritage in the Cleveland area." 16 In 1985 the area's last Hungarian business, a butcher shop, relocated from Buckeye Road to a nearby suburb. 17

Ultimately, preservationists and community developers struggled to navigate the demands of the area's Eastern European heritage, its growing African American population, and increasing community development needs such as housing rehabilitation, commercial revitalization, and affordability. The revitalization of Buckeye as a Hungarian village failed to take hold amid rapid racial change—preservationists and community developers failed to connect preservation to the identity of Buckeye's African American residents and their needs.

Preserving Buckeye in the 2010s

Preservation debates have reemerged in Buckeye in recent years. As residential vacancy rates skyrocketed across Ohio, the nonprofit Western Reserve Land Conservancy created the Thriving Communities Institute to help revitalize the state's urban centers. 18 The institute's fee-based property surveys graded buildings from A (excellent) to F (unsafe/hazard). Buildings graded D or F were often prioritized for demolition. In 2013 the St. Luke's Foundation granted the institute $734,000 to survey an area around the historic St. Luke's Hospital, including portions of Buckeye. The foundation had recently partnered on a massive adaptive reuse project to convert the historic hospital into affordable housing, a charter school, and nonprofit office space. 19 The foundation, along with Cleveland Neighborhood Progress, a community development umbrella organization, sought to use the hospital rehabilitation to anchor neighborhood revitalization and sought the property survey to inform understanding about surrounding property conditions.

Thriving Communities Institute then hired the Cleveland Restoration Society (CRS) to review 1,020 D/F properties in the area, reflecting an implicit understanding that Buckeye possesses unprotected historic resources. CRS conducted a windshield survey of the buildings, with scant attention to social or cultural meaning, and determined that twenty-one (2 percent) of the structures should be prioritized for rehabilitation instead of demolition. Twenty of these were significant for their architectural and historical significance, with the latter attributable to building age rather than social or cultural associations. 20 What this survey illustrates is a preservation practice that overly relies on architectural significance, struggles with cultural and social inclusion, and fails to account for evolving stories of place—in this case, the contributions of the African Americans who have called Buckeye home for nearly fifty years. In Buckeye, preservationists have yet to offer strategies that contribute to neighborhood stabilization and revitalization for the area's existing residents or that go beyond the limitations of architectural heritage.

— FROM SURVEYS TO DEEP ENGAGEMENT

In Cleveland, two survey efforts, conducted thirty years apart (in 1982 and 2012), sought to identify, document, and preserve the city's African American heritage. On their face, both suggest that Cleveland has few significant African American heritage sites—an erroneous conclusion. In fact, what these surveys reveal is that preservationists' attempts to identify non-architecturally significant resources are deeply flawed. In recent years, signs have emerged that preservationists are shifting toward deeper community engagement, hinting at the possibility of a more inclusive, representative, and just future for historic preservation.

"Black History Thematic Resources in Cleveland"
In its first decade, the CLC progressively conferred landmark designation on a handful of African American-affiliated sites, including St. John's AME, Shiloh Baptist Church, Antioch Baptist Church, Lane Metropolitan CME Church, the Afro American Cultural and Historical Society, the Phillis Wheatley Association, and Karamu House. 21 The designation of African American-affiliated sites continued in the 1980s, with preservationists expanding their focus to national-level recognition. 22 In 1981 the state's regional preservation officer prepared the "Black History Thematic Resources in Cleveland" nomination for the National Register of Historic Places. The designation, approved in 1982 and endorsed by the CLC, included eight properties (seven of which were in Central) that represented four areas of African American life: churches, social service agencies, businesses, and social/cultural institutions. FIG. 2 Preservationists framed these buildings as rare survivors of urban renewal, urban decline, and African American out-migration from the central

16
Cleveland Landmarks Commission, meeting minutes, December 10, 1982, 2; Cleveland Landmarks Commission, meeting minutes, January 28, 1983, 5; "Statement of Significance: Proposed Buckeye Road Historic District," undated draft, Robert C. Gaede Papers, box 6, Cleveland Landmarks Commission, 1980–1984, Cleveland Public Library.

17
Thomas S. Andrzejewski, "Buckeye Loses Its Butcher: Last Hungarian Meat Shop Follows Customers to Suburbs," *Plain Dealer*, April 8, 1985.

18
"Thriving Communities: Helping Cities across Ohio Go from Vacancy to Vitality," Western Reserve Land Conservancy, https://www.wrlandconservancy.org/whatwedo/advocacy-and-research.

19
Christine Serlin, "Historic Rehab Finalist: Saint Luke's Manor," *Affordable Housing Finance*, July 1, 2012, https://www.housingfinance.com/developments/historic-rehab-finalist-saint-lukes-manor_o.

20
It is unknown if these twenty-one buildings have been demolished or rehabilitated. In 2015 the City of Cleveland hired Thriving Communities Institute to survey the entire city. Buckeye ranked fifth among all Cleveland neighborhoods in terms of the percentage of D and F properties (9.1 percent of neighborhood buildings). This time, Thriving Communities Institute did not hire CRS to review properties in any neighborhood.

21
Cleveland Landmarks Commission, meeting minutes, March 9, 1973; Cleveland Landmarks Commission, *Descriptive Synopsis of Cleveland Landmarks*, John D. Cimperman Collection

of Cleveland Landmarks
Commission Records,
Michael Schwartz
Library Special Collec-
tions, box 1, Cleveland
Historic Districts and
Landmarks, undated
typescript: 9–10, 13,
19, 20, Cleveland State
University; Cleveland
Landmarks Commis-
sion, meeting minutes,
January 10, 1975;
John D. Cimperman,
"Latest Designated
Landmarks," *Façade* 2
(January 1977): 4; Cleve-
land Landmarks Com-
mission, *1978 Annual
Report* (Cleveland:
Cleveland Landmarks
Commission, 1978), 6;
Cleveland Landmarks
Commission, *1979
Annual Report* (Cleve-
land: Cleveland Land-
marks Commission,
1979), i; Cleveland Land-
marks Commission,
1980 Annual Report
(Cleveland: Cleveland
Landmarks Commis-
sion, 1980), 5; "Karamu
House, a First for Black
Theater Companies
in America," *African
American Registry*,
https://aaregistry.org/
story/karamu-house-
first-black-theater-
company-in-america.

22
Cleveland Landmarks
Commission, *Descrip-
tive Synopsis of Cleve-
land Landmarks*, 28.

23
Eric Johannesen, "Black
History Thematic
Resource," National
Park Service, 1982, 2–3.

24
Stephanie Ryberg-Web-
ster, "Beyond Rust and
Rockefeller: Preserving
Cleveland's African
American Heritage,"
*Preservation Education
and Research* 9 (2017):
7–23.

city.[23] This effort recognized the significance of sites affiliated with the city's African American community, but, at the same time, the inclusion of only eight buildings clearly underrepresents the significance of the city's African American history. Furthermore, National Register listing provided no real protection for these sites, and two have been demolished since the designation.

"Landmarks of Cleveland's African American Experience"

In 2012, to commemorate the fortieth anniversary of its founding, CRS embarked on another effort to survey the city's African American historic resources. Through its "Landmarks of Cleveland's African American Experience" project, CRS sought to identify significant African American heritage sites, promote National Register and/or local designation of those sites, celebrate and communicate the project's findings as a way to help stabilize neighborhoods and attract residents, and commemorate the sites with plaques or markers.[24] A task force of preservation experts and African American civic leaders guided CRS through the process. Using secondary sources and the task force's input, CRS focused their windshield survey efforts on the predominantly African American neighborhoods of Hough, Glenville, Central, Fairfax, Mt. Pleasant, Kinsman, University Circle, and Buckeye. They also conducted a limited survey in the Ludlow neighborhood, which spans the border of Cleveland and Shaker Heights, and in a cluster of communities in the city's far southeast corner (Lee-Miles, Miles-Seville, Union-Miles, Park/Corlett, and Lee-Harvard).

The project's grant funding stipulated that CRS had to complete 150 Ohio Historic Inventory forms. This two-page form is the basis for Ohio's statewide historic survey but provides no systems for protection. The form's brevity facilitates the completion of large-scale surveys but does not encourage deep research or engagement. The target of 150 forms, or 150 individual properties, was an arbitrary goal. The one-year grant period

Property	Local Landmark (year)	Significance	Extant or Demolished
St. John's African Methodist Episcopal (AME) Church	1974	One of the city's oldest African American congregations (est. 1830)	Extant
Shiloh Baptist Church	1974	The city's oldest Black Baptist congregation (est. 1849)	Extant
Cleveland Home for Aged Colored People	n/a	Earliest African American-operated, non-religious social service institution	Extant
Phillis Wheatley Association	1979	Home for single, African American girls and women	Extant
Garrett Morgan House	n/a	Successful African American businessman	Demolished
House of Wills	n/a	Successful African American-owned business, continuously occupying same building since 1941	Extant
Universal Negro Improvement Association	1976	Cleveland home of this nationally-significant institution	Demolished
Karamu House	1980	Nation's oldest Black community theater	Extant

FIG. 2: *Summary of "Black History Thematic Resources" National Register Designation.*

was also a constraint, as CRS had to conduct the background research, convene task force meetings, complete the windshield survey, and prepare all required written reports and documentation within this period. [25]

The project produced disappointing results. The quota-driven effort resulted in historic inventory forms for 91 buildings and one neighborhood of 59 homes in the already designated Ludlow National Register Historic District, an area along the border of Cleveland and Shaker Heights. The inclusion of the Ludlow neighborhood, deemed important for its role in integrating Shaker Heights, seemed more like an attempt to meet the quota of 150 than a good-faith effort to identify African American historic sites. Of the 91 other buildings, only 12 were significant for their affiliation with African American heritage and had designation potential. [26] *FIG. 3* In other words, in a project designed to identify and protect African American historic resources, CRS identified 79 buildings that had no affiliation with the city's African American community or were not eligible for any form of historic designation. The main reasons that buildings did not meet eligibility criteria were a lack of provenance (insufficient available recorded history) and a lack of material integrity (excessive alterations).

CRS's 2012 effort lent credence to perceptions that preservationists place too much value on architecture and material integrity, to the detriment of culturally and socially significant sites. CRS did not engage local residents and prioritized completing an arbitrary number of forms over organically identifying African American heritage sites.

25
Ryberg-Webster, "Beyond Rust and Rockefeller."

26
An additional seven buildings had designation potential but lacked significance associated with African American history. Most of these buildings were significant either for architecture or for their affiliation with Jewish heritage.

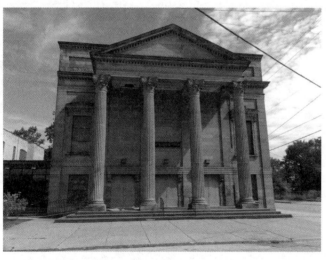

FIG. 3: *Lane Metropolitan CME Church, designated as a local landmark by the Cleveland Restoration Society in 1975 and highlighted in the Cleveland Restoration Society's 2012 survey. Photograph courtesy of the author.*

"The Making of Cleveland's Black Suburb in the City"

The "Landmarks of Cleveland's African American Experience" project, while flawed, elevated local interest in preserving African American heritage, particularly in the city's southeast neighborhoods. In 2016 the councilman for Ward 1, which includes Lee-Harvard, approached CRS about using preservation to stabilize and promote the area. At the same

27
"Cleveland Census
Information 2010,"
Cleveland City Planning
Commission, http://
planning.city.cleveland.
oh.us/2010census/
cpc.html.

28
"Shining a Spotlight
on Lee-Harvard:
Telling Our Story,"
LiveCleveland!,
http://livecleveland.
org/event/shining-
spotlight-lee-harvard-
telling-story.

time, CRS was looking for ways to continue its work protecting African American heritage—the invitation to explore the history of Ward 1/ Lee-Harvard proved opportune. Ultimately, this led to the Restoration Society's "The Making of Cleveland's Black Suburb in the City" project, which continues as of this writing.

Located on the city's southeast side, Lee-Harvard dates to the post-World War II era and resembles many postwar suburbs: small houses along tree-lined residential streets, connected to mid-century thoroughfares and commercial corridors. Along with its neighbors, Lee-Miles and Lee-Seville, Lee-Harvard was built for middle-class African Americans who wanted to leave overcrowded, poorly maintained, and rapidly deteriorating inner-city neighborhoods. The population of Lee-Harvard has remained relatively stable over time, experiencing population decline that is mild compared to that of the city as a whole (22 percent since 1980).[27] Today, Lee-Harvard has an aging building stock and an aging population, with many original residents still living in the neighborhood.

Among CRS's first discoveries were developments built by entrepreneurial African American builder-developers in the 1940s and 1950s. In the mid-twentieth century, African Americans did not have easy access to capital or loans, which made running successful businesses, including home-building businesses, difficult. As CRS staff learned about Arthur Bussey, one such builder-developer, they identified a few streets with an intact collection of his homes. Based on CRS's research and documentation, the landmarks commission approved the Arthur Bussey Development Landmark District in 2016. *FIG. 4* While the district is significant for its social, cultural, and economic history, CRS also emphasized its material integrity "with many properties still exhibiting original mid-century details such as aluminum awnings and wrought iron railings."[28]

Understanding Lee-Harvard's heritage required CRS to adopt new strategies, including community engagement. In fall 2016 CRS sponsored two public events, one at the Harvard Community Services Center, the neighborhood-based community development corporation, and one at

FIG. 4: *Homes within the Arthur Bussey Development Landmark District. Photograph courtesy of the author.*

the Levin College of Urban Affairs at Cleveland State University. These events promoted the area's history and featured scholar Todd Michney, whose recent book, *Surrogate Suburbs*, focuses on the history and development of Cleveland's African American communities, including those in Ward 1.[29] In addition, CRS successfully applied for grants from the Ohio Humanities Council and the National Endowment for the Humanities to support community engagement efforts. With this funding, CRS for the first time implemented documentation strategies including resident storytelling events, oral histories, and archiving neighborhood ephemera such as residents' personal photo albums and scrapbooks.

CRS has now expanded to focus on both Lee-Harvard and Lee-Seville, securing an Ohio History Fund grant in March 2019 to support a publication about African American builder-developers and the heritage of these important and largely overlooked neighborhoods.[30] CRS's work in Ward 1 was the first time it directly engaged with one of the city's African American communities. In a recent blog post, CRS's longtime director, Kathleen Crowther, summarized the shift that the project represented for the organization:

> As a local heritage organization and a Partner of the National Trust for Historic Preservation, our expertise is in architecture, historic styles, and the many methods to preserve older buildings and landmarks. A couple of years ago, Cleveland Restoration Society embarked upon a journey to create deeper meaning in our work by engaging with residents to tell the story of place.[31]

The effort was transformative for CRS in terms of building partnerships, identifying new funders, understanding community significance, and learning inclusive strategies for identifying underrepresented historic places.

— TOWARD AN INCLUSIVE URBAN PRESERVATION

While preservationists have made strides in recognizing the importance of inclusiveness, preservation tools and strategies often still struggle to achieve this goal. In urban African American neighborhoods, such as those in Cleveland, decades of systematic disinvestment, institutionalized racist lending practices, and, often, high concentrations of poverty have produced a materially altered built environment that is seen to lack integrity according to traditional preservation standards. The rich cultural heritage and historic significance of buildings in these communities is then systematically ignored or devalued by mainstream preservationists. To move toward a more socially just and equitable preservation practice, it is imperative to remove barriers to inclusivity, to understand the dynamics and power structures of decision-making, and to craft short- and long-term agendas that foreground inclusivity.

In many cases, funding drives priorities. Historic preservation costs money, whether for research, documentation, nominations, interpretation,

29
Todd M. Michney, *Surrogate Suburbs: Black Upward Mobility and Neighborhood Change in Cleveland, 1900–1980* (Chapel Hill: University of North Carolina Press, 2017).

30
Cleveland Restoration Society, *The Making of Cleveland's Black Suburb in the City: Lee-Seville and Lee-Harvard* (Cleveland: Cleveland Restoration Society, 2019).

31
Kathleen Crowther, "Telling the Larger Story: What Ohio Humanities Funding Has Meant to Us," *Ohio Humanities*, June 26, 2017, http://www.ohiohumanities.org/telling-the-larger-story.

32
"Buckeye Road:
A Hungarian
Neighborhood in
Cleveland," Cleveland
Hungarian Museum,
https://cleveland
hungarianmuseum.
org/buckeye-road-
a-hungarian-
neighborhood-
in-cleveland.

or building rehabilitations. Inclusive preservation requires preservation-ists to spend money differently. Developing survey strategies that make architecture a secondary or even tertiary consideration, when appropriate, would facilitate the identification of underrepresented historic sites. In many cases, it may be more appropriate to redirect budgets for windshield surveys and architectural documentation toward things like community engagement or maintenance and weatherization grants. Preservationists need to seek funding and prioritize projects and grants that further an inclusive agenda. Long-standing relationships with existing funders are a form of power, and preservationists have the ability to press for support that furthers equity goals. Overall, preservationists need to seek out new funders, redirect existing funding where possible, and use their well-established networks to fight any funding biases that undermine the preservation of underrepresented communities and heritages.

Funding decisions, designation approvals, and community develop-ment are political. Underrepresented communities often have a long—and rarely positive—history with urban planning and urban development. Similarly, preservation is often viewed as elitist, and it has long been associated with gentrification. These complex dynamics demand that preservationists directly confront the biases, negative impacts, and dis-criminatory practices of the past. The politics of preservation are highly local and thus require tailored approaches that respond to local conditions and histories. National leadership, such as that of the National Trust for Historic Preservation's African American Cultural Heritage Action Fund, sets a precedent and expectations for the field as a whole. But the real work of breaking down barriers, recognizing value in marginalized communities, and changing the reality (and therefore the perceptions) of what preservation means must occur on the ground in cities, neighbor-hoods, and communities. The formal structures of city government, such as the composition of city councils, also demand that preservationists be willing, at times, to act as political entities, engaging in coalition-building and broader discussions about the future of neighborhoods and cities.

Further, those in the field must confront the tendency to valorize origin stories and nostalgic views of the past, both of which have immense power to erase decades (if not more) of marginalized communities' histories. For instance, in Cleveland, as in many other cities, African Americans were not the "original" settlers of most neighborhoods that are now predominantly African American. When preservationists fail to recognize the layers of urban history, they negate the important contribu-tions of minority residents who faced discriminatory housing practices and severe residential segregation for much of the twentieth century.

Nostalgic views of twentieth-century urban history tend to uplift sto-ries of European immigrants while devaluing those of African Americans. For instance, in 2009 Cleveland's small Hungarian Museum organized an exhibit titled *Buckeye Road: A Hungarian Neighborhood in Cleveland*. The promotional materials described it as "a nostalgic look at the Hungarian community from the early 1900's, through its most vibrant times, to its decline in the 1970's." 32 Buckeye has been a predominantly African American neighborhood for around fifty years, a significant amount of time in its own right and currently just two decades shy of the Hungarian

33

tenure in the neighborhood. By all reasonable forecasts, Buckeye will be an African American neighborhood for much longer than it was Hungarian. Yet powerful, nostalgic narratives negate the lived experiences of African Americans and continue to suggest that African Americans are occupying someone else's space. Any complicity on the part of preservationists in these narratives stands in direct opposition to equity and inclusivity. When it comes to urban neighborhoods, there is a reasonable argument that all residents, over time, have contributed to an area's heritage and that even white flight, racial turnover, and systematic disinvestment are themselves historically significant. Preservationists are often ill-equipped to navigate this type of everyday history, which is not always pretty. Without direct efforts to value the complexity of stories and meaning, preservationists will also be implicated in the othering and dismissal of marginalized people.

33
Jennifer Minner, "Revealing Synergies, Tensions, and Silences Between Preservation and Planning," *Journal of the American Planning Association* 82, no. 2 (2016): 80.

Preservationists must directly address structural barriers to inclusivity inherent in the field and work, in every way possible, to break through them. Architecture and integrity are often the gateways to preservation protections and benefits, but, in marginalized communities, they are an excuse for exclusion. New thinking, strategies, and tools do not require discarding the array of well-established preservation policies and programs. Rather, an inclusive practice demands an expanded toolkit. Removing institutionalized barriers to inclusiveness at the federal level would serve as a model for action by local communities. For instance, the National Park Service could write standards for vernacular residential landscapes where overall community history is more significant than individual buildings' material details; new guidelines could redefine "integrity" to deemphasize (or ignore) materiality when it is not important.

Truly inclusive preservation is possible only in a profession that engages in the difficult and ongoing work of overcoming explicit and implicit biases. Diversifying the profession will require strategies ranging from community heritage projects involving schoolchildren to targeted academic recruitment and the creation of dedicated scholarships and funding to attract minority students. In the short term, consciously crafting diverse preservation commissions and boards can also be effective. To encourage this goal, the National Park Service and/or the National Trust could establish diversity mandates as a precursor for funding eligibility (e.g., for nonprofit boards or local preservation commissions). The faces of those in power matter, and it is well past time for change.

Preservation holds the potential to uplift underrepresented people, communities, and heritages through a practice that prioritizes equity, social justice, and inclusiveness, or what Jennifer Minner calls an "equity preservation agenda."[33] Crafting an inclusive preservation requires understanding and changing the use and distribution of power within the field. It means acknowledging that preservationists are not powerless idealists and that through their work, they have the power to undermine progress toward a more just society—or, preferably, to uplift and shine a light on the full story of our communities, cities, and nation.

How Can Historic Preservation Be More Inclusive?
Learning from New York City's Historic Districts

Ingrid Gould Ellen, Brian J. McCabe,
and Gerard Torrats-Espinosa

Examining Questions of Exclusion

In New York City, the Landmarks Preservation Commission has helped to protect and preserve more than a hundred neighborhoods across all five boroughs since its inception in 1965. However, the neighborhoods designated as historic districts in New York City are home to residents who are more likely to be white and to have higher incomes and higher levels of education than neighborhoods elsewhere in the city. In 2010 the average census tract in a historic district in New York City was 80 percent white and 9.5 percent black, while the average census tract *not* in a historic district was only 43 percent white and almost 30 percent black. Over 90 percent of residents living in historic districts held a college degree, compared to only 33 percent outside historic districts. 1 Previous research suggests that the designation of historic districts widens some of these gaps by accelerating the process of demographic change. 2

— SOCIAL INCLUSIVITY AND HISTORIC PRESERVATION

Historic preservation aims to provide a tangible link to our past. The efforts of preservation advocates and policy-makers in New York City have ensured that historic neighborhoods remain part of the city landscape for generations to come. Preserving historic assets helps to deepen neighborhood identity, to attract visitors to the city, and to ensure a rich, diverse building stock across many New York City neighborhoods. Yet critics contend that historic preservation efforts too often favor certain historical narratives and assets over others. At the global level, researchers charge that non-Western sites are underrepresented on the UNESCO World Heritage List. 3 Even at the local level, diverse histories are not always valued in the preservation process, especially as advocates and public officials focus on historic buildings or their architectural features—giving evidence to concerns about the politics and limits of authenticity in historic preservation. 4

Critics charge that the preservation movement largely serves high-income and white communities who use the designation process against changes that could undermine their housing investments. 5 College-educated, high-income residents may possess better knowledge of the planning process and greater access to the levers of city governance. With these resources, they are able to advocate for historic preservation since they recognize the financial or social benefits of doing so. If they are more politically active than previous residents, or have stronger social connections, they may also be more successful in securing a historic district designation. 6

In response to calls for greater inclusivity and diversity in the preservation process, several national organizations, including the National Trust for Historic Preservation, have launched efforts to diversify the sites that are designated and preserved. 7 One recent example in New York City is the designation of the Stonewall Inn, the site of the 1969 riots credited with launching the modern-day gay rights movement. The site was designated as the first national historic landmark to commemorate the LGBTQ movement and was also declared a New York City historic landmark by the Landmarks Preservation Commission. 8 The designation of the Stonewall Inn explicitly commemorates an important historical and

1
These comparisons are between tracts with *at least* 75 percent of the parcels located within a historic district and tracts that do not include any parcels within a historic district.

2
Brian J. McCabe and Ingrid Gould Ellen, "Does Preservation Accelerate Neighborhood Change? Examining the Impact of Historic Preservation in New York City," *Journal of the American Planning Association* 82, no. 2 (2016): 134–146.

3
Bruno Frey and Lasse Steiner, "World Heritage List: Does It Make Sense?," *International Journal of Cultural Policy* 17, no. 5 (November 2011): 555–573.

4
Sharon Zukin, *Naked City: The Death and Life of Authentic Urban Places* (New York: Oxford University Press, 2011); Lior Jacob Strahilevitz, "Historic Preservation and Its Even Less Authentic Alternative," in *Evidence and Innovation in Housing Law and Policy*, ed. Lee Fennell and Benjamin J. Keys (New York: Cambridge University Press, 2017), 108–131.

5
Edward Glaeser, "Preservation Follies," *City Journal* (Spring 2010), https://www.city-journal.org/html/preservation-follies-13279.html; Brian J. McCabe, "Are Homeowners Better Citizens? Homeownership and Community Participation in the United States," *Social Forces* 91, no. 3 (March 2013): 929–954; Brian J. McCabe, *No Place Like Home: Wealth, Community and the Politics of Homeownership* (New York: Oxford University Press, 2016); Vicki Been, Josiah Madar, and Simon McDonnell, "Urban Land-Use Regulation: Are Homevoters

"Overtaking the Growth Machine?," *Journal of Empirical Legal Studies* 11, no. 2 (June 2014): 227–265.

6
Phillip Kasinitz, "The Gentrification of 'Boerum Hill': Neighborhood Change and Conflicts over Definitions," *Qualitative Sociology* 11, no. 3 (September 1988): 163–182.

7
Erica Avrami, "Making Historic Preservation Sustainable," *Journal of the American Planning Association* 82, no. 2 (2016): 104–112.

8
"The Stonewall Inn," National Trust for Historic Preservation, https://savingplaces. org/places/stone-wall#.XJjqaBNKi9s; Landmarks Preservation Commission, "Stonewall Inn," June 23, 2015, Designation List 483, LP-2574, http://s-media.nyc. gov/agencies/lpc/lp/2574.pdf.

9
Vicki Been, Ingrid Gould Ellen, Mike Gedal, Ed Glaeser, and Brian J. McCabe, "Preserving History or Restricting Development? The Heterogeneous Effects of Historic Districts on Local Housing Markets in New York City," *Journal of Urban Economics* 92 (March 2016): 16–30.

10
McCabe and Ellen, "Does Preservation Accelerate Neighborhood Change?"; Stephanie Ryberg-Webster, "Community Development and Historic Preservation: Exploring Intersections in Seattle's Chinatown-International District," *Community Development Journal* 54, no. 2 (April 2019): 290–309; Brian McCabe, "Protecting Neighborhoods or Priming Them for Gentrification? Historic Preservation, Housing and Neighborhood Change," *Housing Policy Debate* 29 (2019): 181–183; Ted Grevstad-Nordbrock and Igor Vojnovic,

cultural moment in the United States, rather than a piece of architecture worthy of preservation.

Still, despite growing awareness of the need for inclusivity, limited attention has been paid to the types of neighborhoods that are actually designated or the impact of the designation process on neighborhoods and the people living in them. When high-income neighborhoods are designated as historic districts, the designation may help to preserve not only the physical fabric of the neighborhood but also the neighborhood's social and economic composition. By limiting the construction of new buildings or halting efforts to increase density, historic preservation rules can serve as exclusionary supply restrictions. These constraints on neighborhood development often lead to higher housing prices and rents, both citywide and, in many circumstances, within individual districts. They do so by reducing uncertainty about future development and reassuring home buyers that a neighborhood's historic character will be preserved. [9] The requirements for more expensive building materials in historic districts may also translate into higher prices and rents, further limiting the ability of low- and moderate-income households to move in.

While historic designation may help to sustain prices and freeze the demographic composition in initially high-income neighborhoods, observers also worry that it may help to fuel gentrification in lower-income neighborhoods. [10] If the process of historic designation in a low-income neighborhood puts a neighborhood "on the map" and attracts high-income residents, then these policies may accelerate residential turnover, contribute to the rising costs of housing in the area, and displace low-income residents. [11] Furthermore, supply restrictions may make it more difficult to build affordable housing in neighborhoods where it would otherwise have been built.

Preservation in low-income communities raises fundamental concerns about fairness, affordability, and inclusion. While the preservation community should continue to protect historic assets, this work must be done with a sensitivity to the way historic preservation can affect neighborhoods and shape the composition of residents in those communities. Acknowledging the changes that result from historic preservation does *not* mean that such designation should be halted in neighborhoods with valuable historic assets; instead, it demands that advocates and policy leaders couple their preservation goals with efforts to preserve affordable housing and promote economic inclusivity.

— HISTORIC PRESERVATION IN NEW YORK CITY

Established in 1965, the New York City Landmarks Preservation Commission designates historic neighborhoods, properties, and scenic landmarks for protection under the Charter and the Administrative Code of the City of New York. [12] In this capacity, the commission is empowered to preserve historic districts that contain buildings with historic or aesthetic appeal and those that represent unique architectural styles in the city. While designated historic districts may include noncontributing properties, the overwhelming majority of properties included in a historic district are supposed to contribute to the architectural, cultural, or historic character of a designated neighborhood.

Since the establishment of Brooklyn Heights as the city's first historic district in 1965, the Landmarks Preservation Commission has designated over 100 districts across the five boroughs of New York City. By the end of 2014, with the designation of the Chester Court Historic District, the commission had created 114 unique historic districts. 13 Although these designations have occurred in communities throughout the city, they are concentrated in only a handful of areas. In Manhattan, historic districts are located disproportionately on the Upper East Side, the Upper West Side, and portions of the borough south of 14th Street. *FIG. 1* In Brooklyn, historic districts are concentrated largely in the downtown area and in the neighborhoods surrounding Prospect Park. While this concentration maps onto neighborhoods with older, historic buildings, it also suggests that the city's preservation efforts have not been evenly spread across socioeconomically diverse areas.

"Heritage-Fueled Gentrification: A Cautionary Tale from Chicago," *Journal of Cultural Heritage* (forthcoming).

11
Peter Werwath, "Comment on David Listokin, Barbara Listokin, and Michael Lahr's 'The Contributions of Historic Preservation to Housing and Economic Development,'" *Housing Policy Debate* 9, no. 3 (1998): 487–495; Neil Smith, "Comment on David Listokin, Barbara Listokin, and Michael Lahr's 'The Contributions of Historic Preservation to Housing and Economic Development': Historic Preservation in a Neoliberal Age," *Housing Policy Debate* 9, no. 3 (1998): 479–485.

12
Eric Allison, "Historic Preservation in a Development-Dominated City: The Passage of New York City's Landmark Preservation Legislation," *Journal of Urban History* 22, no. 3 (March 1996): 350–376; Anthony Wood, *Preserving New York: Winning the Right to Protect a City's Landmarks* (New York: Routledge, 2007).

13
Through 2014 the Landmarks Preservation Commission also approved seventeen extensions of existing designated historic districts.

FIG. 1: *Historic districts in New York City. Historic districts are shown in black, and their community districts in gray. Community districts in white have no tracts within historic districts.*

— DATA AND METHODS OF ANALYSIS

For this analysis, we utilize data from the US Census Bureau, the New York City Department of City Planning, and the New York City Landmarks Preservation Commission. We rely on census tracts to identify neighborhoods and use data from the decennial census (years 1970 to 2000) and the American Community Survey (five-year estimates of 2010–2014) to describe the socioeconomic status, racial composition, and housing characteristics of New York City's census tracts. Census tracts are statistical neighborhoods that typically contain about four thousand people.

14
New York City
includes fifty-nine
community districts
in total, but only
thirty-two of those
districts include
tracts located within
a historic district.

Drawing on data from the decennial census, we compared the 1970 racial and sociodemographic characteristics of neighborhoods that *would become historic districts* between 1970 and 2014 with the characteristics of neighborhoods that would not become historic districts during that period. In other words, we ask whether, in 1970, neighborhoods that would go on to receive a historic district designation were already more advantaged or home to a higher share of whites than other neighborhoods in the city that would *not* receive a designation. We conducted a simple comparison of means and then also used regression analysis, which allowed us to account for differences in the median age of the housing stock and the share of public housing units in the tract. We restricted our sample to census tracts with more than one hundred residents in all census years between 1970 and 2010.

We also used regression analysis to examine how neighborhoods change following historic designation. We considered the following neighborhood characteristics: total population, percentage of black residents, percentage of white residents, percentage of Hispanic residents, percentage of residents below the poverty line, percentage of adults with a college degree, mean household income, and percentage of housing units that are owner-occu-pied. The regression approach allowed us to contrast changes in tracts that became part of a historic district with changes in tracts that were part of the same community district but outside historic district boundaries. Here, we restricted our sample to census tracts that are located within the city's thirty-two community districts that have at least one tax lot in a historic district by 2014. This left us with 1,003 census tracts in thirty-two community districts. 14 Each of these tracts was observed five times (1970, 1980, 1990, 2000, and 2010), producing a balanced panel with 5,015 tract-year observations. Since we are particularly interested in understanding whether the impact differs for low-income neighborhoods, we examined whether postdesigna-tion changes differ in the 616 neighborhoods that, in 1970, had a household median income below the citywide household median income.

In both sets of analyses, we classified census tracts in four categories, based on the share of tax lots (or parcels) that were inside a historic district: those without any lots in a historic district, those with up to 25 percent of lots in a historic district, those with between 25 and 75 percent of lots in a historic district, and those with more than 75 percent of lots in a historic district. This distinction allowed us to explore both heterogeneity in 1970 demographic differences and the impacts of historic designation based on the land area of the tract that overlaps with a historic district.

— FINDINGS

Our first question was whether neighborhoods designated between 1970 and 2014 differed in their predesignation sociodemographic characteristics from neighborhoods that did not become part of historic districts during that period. Specifically, did neighborhoods that became historic districts between 1970 and 2014 have a more advantaged population than other neighborhoods in 1970? Was the population in these neighborhoods in 1970 whiter than in those neighborhoods that did not become historic districts? Did they have a lower poverty rate or a higher homeownership rate? We compared the 1970 neighborhood characteristics between two types of neighborhoods: those that, over the next four decades, would see most of their lots (that is, more than 75 percent) included in historic districts and those that would not have any lots designated as part of a historic district. FIG. 2

Notably, neighborhoods that would go on to be designated historic districts had a significantly higher share of residents with college degrees and a far higher median income. Designated neighborhoods also had a slightly lower poverty rate in 1970. About 14 percent of households in neighborhoods that would go on to earn a designation lived below the poverty line, compared to almost 16 percent in nondesignated neighborhoods. As for racial composition, neighborhoods that became historic districts by 2014 had a larger proportion of white residents and a lower proportion of African American residents than other neighborhoods. About 79 percent of residents in designated neighborhoods were white in 1970, compared to 71 percent of residents in nondesignated neighborhoods. Approximately 19 percent of residents in designated neighborhoods and 27 percent of residents in nondesignated neighborhoods were African American. Perhaps surprisingly, these neighborhoods also had a lower homeownership rate compared to nondesignated neighborhoods. 15

15 Although we would prefer to separate the white population into non-Hispanic white and Hispanic white, the 1970 census does not enable us to make that distinction.

	% Black	% White	% Hispanic	% Poor	% College	Mean Household Income (in thousands of dollars)	Owner-occupied
Never in historic district (N=1,880)	26.69	71.49	17.94	15.7	8.77	56.15	40.91
	(33.73)	(33.54)	(20.47)	(11.38)	(10.27)	(25.89)	(34.18)
75% in historic district by 2014 (N=33)	19.11	78.96	10.54	13.89	24.11	80.4	20.41
	(27.91)	(27.9)	(8.86)	(8.71)	(13.53)	(47.59)	(20.72)

FIG. 2: *Differences in 1970 demographic characteristics, by 2017 historic district status.*

	-1 % Black	-2 % White	-3 % Hispanic	-4 % Poor	-5 % College	-6 Mean Income	-7 % Owner
1–25% in historic district	1.77	-1.98	-1.52	0.04	2.27**	1.86	-10.15***
	(2.2)	(2.2)	(1.64)	(0.81)	(0.92)	(2.71)	(3.68)
26–75% in historic district	2.21	-1.01	-5.16***	-1.95**	4.75***	11.37***	-9.56**
	(2.26)	(2.26)	(1.69)	(0.83)	(0.94)	(2.78)	(3.79)
76–100% in historic district	-3.58	5.46	-8.54***	-3.53**	7.78***	20.08***	-9.14
	(3.88)	(3.88)	(2.9)	(1.43)	(1.62)	(4.78)	(6.49)
Constant	25.29***	72.22***	16.48***	16.35***	8.33***	55.59***	33.63***
	(1.08)	(1.08)	(0.8)	(0.4)	(0.45)	(1.33)	(1.8)
Observations	1003	1003	1003	1003	1003	1003	1003
Building age & PH controls	Yes	Yes	Yes	Yes	Yes	Yes	Yes
CD fixed effects	Yes	Yes	Yes	Yes	Yes	Yes	Yes

FIG. 3: *Regression-adjusted differences in 1970 demographic characteristics. Levels of statistical significance are as follows: * 0.10, ** 0.05, and *** 0.01. Standard errors clustered by census tract are shown in parentheses.*

Ellen, McCabe, Torrats-Espinosa

16
The decennial census
of 2010 asked when a
housing unit was built.
With this information,
the census reports the
"median year structure
built." We divide the
distribution of median
year structure built
into the following
categories that we
assign to dummy
variables: built before
1930, built in the 1930s,
built in the 1940s,
built in the 1950s, built
in the 1960s, built in
the 1970s, built in the
1980s, built in the
1990s, and built in or
after 2000.

Of course, this simple comparison may be somewhat misleading because not all census tracts are equally likely to be designated as part of historic districts. Historic designation depends on the physical and historical features of neighborhoods, including the age or structural characteristics of their housing stock. Although we recognize that ideas about the historic value of neighborhoods may be culturally biased, we next explored whether the sociodemographic characteristics of neighborhoods that were later designated differed from neighborhoods with similar housing stocks that were not designated. We tested whether these differences held up after controlling for the age distribution of the housing stock and the broader neighborhood. FIG. 3 Specifically, we regressed 1970 demographic characteristics on three dummy variables to capture the share of the housing stock in a census tract that is located in a historic district as of 2014. 16 To account for differences between neighborhoods in the composition of their buildings, we restricted our sample to census tracts in community districts with at least one parcel in a historic district and calculated regression-adjusted means. Because the median age of housing stock in a tract is only a rough proxy for a neighborhood's era of development and architectural style, we also included the community district of the census tract as a proxy for the neighborhood's historic character, although these coefficients are not shown in figure 3.

After controlling for community district and the age distribution of the housing stock, we see that, as of 1970, neighborhoods that would become part of historic districts had more college graduates and higher median incomes, though they had lower homeownership rates compared to other census tracts in the same community district with similarly aged housing stocks. As for racial composition, tracts that would become historic districts had a smaller Hispanic population share and a lower poverty rate compared to other nearby neighborhoods with similarly aged housing stocks. In short, the neighborhoods that would be designated as historic districts over the next four decades typically housed more advantaged residents than other neighborhoods with housing stocks from a similar era.

Next we turned our attention to what happened to the demographic composition of neighborhoods *after* they were designated as a historic district. FIG. 4 We see strong and consistent evidence of change in the socioeconomic status of neighborhoods after some or all of their parcels are designated as part of a historic district. On average, census tracts that include newly designated historic districts saw reductions in the poverty rate and gains in mean income after designation. They also experienced increases in the share of adults with college degrees and in homeownership rates. That said, we see little evidence of racial change after designation, although we do find weak evidence of an increase in the share of white residents relative to nearby tracts outside the historic district. Overall, the population living in census tracts with historic districts became more economically advantaged over time.

Across the board, we see no evidence that these changes were more pronounced in initially low-income tracts. In fact, for some of the characteristics in our analysis—namely, the percentage of college graduates and, to a lesser degree, the median income and the homeownership rate—the postdesignation changes were more muted. Thus, although these findings

FIG. 4: Difference-in-difference estimates of the impact of historic district designations. These regression analyses examine changes in neighborhood characteristics following historic designation. For each dependent variable, we show two sets of results. Odd-numbered columns show average demographic change that followed designation in all census tracts with parcels that are included in historic districts designated between 1970 and 2014. Even-numbered columns examine whether these changes differed in low-income census tracts, which we define as those with median household income below the citywide median household income. Since the regressions include census tract fixed effects, the coefficients on the historic district dummy variables can be interpreted as the changes in population characteristics in the census tract that followed designation. Levels of statistical significance are as follows: * 0.10, ** 0.05, and *** 0.01. Standard errors clustered by census tract are shown in parentheses.

	Log Population		% Black		% White		% Hispanic		% Poor		% College		Log Mean Income		% Owner	
	(1)	(2)	(3)	(4)	(5)	(6)	(7)	(8)	(9)	(10)	(11)	(12)	(13)	(14)	(15)	(16)
HDPost: 1–25%	-0.083 (0.051)	-0.054 (0.049)	1.369 (1.762)	-0.472 (1.471)	-1.738 (1.820)	-1.434 (1.997)	-0.921 (1.110)	-1.925 (1.512)	-0.328 (0.981)	-0.652 (1.067)	1.614 (1.508)	4.009** (1.716)	0.021 (0.034)	0.037 (0.033)	9.548*** (2.692)	11.090*** (2.755)
HDPost: 26–75%	-0.063 (0.051)	-0.072 (0.066)	-1.077 (1.549)	-1.901 (1.618)	2.900* (1.650)	3.087* (1.729)	0.056 (0.969)	-0.151 (1.091)	-2.933*** (0.903)	-2.962*** (0.904)	5.267*** (1.534)	6.217*** (1.771)	0.124*** (0.042)	0.114** (0.044)	13.659*** (2.716)	14.986*** (2.972)
HDPost: 76–100%	-0.050 (0.072)	-0.066 (0.076)	1.715 (2.283)	0.234 (1.785)	1.438 (2.552)	2.236 (2.043)	-0.033 (1.038)	-0.172 (1.057)	-3.417*** (1.127)	-3.627*** (1.221)	7.326*** (1.604)	8.768*** (1.526)	0.160*** (0.046)	0.167*** (0.042)	16.654*** (3.562)	17.645*** (3.794)
Income Below City Median		-0.061** (0.025)		1.526* (0.779)		-3.403*** (1.138)		3.118*** (0.810)		5.460*** (0.518)		-7.416*** (0.773)		-0.296*** (0.017)		0.132 (1.039)
HDPost: 1–25% x Income Below City Median		-0.077 (0.080)		4.328 (2.723)		-0.942 (2.677)		2.676 (1.852)		1.266 (1.510)		-6.204*** (2.129)		-0.066 (0.049)		-3.438 (3.602)
HDPost: 26–75% x Income Below City Median		0.006 (0.073)		2.947 (2.639)		-1.760 (2.526)		1.813 (1.455)		2.140 (1.475)		-5.609*** (1.857)		-0.087* (0.049)		-4.043 (3.613)
HDPost: 76–100% x Income Below City Median		0.170** (0.073)		10.513 (8.127)		-5.506 (9.937)		-0.756 (1.317)		-0.295 (2.891)		-7.577*** (2.426)		0.029 (0.087)		-6.288* (3.347)
Observations		5015		5015		5015		5015		5015		5015		5015		5015
Tract Fixed Effects	Yes	Yes	Yes	Yes	Yes	Yes	Yes	Yes	Yes	Yes	Yes	Yes	Yes	Yes	Yes	Yes
CD-Decade Fixed Effects	Yes	Yes	Yes	Yes	Yes	Yes	Yes	Yes	Yes	Yes	Yes	Yes	Yes	Yes	Yes	Yes

17
Ingrid Ellen and
Brian J. McCabe,
"Balancing the Costs
and Benefits of
Historic Preservation,"
in *Evidence and
Innovation in Housing
Law and Policy*, ed.
Fennell and Keys.

confirm that designated neighborhoods grew more advantaged following the designation of a historic district, they allay concerns that the impacts were more pronounced in neighborhoods that were initially low-income.

Together, these findings begin to chart a path forward that considers issues of equity, diversity, and inclusion. Going forward, planners and preservationists should focus on ensuring that the preservation process captures diverse neighborhood histories. Many New York City neighborhoods are home to rich histories corresponding with different eras, or the changing populations that lived there, and an inclusive preservation process could ensure that these histories are better commemorated and conveyed. Few studies consider how residents, advocates, and preservationists make decisions about where or when to pursue historic designations. Although the historic character of a neighborhood drives designation decisions, characteristics of the local population can also be influential. Gentrification, for example, may expedite the process if newcomers advocate more forcefully for historic preservation. In New York City, we know that many neighborhoods—including many neighborhoods that eventually received designation status—appear on the docket of the Landmarks Preservation Commission and in the sights of preservation advocates years (or decades) before they formally receive designation. Future research should more fully examine how and when the designation process unfolds. Concerns about the timing of historic designation are important for understanding issues of equity and inclusivity, but they have so far received little attention.

Additionally, the gain in socioeconomic status that occurs in historic neighborhoods following designation raises new questions about the effects of preservation. While our findings should ease some concerns about disproportionate impact on low-income communities, they also indicate that neighborhoods across the board tend to see gains in socioeconomic status after designation. Further, we have not fully addressed questions about *who benefits* from the observed changes in historic neighborhoods. Even within neighborhoods, preservation may differentially affect subgroups of residents. For example, since historic preservation appears to accelerate changes that may benefit local homeowners, including rising property values and guarantees against future development, these homeowners may be the primary beneficiaries of the economic impacts of preservation. As property values increase in historic neighborhoods, low-income renters may be effectively shut out of communities by rising rents. Historic preservation policies must be considered alongside other policies aimed at protecting existing residents and ensuring the diversity of New York City's neighborhoods in the long run.

In light of the growing inequality in American cities, our analysis of New York City points to the importance of recognizing the unintended consequences of land-use policies like historic preservation. In our previous research on gentrification and historic preservation, we called for planners and policy-makers to explicitly take stock of the ways that historic preservation limits the production of affordable housing. 17 Since preservation limits the opportunity for new development or increased square footage in designated neighborhoods, we argued that the Landmarks Preservation Commission should offset those changes by upzoning neighboring areas to accommodate additional housing units on noncontributing

43

parcels or in nearby communities. A broader call for inclusivity should reach *beyond* the production of affordable housing to consider other community-level changes that result from historic preservation, such as changes in the types of businesses and commercial establishments that serve neighborhoods before and after designation.

While our analysis describes important issues related to social inclusivity, it also raises important issues that we cannot answer here. First, while advantaged neighborhoods are more likely to undergo designation, this provides only a partial answer to understanding which neighborhoods are designated, why those communities receive historic status, and when that process happens. As we noted above, the historic designation process in New York City often takes multiple years, and neighborhoods are often discussed—either publicly or in preservation circles—for many years prior. Evaluating the timing of this process could help to explain the trajectories of different neighborhoods and the ways that historic and cultural amenities are evaluated. Additionally, analyses of the designation process should account for the different expectations of residents and preservation advocates (and detractors) in pushing for historic status. As they approach the designation process, neighborhood residents may have different ideas about the importance of historic designation or the reasons to push for this distinction. Finally, while we evaluate changes in the racial composition and socioeconomic status of neighborhoods, further research should investigate other changes that result from preservation. From this analysis, we may expect that changes in the composition of neighborhood residents result in changes in commercial establishments, the availability of affordable housing, or the culture of the neighborhood. These community changes may be more pronounced in disadvantaged neighborhoods, even when historic designation results in similar demographic changes.

— REALIGNING THE CONVERSATION

In New York City, efforts to preserve historic buildings and neighborhoods have successfully ensured that the rich cultural and architectural heritage of the city is protected for generations to come. Although more than one hundred neighborhoods are now regulated through the Landmarks Preservation Commission, we have done little to align the conversation about historic preservation with growing concerns about inequality and social inclusion in the city. By asking *which* neighborhoods are designated as historic and how that designation affects those neighborhoods (especially low-income neighborhoods), we hope to broaden the agenda of the preservation community. In order to preserve the diverse history of places like New York City and to ensure that the rich community landscapes reflecting this diverse history are preserved, historic preservation policies should pay explicit attention to whose neighborhoods are designated and who bears the benefits and burdens of those designations.

Historic Preservation and the New Geography of Exclusion

Mark J. Stern

Examining Questions of Exclusion

As historian Max Page has noted, "historic preservation is funda- mentally about bringing old places and living people into contact and dialogue." [1] During periods of rapid social change, one of the challenges is to prevent this dialogue from becoming one-sided, when the places fail to communicate their importance and meaning to the current social realities. This ability of places to insist on their relevance is particularly important in facilitating social inclusion and avoiding social exclusion. Periods of social change can be marked both by the emergence of new dimensions of exclusion and by the persistence of its more durable manifestations, which means they also are times when important histories can be lost.

1
Max Page, *Why Preservation Matters* (New Haven, CT: Yale University Press, 2016), 41.

2
Cybelle Fox, *Three Worlds of Relief: Race, Immigration, and the American Welfare State from the Progressive Era to the New Deal* (Princeton, NJ: Princeton University Press, 2012).

3
Douglas S. Massey and Nancy A. Denton, *American Apartheid: Segregation and the Making of the Underclass* (Cambridge, MA: Harvard University Press, 1993).

4
William J. Wilson, *The Truly Disadvantaged: The Inner City, the Underclass, and Public Policy* (Chicago: University of Chicago Press, 1987).

— MOVING BEYOND A BINARY VIEW OF SOCIAL EXCLUSION

For much of the twentieth century, race and social class merged to produce a binary view of social exclusion. Because African Americans were treated as a subordinate caste—by Jim Crow laws in the South and routine but de facto practices in the rest of the country—they suf- fered multiple forms of exclusion (occupational restrictions, segregated housing, discrimination in public accommodations and schooling) and were subjected to organized extralegal violence. Indeed, a review of mid-twentieth-century literature on social problems would lead one to conclude that to be black was to be poor and to be poor was to be black.

This black-and-white image of the American past has been challenged in recent years, to a great extent through the work of social historians and historic preservationists who have highlighted the fact that African Americans were not the only "other" in twentieth-century America. In her pathbreaking study of the "three worlds" of welfare, Cybelle Fox highlighted a triangular relationship between European immigrants in the North and the Midwest, southern Blacks, and southwestern Mexicans that defined welfare policy during the first half of the twentieth century. [2]

Yet even after the civil rights movement and after the expansion of immigration jolted the system in the 1960s, the binary view of social exclusion persisted. Writing in the 1980s and 1990s, for example, Doug Massey and Nancy Denton argued that those momentous changes had barely changed the system of "American apartheid" that defined a durable system of residential segregation. [3] The "urban underclass" debate— sparked by the work of William J. Wilson, among others—and research in support of welfare reform during the early 1990s reinforced the focus on Black exclusion, adding the concept of *social isolation* to the discussion of racial inequality. [4]

By the turn of the twenty-first century, however, the binary imagery began to give way. One dimension of this shift—where historic preserva- tion work was most prominent—was the demand by other social groups for recognition. Other racial and ethnic groups had followed African Americans in staking a claim to their role in American history, and social movements after the 1960s involved women, LGBT allies and advocates, and groups representing people with disabilities. The debate over inclusion began to shift from a binary to an intersectional perspective, focused on overlapping or crosscutting forms of exclusion.

5
Douglas S. Massey,
Jonathan Rothwell,
and Thurston Domina,
"The Changing Bases
of Segregation in
the United States,"
*Annals of the American
Academy of Political
and Social Science* 626
(2009): 74–90.

6
Michael B. Katz and
Mark J. Stern, *One
Nation Divisible: What
America Was and What
It Is Becoming* (New
York: Russell Sage
Foundation Press,
2006).

7
Martha C.
Nussbaum, *Creating
Capabilities: The
Human Development
Approach* (Cambridge,
MA: Belknap Press
of Harvard University
Press, 2011); Amartya
Sen, *The Idea of
Justice* (Cambridge,
MA: Belknap Press
of Harvard University
Press, 2009).

At the same time, underlying social realities added a new level of complexity. The structural connection of race to social class and economic inequality began to loosen. Douglas Massey and his colleagues—who, a decade earlier, had studied the persistence of American apartheid—discovered that by 2000, racial segregation had declined somewhat while segregation by social class, educational attainment, and ideological stance (that is, liberal versus conservative) had increased. 5 Modest racial integration was accompanied by what Michael Katz and I characterized as *economic differentiation*: the economic status of African Americans, of other racial minorities, and of women was increasingly crosscut by class differences. 6

Intersectionality became the key term as the overlap of race, class, sexual orientation, and gender formed an increasingly complex web of social exclusion. However, the appeal to intersectionality can hide as much as it illuminates. In particular, efforts to highlight the many dimensions of oppression have often left the issue of economic opportunities and their connection to social class understated. Yet it was precisely class oppression—and its ability to cut across other social identities—that was one of the strongest social forces in the late twentieth and early twenty-first centuries.

Intersectionality describes just one of several ways in which the concepts of inclusion and exclusion have become more complex and ideological. In Europe, for example, inclusion has often been used in political debates as synonymous with moving people from welfare into the labor force. In the United States, the increasing popularity of "diversity, equity, and inclusion" programs has often privileged a few types of inclusion while ignoring others. As a result, there are situations like that at my university, where strong "diversity, equity, and inclusion" policies coexist with a median annual household income of undergraduate students' families that exceeds $200,000.

— THE CAPABILITIES APPROACH, INCLUSION,
   AND EXCLUSION

Given the increasing complexity of social exclusion, we need to take a step back and examine these issues through the lens of social justice. To do so, I've found it useful to employ the *capabilities approach* first articulated by philosopher Martha Nussbaum and economist Amartya Sen. 7 The capabilities approach begins with a misleadingly simple question: *what are the opportunities that people need to lead a life they have reason to value?* This idea may come across as a statement of subjective well-being that emphasizes individuals' judgment of what they need. However, the phrase "have reason to value" offers a more objective basis for judging social justice. The capabilities literature has elaborated this concept with a discussion of *adaptive preferences* to point out that marginal and excluded groups often view the idea of justice through their current situation. Those subject to oppression will view sufficient opportunities for a decent life through the lens of their current oppression even if that falls short of a life someone in a more privileged position would "have reason to value."

The capabilities approach seeks to take people's preferences into consideration but also to acknowledge the ways in which past oppression has influenced those preferences. In addition, Sen argues that true *freedom* is the ability to choose the type of life one lives. He uses *capabilities* to describe the choices people have and *functionings* to signify which of these they actually choose.

This counterfactual—what would oppressed people want if they weren't oppressed, what choices could people have beyond the way they actually live—creates a number of empirical challenges for applying the capabilities approach. Most thinking on the approach has translated the ideas of capabilities and functionings into a set of dimensions of well-being (for example, material well-being, political voice, and overall population health outcomes).[8] However, beginning in 2011, the University of Pennsylvania Social Impact of the Arts Project and Reinvestment Fund (formerly the Reinvestment Fund) collaborated to apply this type of approach to urban neighborhoods. We reasoned that national averages—while often illuminating—fail to capture the variation within each country. Furthermore, many elements of well-being are powerfully influenced by social ecology, whether that is the possibility to learn about job opportunities, access to adequate health or educational facilities, or the chance to enjoy cultural or environmental amenities. Our initial work on Philadelphia and New York City was related as well to our interest in the possible role of cultural assets in promoting social well-being.[9]

We chose as our starting point a framework for assessing social well-being by Sen and Joseph Stiglitz, again with a focus on nation-states. We adapted their framework to fit smaller geographies and more inconsistent data. Because some of the measures are dependent on local data sources, the framework for New York City was somewhat different from what we developed for Philadelphia. Although our focus is on the complexity of social well-being, a cursory examination of the data reveals that

8
A majority of this work has focused on differences among nations, typically ranking them on each dimension separately and then generating a summary measure. On most of these scales, the United States ends up as a middling or below middling nation.

9
Mark J. Stern and Susan C. Seifert, "Communities, Culture, and Capabilities: Preliminary Results of a Four-City Study" (Philadelphia: Social Impact of the Arts Project, 2014), https://repository.upenn.edu/siap_ccc/1; Mark J. Stern and Susan C. Seifert, *The Social Wellbeing of New York City's Neighborhoods: The Contribution of Culture and the Arts* (Philadelphia: Social Impact of the Arts Project, 2017), https://repository.upenn.edu/siap_culture_nyc/1.

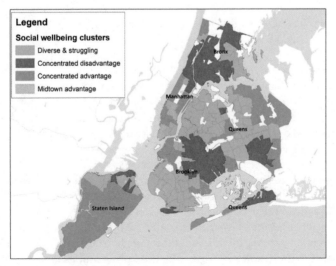

FIG. 1: *Social well-being clusters, New York City. Map courtesy of Social Impact of the Arts Project.*

10
The cluster analysis
resulted in two advan-
taged clusters that we
labeled *concentrated
advantage* and
midtown advantage.
The latter cluster was
distinguished by very
high scores for cultural
assets and social
connections and lower
scores for environmen-
tal amenities.

11
Most of the historic
sites included in our
inventory represent
historic houses (often
associated with a
"friends of" group)
and historic religious
institutions, regardless
of whether they are
officially registered or
designated.

many dimensions are correlated with each other. Of particular note is the fact that economic well-being drives many of the other dimensions. In New York City, for example, housing affordability, health, school effectiveness, security, social connection, and cultural assets are all strongly correlated with economic well-being. These patterns emphasize how much social class determines one's ability to live a life one has reason to value.

Furthermore, from a spatial standpoint, the different dimensions of well-being come together in a distinctive pattern, which we've characterized as the *new geography of social exclusion*. In particular, we've identified two clusters of exclusion. The first, and most obvious, are places we've identified as areas of *concentrated disadvantage*. These neighborhoods essentially have low scores on virtually all dimensions of social well-being. *FIG. 1* A second cluster of neighborhoods—which we've labeled *diverse and struggling*—combine low economic well-being and severe housing burden with a mix of other positive and negative characteristics. In contrast to neighborhoods with concentrated disadvantage, these sections of the city score better on school effectiveness, security (lower crime rates), and personal health. 10

The economic status of individuals and households—whether we label it social class or economic well-being—drives much of the social exclusion we see in the twenty-first-century city. But within this overall pattern of class oppression, we need to be sensitive to the mitigating conditions that may account for communities that "exceed expectations" in the context of economic disadvantage. That is to say that low-income communities typically have poor results for personal security, health, and school effectiveness, so when we find low-income communities that do better than most, it suggests that they possess some resources that account for their exceptional outcomes.

A variety of concepts that have gained traction in urban sociology over the past generation—such as *social capital* and *collective efficacy*—suggest that even in poor communities, the development of relationships or shared expectations among community residents can serve a mitigating function, reducing the link between social class and other dimensions of well-being. However, in our own work, we've focused on the role of cultural engagement at the neighborhood level and studied the ways that community-based cultural resources—including historic preservation sites and organizations—both reinforce and mitigate the impact of exclusion on social well-being. 11

— CULTURE AND SOCIAL EXCLUSION

Cultural engagement is an important dimension in our conceptualization of social well-being. Indeed, between our two efforts to measure cultural assets across Philadelphia (in 1997 and 2011), we discovered that the correlation between the presence of these assets and economic status had increased sharply. For example, between 1997 and 2011, and controlling for ethnic composition, economic diversity, and household diversity, the explanatory power of educational attainment (eta-squared) increased from 12 to 23 percent. This shift resulted from the expansion of cultural resources in affluent neighborhoods and their decline in poor and middle-income neighborhoods. 12

One measure of the latter trend was the "mortality" rate of community-based arts groups. While the overall disappearance of cultural organizations is quite impressive—only half of all cultural groups in our 1997 nonprofit cultural inventory could still be found in 2011—the survival rate was much lower in predominantly black neighborhoods, only 35 percent. Similarly, while 52 percent of historic sites across Philadelphia survived over this period, those in predominantly black and Hispanic neighborhoods had a survival rate of only 30 percent (seven of twenty-three sites). 13 Although we don't have change-over-time data for New York City, the distribution of nonprofit cultural institutions in 2014–2016 makes clear that the most privileged neighborhoods in the city also enjoyed the greatest concentration of cultural assets. *FIG. 2*

Yet, while the dominant narrative of culture and social exclusion is one of increasing inequality, this is not the only story. In New York, we identified three types of *cultural clusters: high market clusters*, which are well-off neighborhoods with a much higher than average number of cultural assets; *market clusters*, which are well-off neighborhoods with about the number of cultural assets we would predict based on their economic status; and *civic clusters*, which are low- and moderate-income neighborhoods with more cultural assets than we would predict based on their economic status. *FIG. 3* These civic clusters take on added importance when we associate cultural assets with other social indicators of neighborhood well-being. Because of the strong correlation between economic well-being and cultural assets generally, statistical control tends to reduce the relationship between culture and social well-being.

Indeed, in both New York City and Philadelphia, we discovered statistically significant relationships between several dimensions of

12
Mark J. Stern and Susan C. Seifert, "Cultural Ecology, Neighborhood Vitality, and Social Wellbeing—A Philadelphia Project" (Philadelphia: Social Impact of Arts Project, 2013), https://repository.upenn.edu/siap_cultureblocks/1.

13
We want to thank Leah Reisman for revising our database. These figures are based on her version of the database.

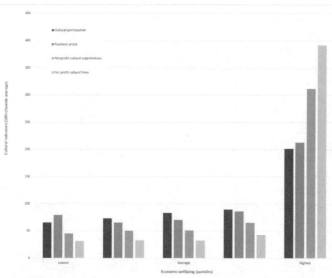

FIG. 2: Distribution of cultural assets by economic well-being, New York City block groups, 2014–2016. Chart courtesy of Social Impact of the Arts Project.

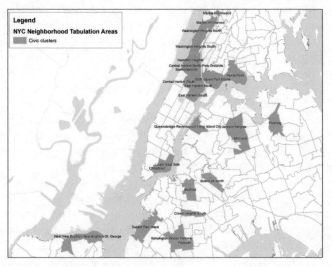

FIG. 3: *Cultural cluster neighborhoods, New York City, 2014–2016.*
Map courtesy of Social Impact of the Arts Project.

social well-being and the Cultural Asset Index. This was especially the case in low- and moderate-income neighborhoods. For example, in New York City, in the bottom 40 percent of the income hierarchy, we found the following differences in social well-being between neighborhoods with the fewest cultural assets and those with the most:

- Diabetes and obesity: 4–5 percent lower
- Teen birth rate: 25 percent lower
- Felonies: 18 percent fewer
- Cases of indicated abuse or neglect: 14 percent fewer
- Top-level scores on standardized tests in English and language arts and math: 17 percent higher

In short, the presence of cultural assets in low- and moderate-income neighborhoods was associated with significantly better social well-being. Still, for the most part, the well-being of these neighborhoods remained below the citywide average. In other words, although the presence of cultural assets corresponds with a reduction in the impact of structural social exclusion, it does not erase the process and practice of exclusion.

— WHY CULTURE MATTERS:
THE IMPACT OF INSTITUTIONAL NETWORKS

Although it is important that cultural assets are associated with a measurable improvement in social well-being, it raises the question of exactly how this improvement works. Here we draw from the extensive literature on *social capital* and *collective efficacy*. The evidence suggests that cultural engagement is, in effect, a form of community engagement that builds relationships within and between neighborhoods. To cite just one example, Roger Sanjek, in his book *The Future of Us All: Race and Neighborhood Politics in New York City*, found that in the Queens neighborhoods he studied, cultural events and civic rituals were a critical element in forging a neighborhood identity that transcended racial and ethnic divides. This point was reinforced by our own fieldwork and interviews for the University of Pennsylvania's Social Impact of the Arts Project study of New York City. [14]

From a broader perspective, we were able to study the types of institutional networks that New York City cultural organizations forged through the various sites where they ran programs. The NYC Department of Cultural Affairs compiled a database of approximately eight thousand program sites as part of its oversight of approximately one thousand grantees. As with our previous findings, we found that low-income neighborhoods had fewer and weaker connections to cultural organizations in other parts of the city but that civic clusters enjoyed stronger and more diverse regional networks. [15]

The program site analysis allowed us to address the question of whether mapping cultural facilities and administrative offices meant we were underestimating the cultural opportunities available in lower-income neighborhoods. If we were to use data on program sites, some skeptics suggested, a much more equal portrait would emerge. In fact, this is not true. Overall, off-site programs funded by the City of New York were as likely to take place in higher income neighborhoods and much less likely to be located in low-income neighborhoods. Furthermore, low-income neighborhoods had fewer connections with cultural providers in the rest of the city. In addition, the connections they did have were less likely to be with cultural organizations or with other organizations in or near the neighborhood and more likely to be one-time programs with institutions like senior centers or libraries—that is, types of interactions that were often a one-time event rather than an ongoing relationship.

In contrast, civic clusters—lower-income neighborhoods that are exceeding expectations with respect to social well-being—report a greater number of Department of Cultural Affairs grantees, program sites, and linkages. What is more, the nature of those links is more varied. A higher proportion of linkages is within the neighborhood, which strengthens the social ecology, and those linkages are more likely to be to another cultural organization. In other words, in contrast to other low-income neighborhoods, civic clusters display a balance of bridging and bonding connections. These findings are indicative of the ways in which culture more broadly forges relationships that build the civic infrastructure of urban communities. At the same time, they reinforce the point that the capacity to strengthen neighborhoods is frustrated to a great extent by the unequal distribution of resources across the city.

How we remedy this aspect of social exclusion is not altogether straightforward. At the very least, cities (ideally supported by both state and federal governments) should take responsibility for addressing the shortfall of cultural opportunities in low-income neighborhoods. For example, New York City could assure that funding strategies for its three public library systems favor disadvantaged neighborhoods both in terms of their budgets and by expanding capacity to build connections

14
Roger Sanjek, *The Future of Us All: Race and Neighborhood Politics in New York City* (Ithaca, NY: Cornell University Press, 1998).

15
Mark J. Stern, "Social Networks and Inequality in New York City's Cultural Sector" (Philadelphia: Social Impact of the Arts Project, 2017), https://repository.upenn.edu/siap_culture_nyc/5.

within their neighborhoods and across the city. A similar approach could be used in prioritizing possible historic sites for designation. This strategy could be complemented by increasing focus on civic clusters. These neighborhoods currently mitigate the broader social exclusion of low-income neighborhoods. Targeting resources to civic clusters could both improve their effectiveness and, in doing so, ideally promote social and cultural inclusion in neighboring communities.

— THE COMPLEXITY OF SOCIAL EXCLUSION

We began this paper with Max Page's observation that historic preservation is a conversation between old places and living people. Yet, by incorporating a discussion of the role of social exclusion and inclusion, that conversation becomes a good deal more complex. Several years ago, while doing qualitative study of cultural districts in Seattle, we spent a lot of time in the Chinatown-International District. As an American historian, of course, I had studied the internment of Japanese Americans during World War II. However, it was only in visiting the Wing Luke Museum of the Asian Pacific American Experience, drinking tea at the Panama Hotel, browsing KOBO at Higo (formerly Higo Variety Store), and walking the streets of what for a half century was known as Japantown (Nihonmachi)—that the scar of those events fully registered for me.

Memory is oftentimes the uninvited participant in the conversations that Page highlighted. But to treat memory as a single participant still gets it wrong. My synthetic memory of Japantown must share the table with the memories of the Japanese Americans who were deported, as well as those of the African American migrants who moved into the spaces left vacant in the wake of the internment. The deported Japanese Americans and the African Americans who took their place were both visible ethnic/racial groups, but for the most part they suffered exclusion on other dimensions of well-being as well. Capturing the complexity of social exclusion remains a significant challenge both for identifying historic sites for designation and for including more voices in their realization. The risk and opportunity of historic preservation is to make room for all those memories without pushing any out of the way.

We need a multidimensional concept of social exclusion that makes room not only for the Japanese American, African American, and European American perspectives but also for marginalization based on health, educational opportunity, or personal security. One perspective that often gets lost in these conversations, then, is that of social class, the results of which are magnified by the disparities in health care, education, environment, community amenities, and political voice that are connected to it. Social class is an enduring form of exclusion and encompasses an important set of memories that we should take care not to lose.

Telling the Full American Story: Insights from the African American Cultural Heritage Action Fund

Brent Leggs, Jenna Dublin, and Michael Powe

Examining Questions of Exclusion

"The Negro's life and labors are inseparably entwined with the life and ideals of the American Nation—and at this storehouse shall establish our claim to immortality." With these words over a century ago, Mary B. Talbert and the National Association of Colored Women launched a national campaign to save Frederick Douglass's home in Washington, DC, thereby inaugurating the Black preservation movement in the United States. Douglass's home, Talbert argued, could be "a hallowed spot, where our boys and girls may gather during the years to come, and receive hope, and inspiration, and encouragement to go forth like Douglass, and fight to win." [1]

Fast-forward to today, and both the opportunity and the need to preserve the stories, struggles, and achievements of diverse Americans are no less compelling. Today, as then, our culture is embodied in old places and the history we keep. By preserving Americans' full culture and history in its material form, we celebrate the tremendous impact that a broad range of Americans have made to the life of our nation—its politics, society, culture, art, ideals. We weave these stories into the American tapestry, carrying them forward into our contemporary debates and transmitting them to the future.

The work to save the home of Frederick Douglass is a notable exception to the broader historic preservation movement, which has primarily focused on saving landmarks associated with famous, predominantly white and male, industrialists, wealthy farmers, or former presidents. The absence of public spaces, historic sites, and monuments dedicated to the achievements and lived experience of groups subject to oppression, both historically and in the present day, continues to marginalize communities that are essential and inextricably tied to American identity. In failing to take an inclusive approach to preserving and amplifying the voices and places of our full history, the stories of women, immigrants, native peoples, and enslaved and free persons of color have been excluded from mainstream narratives, and tangible evidence of them has been disproportionately lost, sending powerful and enduring signals about who is valued and who belongs in our society, and propagating legacies of racially motivated erasure.

These deficits have far-reaching consequences. "Without a thorough reckoning with the complex and difficult history of our country," Darren Walker, president of the Ford Foundation, has said, "especially when it comes to race, we will not be able to overcome intolerance, injustice, and inequality." [2] This imperative is one of the many reasons that, in recent decades, preservationists have worked to expand our horizons, unearth a fuller understanding of America's diverse past, and reconstruct our national identity so that it more closely aligns with who we really are as Americans—a diverse people who, despite our complicated and sometimes difficult past, are stronger because of that diversity. As the historian David McCullough once reminded a group of preservationists, "History is no longer a spotlight. We are turning up the stage lights to show the entire cast." [3]

To help rectify these long-standing disparities, the National Trust for Historic Preservation, an organization chartered by Congress in 1949 to save America's historic places and to engage the public in the project

1
"Save the Frederick Douglass Home!," *Washington Bee*, January 6, 1917, 2.

2
Walker quoted in National Trust for Historic Preservation, "National Preservation and Philanthropic Groups Partner for $25 Million Funding Initiative to Transform Our Nation's Cultural Landscape," November 15, 2017, https://savingplaces.org/press-center/media-resources/national-preservation-and-philanthropic-groups-partner-for-25-million-funding-initiative-to-transform-our-nations-cultural-landscape.

3
McCullough quoted in Stephanie Meeks and Kevin Murphy, *The Past and Future City: How Historic Preservation Is Reviving America's Communities* (Washington, DC: Island Press, 2016), 163.

of preservation, has committed to tell the full breadth of American stories. In the past eight years, through our National Treasures program, we have advocated for the preservation of more than ninety nationally significant places that reflect a diverse range of histories. At our twenty-eight National Trust historic sites, we continue the ongoing work of not only expanding their narratives to incorporate the experiences of all their diverse inhabitants but also creating inclusive experiences that serve and engage the broadest possible audiences.

In the wake of the tragic events in Charlottesville, Virginia, in 2017, when white nationalists and their sympathizers rallied around a statue of Thomas Jefferson to spread an appalling message of divisiveness and hate, we have redoubled our efforts to expand the American narrative and tell a broader and truer story of our nation, one in which African Americans and other social, cultural, and economic groups are actors in history rather than spectators.

And so, in November 2017, the National Trust created the African American Cultural Heritage Action Fund. This initiative is focused on elevating the remarkable stories that describe centuries of African American activism, achievement, and community. By actively linking historic preservation with justice, equity, and activism, the Action Fund is underscoring the role of cultural preservation in telling our nation's full history and empowering activists and diverse communities to advocate on behalf of America's historic places. In the past two years, the National Trust invested $2.7 million across thirty-eight grants to preserve a diverse and national collection of places and stories and launched four new National Treasure advocacy campaigns to honor historic icons like Nina Simone and John and Alice Coltrane. Additionally, at our own National Trust historic sites, we have created new exhibitions and works of art focused on the experiences of African Americans, expanded our connections with descendant communities, and established best practices for this work, while also reclaiming spaces where African Americans lived and worked to tell their stories.

Through this work, the Action Fund is shifting the national conversation about the significance of African American history. By protecting and preserving more stories of Black contributions to our nation, we hope to foster truth, healing, and reconciliation. Just as important, we want to inspire a new generation of diverse activists to take up the standard and recognize preservation as a tool for social justice in their own communities. To this end, the Action Fund is exploring new approaches to strengthen our urgent moral imperative and expand our professional toolkit in collaboration with an esteemed National Advisory Council and a cadre of emerging and established artists, scholars, and community leaders. In communities across the country, we have already seen firsthand that preservation can be redemptive, holistic, and transformative, and that working to create an American historical landscape that speaks truthfully about who we are can change how we relate to one another as diverse citizens and neighbors in profound and positive ways.

— CULTURAL HERITAGE AND DISPLACEMENT IN HISTORICALLY AFRICAN AMERICAN NEIGHBORHOODS

4
Preservation Green Lab, *Older, Smaller, Better: Measuring How the Character of Buildings and Blocks Influences Urban Vitality*, National Trust for Historic Preservation, 2014, http://forum.savingplaces.org/connect/community-home/librarydocuments/viewdocument?DocumentKey=83ebde9b-8a23-458c-a70f-c66b46b6f714; Preservation Green Lab, *The Atlas of ReUrbanism: Summary Report*, National Trust for Historic Preservation, 2016, http://forum.savingplaces.org/viewdocument/report-atlas-of-reurbanism-buildi.

As a component of the African American Cultural Heritage Action Fund, the National Trust's Research and Policy Lab is conducting new research on the connections between preservation, cultural heritage, and displacement in historically African American neighborhoods in ten cities across the United States. Years of complex economic factors, structural racism, and systemic divestment and neglect have resulted in the disproportionate presence of vacant and dilapidated buildings in African American neighborhoods across the country today. Eager to erase signs of disrepair, city-led initiatives often seek expedient solutions through indiscriminate demolition and condemnation—erasing, along with it, irreplaceable physical connections to community identity. As historic structures age, the challenges of preserving them and the neighborhoods they anchor multiply. Preservation asks if there is an alternative to large-scale demolition and promotes development that is sensitive to the values of vulnerable and impacted communities. To drive social innovation and action, we are conducting targeted, place-based research to inform new arguments for creating more just American cities, where communities of color will benefit from responsible and inclusive preservation policy and practice.

Our work seeks to address the following questions:
- How does the changing physical and social character of urban neighborhoods influence housing affordability and displacement in cities with significant African American populations and in neighborhoods with significant African American history?
- How do the challenges facing historically African American neighborhoods compare to the challenges facing cities as a whole? Do historically African American neighborhoods face especially acute or severe threats?
- What existing and new tools could help cities to leverage their historic assets in support of improved social, environmental, and economic outcomes? How might the preservation and reuse of older, smaller, and historic buildings foster more racially just and equitable communities?

The Cultural Heritage and Displacement in Historically African American Neighborhoods study builds upon the Research and Policy Lab's expertise in statistical modeling, spatial mapping, and policy analysis established in previous studies that linked older buildings and blocks to higher social, economic, and environmental resilience.[4] The lab is expanding this research through analysis of ten cities with significant African American history and populations: Atlanta, Birmingham, Chicago, Los Angeles, Louisville, New York, Oakland, Philadelphia, St. Louis, and Washington, DC. Using spatial analysis of secondary data, the study documents the economic, demographic, and real estate changes that occurred in these cities between 2009 and 2016 and assesses how building age, new development, demolition, and other aspects of the built environment have influenced displacement pressure.

Though the research focuses on historically African American neighborhoods, we explore social and economic dimensions of exclusion alongside race. Our primary measure of economic displacement in the study combines data on the changing cost of rental housing and the changing demographic profile of a census tract. We observed the intersections of this economic displacement index alongside each census tract's potential status as a historically African American place. Furthermore, we worked with ten research fellows to better understand the perspectives of residents of historically African American neighborhoods and perceptions of neighborhood change, regardless of the specific mechanism or mode of exclusion.

Insights into the Dimensions of Exclusion

Our spatial and statistical analysis clearly demonstrates three broad findings: First, the number of African American residents in cities and urban neighborhoods has diminished in recent years, and the decline is most precipitous in historically African American neighborhoods. Second, historically African American neighborhoods are underrepresented in local and national historic designation programs. And third, some of the most commonly used tools of historic preservation—historic district designation and Federal Historic Tax Credits—sometimes exacerbate challenges of affordability and displacement.

In many parts of the country, the African American proportion of cities' populations declined between 2009 and 2016. In aggregate, the ten cities included in the study experienced a net increase in total population of about 215,000 people between 2009 and 2016, but at the same time, these cities experienced a net *decrease* of more than 200,000 African American residents. Between 2009 and 2016, the African American proportion of the population declined in eight of the ten study cities. (Louisville and Philadelphia are the exceptions.)

The changes in the proportions of African American residents citywide are modest when compared to changes within those cities' historically African American neighborhoods, where the population changes were much more pronounced. In this study, we defined historically African American neighborhoods as census tracts where there were majority African American populations in at least four of the past five decennial census counts (1970–2010). The proportion of Black residents dropped in the historically African American neighborhoods of nine of the ten study cities. In half of the cities studied, the proportion of Blacks in the population of historically African American neighborhoods declined by greater than 10 percent between 2009 and 2016. Chicago's historically African American neighborhoods lost more than 95,000 Black residents. In New York, historically African American neighborhoods lost nearly 50,000 African American residents. Historically African American neighborhoods in the two California study cities, Los Angeles and Oakland, lost 12 percent and 18 percent of their African American populations, respectively.

By working from an operational definition of historically African American neighborhoods and by comparing the locations of such census tracts to local and National Register historic district information, we are able to statistically assess the degree to which there are disparities between historically African American neighborhoods and other neighborhoods in the study cities. We find that local historic districts have been established less frequently in African American neighborhoods compared to other neighborhoods in seven of the ten study cities and that National Register historic districts are less commonly found in historically African American neighborhoods in eight of the ten study cities. Racial disparities in local designation are especially pronounced in Washington, DC, where 30 percent of historically African American tracts intersected a local historic district, compared to 90 percent of all other DC tracts; and in Oakland, where 25 percent of all historically African American tracts intersected a local historic district, compared to 41 percent of all other tracts. The historically and culturally significant places in these neighborhoods that are currently undesignated and unprotected may face even greater threat of demolition as the local African American populations confront displacement.

Our findings also raise questions about the impacts of historic district designation on housing affordability and economic displacement. Using spatial regression analysis, we assessed the impact of historic district designation status—along with an array of other built environment, development activity, and demographic measures—on economic displacement, where economic displacement was defined as a proportional increase in rent, decrease in low-income households, and decrease in adult residents without college degrees. We find that the proportion of land in a tract that falls within a local historic district serves as a significant predictor of economic displacement in three of the ten study cities: New York, Oakland, and St. Louis. We did not find statistically significant links between National Register historic district designation status and economic displacement in any of the ten study cities.

While we attempted to remove any historic districts designated after 2009 from our analysis, we did not measure fluctuations in the housing market or demographic trends prior to 2009, nor did we carefully match census tracts intersecting historic districts with similar census tracts that did not. Given this, our methodology does not allow us to demonstrate any causal relationship between historic district designation and subsequent economic displacement. Nevertheless, the findings suggest that preservationists interested in mitigating impacts on affordability and neighborhood change should tread lightly and think critically about the potential for unintended consequences, particularly in urban neighborhoods where displacement is of great concern.

Insights from New Preservation Voices

Given that much of the statistical analysis portion of the research project was managed by the National Trust's Research and Policy Lab using secondary data, we had to look elsewhere for local, city-specific insights and perceptions. To gain those perspectives and incorporate different voices and backgrounds into the work, we sought ten emerging scholars with personal experience in each study city to research the relationships between affordability, displacement, historic preservation, and planning at the neighborhood level. During summer 2018, this group of research fellows got to work. 5 The fellows brought a diversity of academic disciplines to the work, ranging from historic preservation to sociology and museum studies, which made the case studies even more varied in terms

5
The research fellows were Shaonta' Allen (University of Cincinnati), Julia Cohen (University of Pennsylvania), Akilah Favors (University of California, Berkeley), Jeran Herbert (Alabama A&M University), Ni'Shele Jackson (Wellesley University), Emily Junker (Columbia University), Kaelyn Rodriguez (University of California, Los Angeles), TK Smith (Saint Louis University), and Theodore Wilhite (University of the District of Columbia).

6
Mark Riley and David
Harvey, "Landscape
Archaeology, Heritage
and the Community
in Devon: An Oral
History Approach,"
*International Journal of
Heritage Studies* 11, no.
4 (2005): 269–288.

7
Iago Otero, Marti
Boada, and Joan David
Tabara, "Social-
Ecological Heritage
and the Conservation
of Mediterranean
Landscapes under
Global Change: Case
Study in Olzinelles
(Catalonia)," *Land Use
Policy* 30 (2013): 25–37.

of orientation and focus. Each fellow also interviewed local stakeholders to the greatest extent possible to ensure that the case studies captured what was happening "on the ground." An important aspect of social inclusion in historic preservation is diversifying who defines the values ascribed to older places and how historic preservation can serve different purposes— such as the ways it can promote social justice by amplifying marginalized stories, preserve affordable housing, and foster economic development without displacement.

For example, research fellow Shaonta' Allen elected to analyze local social media content to examine how anticipated development is affecting West Louisville and how residents envision the neighborhood's future. From the perspective of residents, sociocultural displacement was occur- ring in West Louisville long before signs of economic displacement began to appear. In the case of West Louisville, residents assert that long-term disinvestment in the historic neighborhood park system and the current disparate policing of African Americans who use the parks are at odds with the ways these small pockets of greenery have served as important places for gathering, celebrating, and community building among residents.

In another case, fellow TK Smith interviewed St. Louis residents and historians about their memories of historically African American neighbor- hoods that were demolished for the construction of buildings for Saint Louis University. Thousands of residents were made homeless without adequate support for relocation, and campus resources remain overwhelmingly exclusive to students although the surrounding community is in need of complex social and financial repair. The neighborhood of Midtown has a long history of transformation, and Smith's oral histories demonstrate that its African American communities were not completely vulnerable to decision-making by large entities like a university but possessed levels of agency and political power to resist the taking of the neighborhoods as long as they could. Much like the oral histories conducted by Mark Riley and David Harvey with individuals who farmed and worked land in southwest- ern England around World War II, Smith finds that oral histories derived from people's interactions with specific places and physical landmarks can challenge dominant narratives in terms of who is most entitled to occupy places and who knows best what the future of the area should be. 6

As a new generation of scholars, from diverse backgrounds, the fellows listened to community members and did not bring preconceived expectations. A number of findings from the fellows' case studies may be unique examples of the "powers of heritage" and "memory work" identified in the literature review. Heritage, more broadly defined, can be considered as the exchange of skills and adaptive knowledge through physical objects, such as landmarks, and through intangible social practices, like songs, stories, and religious celebrations. 7 Through the fellows' meticulous and conscientious research, the knowledge exchanged through heritage here demonstrates personal experiences of vulnerability and local strategies used to resist the quickening pace of gentrification and the loss of affordable housing in historically African American neighborhoods.

Given the findings that African American neighborhoods are under- represented in historical designation and that some traditional preservation tools may exacerbate issues of affordability and displacement, it is clear that additional research is needed to better understand the potential for preservation-based solutions. Future work should explore the practices that local stakeholders are undertaking to make the best promises of historic preservation—like economic rehabilitation, sense of shared identity, and reconciliation—viable in diverse communities.

Toward a More Inclusive Future

To build a more inclusive preservation practice and support more inclusive outcomes through preservation, the National Trust, through the Action Fund, has engaged diverse stakeholders of historically African American neighborhoods and emerging scholars working on these issues. By sharing their perspectives with broader preservation audiences, we can collectively understand the many ways that the practice of preservation and its meaning (whether positive, negative, or absent) affect our communities and daily lives. Spatial data and statistical analysis can highlight opportunities for preservationists to address racial disparities in historic designation and reimagine preservation practice as a force supporting strong communities rich with culture and opportunity.

This work is sometimes uncomfortable, and its challenges are often complex, but we believe these discomforts and manifold complications represent important and productive grounds for shaping a stronger preservation movement and a more just society. We believe an inclusive future requires inclusive public policy and public financing, where targeted revitalization and investment address the inherent social and economic disparities in cities. Through place-based research, creative public policy, and socially driven development, we can demonstrate the unique role of cultural preservation and professional practice to more effectively drive social change and social innovation in underserved communities of color.

Of course, this work is far from complete. Our research to date serves as a conversation starter, raising difficult questions for preservationists and for communities experiencing displacement. In the face of exclusion, how might preservationists think differently about the standards set by the secretary of the interior, the notion of integrity, or the value of intangible heritage? How might preservationists better address physical, social, and cultural preservation in tandem? To uncover and understand what is truly needed in neighborhoods experiencing displacement and disinvestment, the National Trust is committed to partnering and engaging with the field and multidisciplinary community-based organizations and institutions.

— Examining Questions of Exclusion
— Shifting Policy Toward Inclusion
— Challenging and Redefining Narratives
— Connecting to Community Development

Serving All Americans: The Case for Relevancy, Diversity, and Inclusion in the National Park Service

An interview with Sangita Chari

Shifting Policy Toward Inclusion

ERICA AVRAMI
As the program manager of the National Park Service (NPS) Office of
Relevancy, Diversity, and Inclusion, you are deeply engaged in questions of
cultural heritage and social inclusion. What led you to this work?

SANGITA CHARI
When I think about how I arrived here—how inclusion, justice, and equity
became guiding concepts for what I do—I'd have to start with my own
personal experiences growing up. My parents were two of the very, very
early immigrants from India to the United States. My father came in the
early 1960s, so until college, I was the only person from India at school, at
the playground, in Girl Scouts, in the grocery store, anywhere. In everything
I did, I was the only person with Indian heritage, and oftentimes there
might have been only one or two other people of color. Growing up in the
United States, isolation was just a part of who I was. It didn't really occur
to me as a child that there was any other way to be as an American, other
than when we would go to community events and I would be with other
Indians. I have a very strong memory of what that felt like—the comfort
of being around people who understood me on a deeper level—even if I
didn't have the words for what that meant. My parents also lived in the
Middle East for a number of years, and there I had a different experience
of being the "other," but this time being very, very aware of economic and
social hierarchies, and where people from India fell in that order. There
was a very obvious sense of racism and mistreatment. So I always held onto
these two experiences, one of racial isolation as a child, and one of seeing
blatant discrimination that was really harmful, and having a visceral sense
of that—not just watching, but really owning that in my heart.

I have a degree in anthropology, and I studied international relations.
I have always, throughout my career, worked in arenas where I had the ability to address issues of inclusion, whether it was at Amnesty International
as a youth organizer or with the United Way of Metropolitan Atlanta,
where I was part of a groundbreaking team that was looking to reshape
the way United Way worked with the nonprofit organizations it served. I
was part of a movement away from being strictly a funder to really being
a community-building institution. We were looking more broadly at our
influence as a relationship broker—with state government, with county
government—to see what we could do on the ground through organizing
and bringing people to the table, really expanding the notion of what an
institution is within a community.

Working in museums, where I was a grant writer and employed in
different positions, enabled me to understand the power of cultural institutions to shape identity. My master's thesis, where I looked at interracial
relationships between Indo-Trinidadian women and Afro-Trinidadian
men, allowed me to see how what seems like a personal relationship actually has an enormous impact on identity, on politics, and on the way that
groups interact with each other—how just that very personal relationship
can really disrupt power dynamics.

All of that brought me here to the National Park Service, where I spent
five years as the grants coordinator for the national Native American Graves
Protection and Repatriation Program. In that time, I was able to draw on

all the work I had done around community grant making, as well as my interest in human rights, for one position where all of that was at play. It really solidified my understanding of heritage, especially of heritage being connected to identity, and being connected to one's sense of dignity and inclusion within a larger society.

> *Through a dedicated Office of Relevancy, Diversity, and Inclusion, how is the NPS seeking to change its internal institutional dynamics as well as its relationship to the public?*

My NPS position, program manager for relevancy, diversity, and inclusion, is relatively new, and it is certainly very unusual in the Department of the Interior. The former director of the National Park Service, Jon Jarvis, shepherded the NPS through its centennial in 2016. He was really trying to break open this notion that parks are isolated, boundary-defined places where people are visitors, to help people really see parks as embedded in the American landscape, and to help us at the NPS see that our responsibility was to all citizens, whether they came to the parks or not. Former NPS deputy director Mickey Fearn asserted that if we were truly going to embrace relevancy, diversity, and inclusion as guiding principles and as a way of working, we needed to embed them into the infrastructure of the National Park Service, which meant that these ideas needed to have a home and a full-time employee on a team that had resources and access.

As a direct report to the associate director for what is now called Workforce and Inclusion, the office has always had a measure of independence. Not being tied to formal human resource or EEO structures allows for greater flexibility. When it's a leadership issue, I can engage at that level. When it's a research and data analysis issue, I can look at it from that angle. When it's a training issue, I can look at it from that angle. I'm not siloed into one particular perspective, and that's been really, really helpful because it's allowed me to be nimble and evolve with the culture.

> *In many respects, you are not only transcending bureaucratic silos, you are transcending different concepts of community—the people who work for the NPS, the people who visit national parks, the people who live around parks, and even, as you said, everybody who is living in the country. Within the broad mission of the NPS, how is this mandate communicated, and how is it interpreted by staff?*

To be totally honest, it depends on whom you talk to. I'm seeing a lot of forward movement, particularly as times change and we see new faces. There are those who are really in alignment with this office, who see the benefits of it and want to work with us. They are the innovators in the NPS. They are putting these concepts into practice and challenging themselves to think about how they're interacting in the community—who's not there, who is. How are you engaging with everyone, and how are you having those conversations internally?

But the NPS operates over four hundred sites, each with its own management structure. We're highly decentralized, and so it really depends on having the leadership to support that work, because it takes a fundamental shift in time, energy, and resources to work that way. Without leadership on board, it's a struggle. We also have a very tenured workforce. Many staff members have spent their entire career with the NPS, and the cultural norms, systems, and processes in place support a particular way of working, so opening up to new ways of doing things can sometimes be a challenge.

Where I find myself, as an office, working most is in challenging the workforce of the NPS to consider how we ensure the integrity of our mission, our values, and what we want to do. Several times, in the six years now that I've been in this position, that has come to a head. People have said, "We can't tell this story with any integrity if we don't look internally." For example, another significant area of concern is our workforce demographics. Our workforce is over 80 percent white. How does that impact our integrity as an agency to tell the story of civil rights? Those are the kinds of questions and conversations that can happen because of this office. It creates the space for the organization to have critically important, if uncomfortable, conversations.

A related dialogue came to a head with the sexual harassment case at the Grand Canyon in 2016. In 2017 the National Park Service conducted its first survey to assess employee attitudes, behaviors, and perceptions of harassment within the work environment. The results showed that nearly 40 percent of employees had experienced some form of harassment or assault behaviors in the twelve months preceding the survey. The survey speaks to the effort needed if we are to align our values and norms with our mission. How do you maintain integrity with an external audience when integrity within the institution is compromised? What is it about the way we are set up that allows for a culture where harassment can not only exist but, in some cases, even thrive? What is underlying this system?

While people may not see harassment as an issue of diversity and inclusion, I see it as extreme exclusion. The secretary of the interior is committed to creating an ethical work culture, one that is transparent and accountable, where harassment is not tolerated. He has reiterated the importance of that to our field employees in particular. The conversation over time has changed and shifted, but if you look underneath that, there's been a steady march toward the root cause of these issues, which is the fundamental operational structure of the National Park Service.

> *There is a powerful sense of accountability in this approach: in order to pro- mote diversity and inclusion, the NPS must understand the relationship of its internal system to its ability to externalize these shared values. As you continue these efforts internally, how do you see it working externally, toward empowering other communities and serving multiple publics and diverse narratives?*

The National Park Service is doing amazing and important community work throughout the country and territories. We are continually looking for ways to lift up and highlight this work. What I'm looking for is the tipping point where it goes from these localized, disparate opportunities to a funda- mental operational norm where the policies, the structures, the programs, the way we hire people, and the way we engage with communities creates permanent, meaningful, lasting change. It's about asking the question in a different way. For example, when we hire people into a park, particularly at the superintendent level, are we consistently considering what it would look like to have a meaningful, sustained, engaged connection to the community the park is in? Are we hiring somebody who has knowledge of that community or who has a commitment to that community that will be sustained? And when we hand off the park from one superintendent to the next, is that commitment being preserved? Have we really looked at what our values are and integrated them into our hiring practices?

It's not just about discrete projects; it's about an actual ongoing relationship that grows and evolves. I think we still don't have the infrastructure in place to ensure that that's happening, to expand all of these examples from discrete projects into a way of working that redesigns our relationships to communities.

> *Much of this work toward community-oriented impact is understandably focused on the sites that the National Park Service operates. In the realm of preservation, the NPS plays a significant role in communities far beyond the national parks themselves, as it is the agency that largely oversees the federal preservation system. Can you speak to some of the challenges and opportunities of promoting inclusion in preservation policy beyond the sites for which the NPS is directly responsible?*

We are starting to think about barriers to engaging communities of color that exist in legislation and in the policy process. One way we are working to expand the way we think about preservation is through theme studies, such as the American Latino Heritage Initiative and the LGBTQ Heritage Initiative. That's been a very deliberate attempt to expand the story, create an avenue for a more diverse group of people to engage in the process, and start to really diversify the spaces that tell the full breadth of the American story.

I believe the NPS has an opportunity, at the national level, to fundamentally change the concept of what it means to preserve and to shift the language of the dialogue around preservation. We have success stories, stories of working with community partners to figure out: "How do we bring the language of preservation to you so that you know that you can even join these processes?"

It means looking systematically at the barriers in the laws, in the process. Who's on the panels? What kinds of projects are coming to life? What are the barriers to those projects' success? How do you start having conversations that open up space for other kinds of projects to move forward? How do you provide technical assistance in ways that even the playing field?

The inclusion of marginalized communities may be in the spirit of legislation, of laws, of acts. But that does not mean it is reflected in the written documents or in the processes those documents produce. It's a practice of privilege to pick and choose when to act in the spirit of something and when to limit actions to a specific interpretation of the written word. One of the biggest challenges, from my perspective, is that telling the more accurate story—the one that's more inclusive, the one that is potentially less happy—takes a great deal of skill. It takes a willingness to look beyond the obvious, it takes resilience, and it takes the ability to weather pushback when the public is challenged to rethink its assumptions, and that's a very real challenge in the National Park Service.

The National Park Service is a highly mission-driven organization. And so, for us, it's really about challenging people to think about what the mission of the NPS is and how the work that we do must change if we're truly going to preserve and protect for future generations. Who are those future generations, and what is the work that needs to be done?

Looking at this from the perspective of underrepresented publics rather than that of the NPS, what do you see as key issues that will help these communities enhance their agency in preserving their heritage and engage in the federal preservation system? And what can preservationists do to support such efforts?

It's about that visionary mindset, not just on the part of the preservation community but within underrepresented communities as well. The community has to understand the connection between preservation and the benefit it has to the community. As much as preservation is about place, it's actually a very intangible concept, particularly if it's competing against more commonly understood benefits such as good schools, health care, or economic viability. Preservation and identity should go hand in hand, the firmer you are in your identity—frankly, that's the foundation to the economics, to the education, to everything else. At least that's what I have found personally. The more I know who I am, where I come from, who my people are, the more engaged I am in the rest of the world, and the more open I am to diversity and to new ideas and new ways of thinking.

It's about helping communities see the "why" behind preservation. I think if the preservation field is willing to engage in that question and accept an equal relationship with the local community, it could be a powerful partner. If the local community is not engaged, it may be because they don't even know that preservation is a possibility. In addition, the preservation field may not be a very compelling community to be part of, especially for younger people. As long as the field is dominated by a way of thinking that outsiders find to be stifling, people will not engage. If the preservation community itself is, frankly, not fun, is not interesting, is not curious, is not willing to try something different, is not willing to let go of stuff that actually only they care about, it doesn't matter what they do. They're not going to create the change they want. And honestly, with technology and with everything else that's advancing at this incredible pace, I think these marginalized communities are going to get what they need in different ways. And then the preservation field risks obsolescence.

Because of my work at the NPS, I'm knee-deep in thinking about systems and operations. Diversity and inclusion are really about dismantling the specific ways in which we have operated that are detrimental to everybody. And I think that that's where the conversation gets exciting, because then it's not about terms we ascribe to one another—the white man or the straight person or the person who grew up with affluence as opposed to the "other." What it becomes about is our capacity to create the change needed to break down silos, to create deliberate connections, and to solve problems that may have felt entrenched but really just needed a new perspective and a willingness to change.

Los Angeles's Historic Contexts:
Pathways to Inclusion in Preservation

Janet Hansen and Sara Delgadillo Cruz

Shifting Policy Toward Inclusion

Historic contexts, and the heritage surveys they inform, are the foundation of municipal preservation programs. But too often these tools, even today, reflect a limited set of community interests, are overly tied to aesthetics, and focus on buildings and monumental architecture. However, preservation practice is slowly shifting to be more inclusive of ethnic, social, and cultural values and to encompass heritage resources that reflect these values. In Los Angeles, SurveyLA fueled efforts to engage all Angelenos in the city's heritage preservation program. [1] This citywide heritage survey included a wide range of historic themes to reflect multiple narratives and directly involve the community in telling these stories. Now the survey framework and results are not only accelerating the designation of resources that represent the city's diversity, but also support broader preservation planning goals and objectives to celebrate and protect these historic community resources.

1
SurveyLA, the first citywide survey of Los Angeles, was a grant-funded multiyear partnership between the City of Los Angeles and the Getty Foundation.

2
See "Elements of Survey Planning," in *Guidelines for Local Surveys: A Basis for Preservation Planning* (Washington, DC: National Park Service, 1977), https://www.nps.gov/nr/publications/bulletins/nrb24/chapter1.htm.

— VOICING DIVERSITY THROUGH HISTORIC CONTEXTS

Historic contexts are narrative, technical documents that guide the survey and evaluation of heritage resources. They are not intended to be definitive histories; rather, they are place-based and relate to heritage resource types—buildings, structures, objects, sites, landscapes, and districts that represent important themes in the history and development of a geographic area. Although the relationship between surveys and historic contexts is explained in the 1977 National Park Service (NPS) publication *Guidelines for Local Surveys: A Basis for Preservation Planning*, the use of historic contexts has been recently reinvigorated, rediscovered, and (in some places) newly discovered as a means to incorporate places associated with ethnic and cultural histories into survey work and preservation planning. [2]

Spanish Colonial and Mexican Era Settlement, 1781–1849

Pre-Consolidation Communities of Los Angeles, 1862–1932

Residential Development and Suburbanization, 1880–1980
- Deed Restricion and Segregation
- Ethnic Enclaves

Commercial Development
- Commercial Identity

Public and Private Institutional Development, 1850–1980
- Religion & Spirituality
- Community Organizations, Social Services & Insitutions
- Civil Rights – Ethnic and Gender Equality

Industrial Development, 1850–1980
- Labor History

The Entertainment Industry, 1908–1980

Architecture and Engineering, 1850–1980

Cultural Landscapes, 1850–1980
- Japanese Landscapes

FIG. 1:
The nine contexts that make up the Los Angeles Historic Context, with representative themes that inform the ethnic and cultural contexts.

3
SurveyLA incorporated evaluation standards using local and state designation criteria as well as National Register of Historic Places criteria.

4
The 1780s are the beginning of the period of Spanish and Colonial Era settlement; 1980 is the established end date for SurveyLA.

5
The Chinese American context was initially completed in 2013 but was not published at that time. Under the later "Asian Americans in Los Angeles" National Park Service Underrepresented Communities Grant (2016–2018), the context was further developed and then published. See: "Historic Themes," Los Angeles City Planning, https://planning.lacity.org/preservation-design/historic-resources/historic-themes.

The Multiple Property Documentation (MPD) approach established by the NPS provides a framework for developing contexts relating to ethnic and cultural histories and is in use by both public and private heritage agencies and organizations throughout the United States. This approach uses one or more historic contexts to streamline the nomination of related properties to the National Register of Historic Places. Using the MPD approach, each context establishes significant themes and topics relating to ethnic and cultural histories, identifies important property types, and provides specific guidance or eligibility standards to guide evaluation and designation. Often, resources significant for their association with social, cultural, or ethnic history are unremarkable for their physical appearance. The heritage value of these resources is based less on physical attributes and more on the strength of the association with a particular theme.

— ETHNIC AND CULTURAL DIVERSITY IN LOS ANGELES'S HISTORIC CONTEXTS

Development of Los Angeles's historic context began in 2007 with the inception of SurveyLA and the adoption of the MPD approach. 3 The historic context covers the area within the geographic boundaries of the incorporated City of Los Angeles and the period from 1780 to 1980. 4 During the planning of the survey, the contexts and related themes were defined in broad terms, with the intent to refine, revise, and elaborate as the field surveys progressed. One of the most challenging aspects of this early phase was creating a structure for a context that integrated ethnic and cultural histories citywide. Los Angeles is a large, complex, and diverse city with more than 140 nationalities now represented in the population. While it is common practice in the preservation field to write stand-alone narratives for ethnic and cultural themes, this approach fails to take intersectionality into account and does little to convey the complexity of immigration, settlement, and migration patterns in Los Angeles. Different groups have settled and moved throughout the city over time, leaving unique and layered imprints on the built environment. Because of these overlapping histories, SurveyLA's ethnic and cultural themes are published separately yet are purposefully integrated within the larger framework of the city's historic context. *FIG. 1*

The *Chinese Americans in Los Angeles* historic context, the first to be taken on, was a testing ground of sorts for integrating ethnic and cultural themes into the overall framework of the context as well as for implementing a format that could be used consistently. It was also useful for designing an outreach approach to involve diverse communities as stakeholders in the process of context development. Although these early efforts were rudimentary at best, they served as the starting point for the more thoughtful efforts to come. The city subsequently published contexts relating to Los Angeles's lesbian, gay, bisexual, and transgender (LGBT) community, and its Jewish, Latino, Chinese, Japanese, Korean, Thai, Filipino, and African American populations. Labor history overlaps with these ethnic and cultural histories and also covers the socioeconomic topic of worker housing. 5 *FIG. 2*

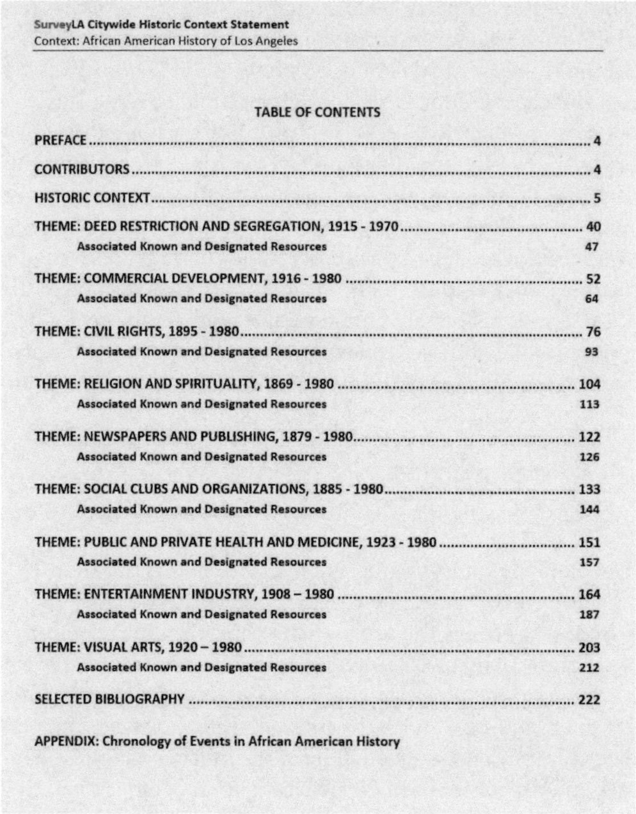

SurveyLA Citywide Historic Context Statement
Context: African American History of Los Angeles

TABLE OF CONTENTS

FIG. 2: African American History of Los Angeles Context *table of contents. Courtesy of Los Angeles City Planning.*

While ethnic and cultural contexts are meant to be inclusive of diverse and underrepresented communities, contexts themselves can be exclusionary when not all groups are recognized. Several considerations were taken into account to set priorities for completing ethnic and cultural contexts for Los Angeles. First, the period covered by the historic context ends in 1980. This means that populations only more recently present in Los Angeles have not been as well represented in SurveyLA and that the resources identified for other, longer-established groups generally date from before 1980. However, because the overall framework is designed to be expandable, more contexts will be added over time to take into account these new populations, recent histories, and additional themes and property types not yet known. [6]

A second consideration in prioritizing contexts was limited funding. Ethnic and cultural contexts were wholly funded by grants from the California Office of Historic Preservation and the NPS. [7] Grant cycles ranged from one to two years with a limited amount of funds available during each cycle. In addition, the grants required a substantial match; with no cash match available, this meant in-kind city staff time. [8] As a result, the city generally took on only a single context per year, which restricted the number that could be completed as part of the larger

6
Additional themes and property types may include intangible cultural heritage.

7
Context development was not included in the SurveyLA grant agreement between the city and the Getty Foundation.

8
Los Angeles City Planning contracted with heritage preservation consultants to write the contexts under the direction of the Office of Historic Resources.

9
Field surveys
were conducted
from 2009 to 2017.
Context development
and refinement
continued afterward.
The final ethnic and
cultural themes were
published in 2018.

10
As implied by this
statement, there is
naturally a degree of
overlap in the ethnic
and cultural contexts.
These overlaps
are referenced for
the reader in the
introduction section
of the narrative
contexts.

11
Historic Resources
Group for the City
of Los Angeles,
*Women's Rights
in Los Angeles*,
Los Angeles City
Planning, Office of
Historic Resources,
September 2018.

SurveyLA project. 9 A final consideration in prioritizing contexts was the expected number of eligible resources under local, state, and national designation programs.

Research for developing the city's ethnic and cultural contexts brings unique challenges. Most notably, the body of existing scholarship differs greatly among the contexts. The historical experiences of Thai Americans in Los Angeles, for example, remain largely untold, primarily due to the community's arrival in the 1950s. Also, many sources are available only in the native language. Some topics, such as Korean Americans in the performing, visual, and literary arts, have not yet been well documented in English. While in a few cases interpreter services were used, the contexts relied primarily on English-language sources. Research for the women's rights context brought to light a number of issues that underscore the difficulties in equitably representing all populations within a single topic. 10 As explained in the introduction to the *Women's Rights in Los Angeles* context:

> Presenting a history of women's rights in Los Angeles has several challenges. First, the documentation of women's history has historically been underreported in traditional media. Second, the activities of women of color were documented and reported even less by traditional media, and archival materials from the clubs and organizations for women of color have largely been lost to history. Third, the contributions of Los Angeles women to the suffrage movement have often been overlooked by scholars focused on the east coast or northern California and its cache of archival materials.
>
> Lastly, women's history has been written primarily by white women, without acknowledgment that the forms of oppression experienced by white middle- and upper-class heterosexual women were different from those experienced by women of other ethnicities, cultural backgrounds, and sexual orientations. This results in an incomplete telling that fails to take intersectionality into account. Documented examples of the participation of women of color are included here, but likely represent a small sample of their actual contributions. As a result, these examples should be viewed less as a comprehensive telling of the story and more as inspiration for additional scholarship in the future. 11

Telling the stories of ethnic and cultural places requires broad-based outreach programs that engage all segments of the population to identify important places, as well as to write and review narrative contexts. For each of Los Angeles's ethnic and cultural contexts, outreach strategies included the identification of key individuals, institutions, and organizations. Early involvement by these experts helped guide themes, establish relevant periods of significance, and identify geographic areas where resources may be present. This involvement focused research and reconnaissance efforts and ultimately informed the field surveys.

Over time, outreach strategies evolved to include varying and flexible approaches, including the following:

- Asking for assistance from scholars and students at colleges and universities with specialized ethnic and cultural studies programs.
- Engaging community/topical experts to work with survey teams as part of the research and reconnaissance tasks.
- Organizing public meetings and workshops, facilitated by city staff and context consultants, to explain the overall purpose and objectives and to outline a plan for public participation.
- Creating historic context advisory committees composed of stakeholders, community leaders, scholars, neighborhood and topical experts, and others to promote community interest, identify important themes and relevant cultural resources, and review and provide input on context drafts and other deliverables.
- Partnering with communities and heritage organizations to promote widespread and long-term use of the historic contexts.

— ASIAN AMERICANS IN LOS ANGELES: A CASE STUDY IN COMMUNITY PARTNERSHIPS

The Office of Historic Resources (OHR) received a National Park Service Underrepresented Communities Grant to produce the historic contexts for Los Angeles's Asian American communities, specifically the Chinese, Japanese, Korean, Filipino, and Thai American communities. Geographically, the contexts cover the history and development of five Los Angeles neighborhoods that have been designated as Preserve America Communities: Little Tokyo, Thai Town, Historic Filipinotown, Koreatown, and Chinatown—but the contexts also include other areas in the city where these groups have settled and lived.

The contexts were completed in partnership with Asian American community leaders, scholars, and activists, with the help of a diverse project advisory committee and a series of public meetings and workshops. The project resulted in five discrete contexts that are part of the city's historic context, as well as a National Register of Historic Places Multiple Property Documentation Form titled "Asian Americans in Los Angeles, 1850–1980" and an associated individual National Register nomination for the Filipino Christian Church. *FIG. 3*

FIG. 3: Filipino Christian Church, 301 North Union Avenue, Historic Filipinotown. Image courtesy of Los Angeles City Planning.

12
Koyoshi Uono, "The Factors Affecting the Geographical Aggregation and Dispersion of the Japanese Residents in the City of Los Angeles" (master's thesis, University of Southern California, 1927).

The collaboration of the city, project advisory committee, and community members throughout the two-year grant period resulted in the Asian Americans in Los Angeles Historic Context Symposium in October 2018. Held at the Filipino Christian Church, the event was cosponsored by the city and Asian and Pacific Island Americans in Historic Preservation. The intent of the symposium was not to celebrate the end of the grant project but rather to promote continued partnerships with the city and to encourage future community action. At the same time, the symposium offered an opportunity to follow up on the usefulness of contexts in identifying cultural resources, guide the formal designation of eligible properties, and potentially identify other means through which community heritage resources could be safeguarded.

— REDISCOVERING LOS ANGELES'S DIVERSITY

Research, reconnaissance surveys, and outreach efforts associated with context development have led to the rediscovery of significant ethnic and cultural places. Research for the Japanese American context, for example, uncovered a 1920s map of Uptown, a little-known enclave. 12 This turn-of-the-twentieth-century community was located east of downtown in what is today part of Koreatown. Further research identified a number of intact resources in the area relating to the early Japanese community, notably rooming houses for day laborers and gardeners. *FIGs. 4–5*

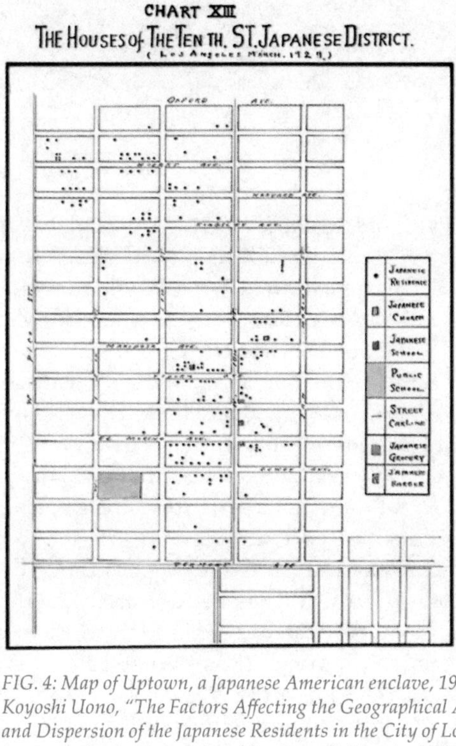

FIG. 4: Map of Uptown, a Japanese American enclave, 1927. From Koyoshi Uono, "The Factors Affecting the Geographical Aggregation and Dispersion of the Japanese Residents in the City of Los Angeles" (master's thesis, University of Southern California, 1927), 130.

77

FIG. 5: *Rooming House/Obayashi Employment at 564 North Virgil Avenue and Joyce Boarding House at 560 North Virgil Avenue. Image courtesy of Los Angeles City Planning.*

FIG. 6: *San Pedro Jewish Community Center at 1903 South Cabrillo Avenue. Image courtesy of Los Angeles City Planning.*

13
In 1961, the museum was divided to form the Los Angeles County Museum of History and Science and the Los Angeles County Museum of Art.

14
The Gay Liberation Front was founded in New York City in 1969 after the Stonewall riots. Kight was one of the founders of the Los Angeles chapter.

Other examples include the residence and studio of Beulah Woodard (1432 East 49th Street), a key figure in the African American visual arts community from the 1930s through the mid-1950s. Woodard was known for her sculptures; her 1935 solo exhibition at the Los Angeles Museum of History, Science, and Art made her the first African American artist to be featured at this public institution. 13 She helped create the Los Angeles Negro Art Association in 1937 and remained a key figure in the African American visual arts community until her death in 1955. The Morris Kight residence (1822 West 4th Street) was an important find for the city's LGBT history. Kight was a notable figure in the gay liberation movement, and the house also served as the founding location and early headquarters of the Los Angeles chapter of the Gay Liberation Front. 14 Another important discovery was the San Pedro Jewish Community Center (1903 South Cabrillo Avenue), dedicated in 1935, which traces its roots to the San Pedro Jewish Sisterhood. The sisterhood sold this property in 1955, after which it served as the Yugoslavian Women's Club and then the Italian American Club, evidencing the layering of ethnic and cultural histories over time. FIG. 6

15
The Historic-Cultural
Monuments program
is managed by the
Los Angeles City
Planning, Office of
Historic Resources.
The Cultural Heritage
Commission
recommends
and forwards
nominations to
the city council for
designation.

16
City Ordinance
121,971, Section 3,
approved May 1962.
Though the content
remains the same, in
2018 the Monument
Definition was
revised to Monument
Designation Criteria.
Ordinance No.
185472 amending
Section 22.171 of
Article 1, Chapter
9, Division 22 of
the Los Angeles
Administrative Code.

17
The National Register
has a fifty-year age
requirement for
eligibility, although
there is a Criteria
Consideration for
properties not yet
fifty years of age
but of exceptional
importance.

18
Currently, the
city does not hold
statistical analysis
data on the number
of Historic-Cultural
Monuments
associated with
ethnic and cultural
histories.

19
Historic-Cultural
Monuments can
be nominated and
designated despite
owner objection.

Although equitable inclusion of all communities in historic preserva-tion programs requires going beyond property designation, designation itself can be a significant step in integrating a wider range of histories and community narratives into planning initiatives. One of the logical outcomes of SurveyLA and the expansion of historical contexts has been to increase recognition and designation of properties associated with groups underrepresented in the city's list of Historic-Cultural Monuments and in the National Register of Historic Places. 15

While Los Angeles's Cultural Heritage Ordinance, adopted in 1962, did not specify criteria for designation of city Historic-Cultural Monuments (HCM), it did provide a definition that clearly addresses social and cultural history:

> For purposes of this ordinance, an historical or cultural monument is any site… building or structure of particular historic or cultural significance to the City of Los Angeles, such as historic structures or sites in which the broad cultural, political, economic or social history of the nation, state, or community is reflected or exemplified, or which are identified with historic personages or with important events in the main currents of national, state or local history, or which embody the distinguishing characteristics of an architectural-type specimen, inherently valuable for a study of a period style or method of construction, or a notable work of a master builder, designer, or architect whose individual genius influenced his age. 16

Although the ordinance was adopted prior to the National Register of Historic Places program, Los Angeles's designation criteria generally align with those of the National Register. But there are important differences. Los Angeles's criteria do not include "integrity," a set of standards by which a property is determined to "convey significance," and do not have an age requirement. 17 This gives the city leeway to recognize resources associated with more recent histories and those based on associative values rather than material or architectural integrity.

While the percentage of resources associated with ethnic and cul-tural histories is small in relation to the total number of city monuments, there are examples that demonstrate the city's early recognition of under-represented histories. 18 Importantly, the Los Angeles ordinance states that "any interested individual may apply for the proposed designation of a Monument." Most Historic-Cultural Monuments are, in fact, nomi-nated by property owners or interested individuals and organizations. 19 The Dunbar Hotel (HCM no. 131), designated in 1974, is evidence of these early inclusion efforts. Built in 1928, the hotel played a significant role in the social and political history of the thriving African American community along the Central Avenue corridor in the first half of the twentieth century. Commissioned by Drs. John and Vada Somerville, the property hosted the first national convention of the National Association for the Advancement of Colored People, and in the 1930s, the hotel's nightclub served as the stage for a multitude of internationally acclaimed jazz musicians.

Designation of the Kinney-Tabor House (HCM no. 926) in 2008 illustrates an important shift in the recognition of properties of ethnic and cultural importance. The original nomination in 1968 was denied because the building was not in its original location and the house had been altered. Irving Tabor worked for Abbot Kinney, who developed Venice, California. After Kinney's death and his widow's subsequent move to a convalescent home, the house was gifted to Tabor. In 1925 he tried to move in but was restricted by racial covenants and the objections of neighbors. Tabor therefore moved the house to Oakwood, an African American enclave in Venice. The 2008 nomination recognizes the importance of both Abbot Kinney and Irving Tabor as owners of the property and treats the house relocation as a significant event for both local history and the area's African American community. FIG. 7

Publication of the ethnic and cultural contexts is increasing public interest in new designations. The Tom of Finland House (HCM no. 1135)

FIG. 7: Kinney-Tabor House, 1310 South 6th Avenue, Venice. Image courtesy of Los Angeles City Planning.

FIG. 8: Edward Roybal Residence, 628 South Evergreen Avenue, Boyle Heights. Image courtesy of Los Angeles City Planning.

20
The nominations were prepared under the direction of the California Office of Historic Preservation and Los Angeles City Planning using NPS Underrepresented Communities Grants.

21
The nomination was made on behalf of Save Beverly Fairfax, an advocacy organization. In 2015 SurveyLA recorded the Orange Grove Avenue-Gardner Street Multi-Family Residential Historic District with roughly the same boundaries as the Beverly Fairfax Historic District. The Jewish History context, published in 2016, provided additional information to support the district's historical associations.

was identified in the LGBT context under the theme "Queer Art" as the Los Angeles-based home and studio of gay erotic artist Touko Laaksonen, more commonly known as Tom of Finland. The artist resided at the house during the last ten years of his life, during which he gained international recognition. The property is also the headquarters of the Tom of Finland Foundation. Forsythe Memorial School for Girls and the Edward Roybal Residence, both in Boyle Heights and listed in the National Register, were identified through research conducted for the statewide *Latinos in Twentieth Century California* context. 20 *Latino Los Angeles* followed on the heels of this context. The Forsythe School is an example of early Protestant outreach and church-based Americanization efforts in the form of social services, settlement houses, and schools. The school is also significant for its association with Japanese American history in Los Angeles. Known as Evergreen Hostel, the building was used in the period immediately following World War II as temporary living quarters for Japanese Americans. Although this association was noted in the National Register nomination, it was not included as a reason for significance. This omission underscores the need to amend existing nominations to address multiple narratives.

Another example is the Roybal Residence, home of Edward Roybal, champion of civil rights and equal access to education, health care, and housing. In 1949 Roybal became the first Mexican American to be elected to the Los Angeles City Council since 1883. In 1962 he was elected to the US Congress, making him the first California Latino elected to the House of Representatives in the twentieth century. FIG. 8

A third National Register designation is the Beverly Fairfax Historic District. Nomination of the district was a result of SurveyLA fieldwork and the Jewish History context. 21 The district is composed mostly of multifamily residences and is significant for the quality of its Period Revival-style architecture, as well as for its association with Los Angeles's Jewish history. The residential neighborhood played a key role in the westward shift of Los Angeles's Jewish population starting in the 1920s and was also critical to the establishment of Jewish businesses and institutions in the area. By the end of the 1940s, the district was firmly established as the residential anchor of Los Angeles's Jewish community. FIG. 9

FIG. 9: *North Stanley Avenue, Beverly Fairfax National Register Historic District. Image courtesy of Los Angeles City Planning.*

FIG. 10: Houses constructed for Goodyear Gardens, South Los Angeles. Image courtesy of Los Angeles City Planning.

SurveyLA field efforts in South Los Angeles uncovered the Goodyear Gardens neighborhood, a rare example of affordable worker housing located near factory jobs, developed and built by the Goodyear Tire & Rubber Company. In the 1920s Goodyear hired architects Sumner Hunt and Silas Burns to design the single-family houses in modest interpretations of popular architectural styles of the day. Goodyear Gardens remained largely occupied by workers and their families through the mid-twentieth century. While the neighborhood is not sufficiently intact to become a historic district, four representative residences have been locally designated (HCM nos. 1033–1036). *FIG. 10*

Moving forward, Historic-Cultural Monument nominations can be more representative of the city's diversity. The types of resources now being considered are more complex than those previously considered for the Historic-Cultural Monument program. The historic contexts, and their eligibility standards, encourage the designation of properties important for their associative qualities rather than their physical attributes.

— BEYOND DESIGNATION:
PLANNING CHALLENGES AND OPPORTUNITIES

While SurveyLA findings facilitate the designation of resources that better represent the city's diversity, perhaps more importantly, they are provoking discussions of how the data can serve larger citywide efforts. From the outset, the findings informed planning policies, goals, and objectives; survey results are now being tied to broader initiatives to celebrate neighborhood diversity and cultural identity and inform the vision for neighborhoods into the future.

A challenge and opportunity for Los Angeles is to integrate the results with programs and services led and provided by other city departments.

22
The Historic-Cultural Monuments program was overseen by the DCA prior to its move to Los Angeles City Planning in 2004.

23
SurveyLA identified murals and other public art as historic resources eligible for designation. DCA manages the registration of new and existing murals.

There are opportunities for interdepartmental collaboration in meeting the broader goal of telling the stories of all Angelenos. For example, there is an overlap between the work of the OHR and the Department of Cultural Affairs (DCA), which manages programs that support arts and cultural activities. [22] In practice, interdepartmental collaboration is often hindered by large and dispersed city offices, scarcity of staff time, and the difficulty of allocating funding for joint programs or projects. Areas of immediate opportunity are the city's mural program and the conservation of historic murals and public art. Both departments have an interest in and responsibility for the promotion of these resources; however, mural registration is an activity solely administered by the DCA. [23]

Still, strides are being made. Heritage resources are now taken into account during the process of updating the city's thirty-five community plans. Part of the Land Use Element of the City's General Plan, these plans guide the future growth and development of Los Angeles neighborhoods citywide. Planners are familiarized with SurveyLA findings for their geographic area—that is, the broad historical patterns of settlement, migration, growth, and development that shaped the social and built environment of neighborhoods over time. For the planners, the findings can demystify heritage resources. Understanding that heritage resources need not be exemplary architectural specimens—or buildings, for that matter—challenges planners to craft policies that sustain and celebrate community heritage in ways that serve the growth and well-being of neighborhoods.

Achieving Equity through Heritage Preservation: Lessons from the Margin for the Center

An interview with Donna Graves

Shifting Policy Toward Inclusion

ERICA AVRAMI
Your work of almost thirty years has focused on creating a more inclusive record of US history in the public realm. How has your practice as a public historian and preservationist changed over those three decades?

DONNA GRAVES
I came to preservation with a background in American studies, specifically social history and art history; my early career was as a museum curator. Museums in the 1980s were not thinking about audience and place in as broad a way as I like to think about them, so I ended up going back to school in urban planning at UCLA, where I was able to pursue my interest in cities, urban history, and social justice. While I was there, I served as executive director of the Power of Place, a nonprofit founded by historian and architect Dolores Hayden. The project focused on downtown Los Angeles and broke ground by attempting to portray a more comprehensive view of the city's histories. We worked to recover and highlight the experiences of working women and men of many races and ethnicities who had been instrumental in building LA but were not visible in the popular narrative of the city at that time, which instead focused on suburbs and freeways and Hollywood. The Power of Place was really foundational in helping me think about a more inclusive way of looking at urban history and about how that history could be documented and conveyed. *FIG. 1*

FIG. 1: Biddy Mason: Time and Place, *by Sheila de Bretteville, 1991, Los Angeles. The Power of Place developed a multipart project recognizing Biddy Mason, who was born into slavery in Mississippi, won her freedom in California, and became a community leader. Photograph by Don Barrett, Flickr/Creative Commons.*

But I also came to see the limitations of our methods as a very small organization. At UCLA we were firmly based in academia, and we didn't really develop strong partnerships with community members. Ever since then, my practice has relied on forging strong relationships and collaborating with individuals and organizations affiliated with the relevant histories. The goal of "Preserving California's Japantowns" was to try to knit back

1
"Preserving
California's Japan-
towns," California
Japantowns,
https://www.
californiajapantowns.
org/preserving.html.

2
"LGBTQ Historic
Context Statement,"
San Francisco
Planning,
https://sfplanning.
org/project/lgbtq-
historic-context-
statement.

into public memory the communities that had been built before World War II, before all people of Japanese descent were forcibly removed and incarcerated. 1 There were dozens of prewar Japantowns, and documenting them required support from many, many Japanese American individuals and groups throughout the state and sponsorship from the California Japanese American Community Leadership Council. FIG. 2

FIG. 2: Post Street, San Francisco, 2007. Like much of San Francisco's Japantown, Post Street is a mix of historic vernacular buildings inhabited by Japanese immigrants and their children prior to World War II and more "Japanese-themed" buildings from the postwar decades. Photograph by Donna Graves.

I've now also worked for about two decades with residents and community organizations in Richmond, California, at first to develop a monument to women's labor during World War II at the Richmond Kaiser Shipyards—the biggest shipyard facility in the world, located in a small town in the San Francisco Bay Area. That monument project grew into a national park and became the Rosie the Riveter World War II Home Front National Historical Park, which looks at the complex social changes that occurred during World War II and the resonance of those changes today.

For the last five years, I've also been working on projects related to LGBTQ history. First, I coauthored the most intensive citywide study of queer history in the US for the City and County of San Francisco with architectural historian Shayne Watson. Because we wanted to ensure that our report reflected the diversity of queer lives, we needed to work closely with a diverse advisory committee and with groups and individuals whose stories are underrepresented in LGBTQ histories. Unlike so many planning reports, we also worked to make the final document as reader-friendly as possible for nonpreservationists. 2 We created a step-by-step guide for documenting, evaluating, and nominating historic LGBTQ properties. That effort spun off into other projects that included writing a chapter for the National Park Service's LGBTQ National Theme Study, nominating a few buildings to the National Register, developing an exhibit about queer history for Rosie the Riveter National Historical Park, and several others.

I feel that the work I've done on social inclusion relies on establishing deep and long-term connections, not just parachuting in and out. For me, this more engaged method helps to surface histories that have been marginalized or erased. There's a level of trust-building and repeated exposure to topics and people and stories that enables more powerful projects.

The project I'm working on right now that's really challenging me is in Pennsylvania. It's with Temple University's Institute on Disabilities. I'm part of a team of artists and disability experts who are working to document and convey the history of residential institutions in Pennsylvania for people with intellectual disabilities and to capture the lived experiences of the dwindling number of people who still live in those institutions, before they're all closed. While I feel strongly about the importance of how you collaborate with communities across many aspects of difference, this project is one where the task of capturing and conveying the experiences of people who communicate very differently, and often not verbally, is an incredibly interesting and challenging aspect of this work. It's making me think really hard about how we understand place and how we learn to understand other people's experiences of the places that matter to them.

3
"Five Views: An Ethnic Historic Site Survey for California," California Department of Parks and Recreation, Office of Historic Preservation, December 1988, https://www.nps.gov/parkhistory/online_books/5views/5views.htm.

4
Donna Graves, "The Legacy of California's Landmarks: A Report for the California Cultural and Historical Endowment," California Cultural and Historical Endowment, September 2012, http://resources.ca.gov/docs/cche/TheLegacy_of_CaliforniasLandmarks.pdf.

As you have progressed on your own professional arc, how have you seen the field of historic preservation evolve with respect to social inclusion?

Painfully and slowly. Like some others in the preservation field, I was weaned on a very influential project called "Five Views: An Ethnic Historic Site Survey for California," which was conducted in the early 1980s by our State Historic Preservation Office (SHPO) and was funded by the National Park Service (NPS). [3] I look at that as a watershed moment, when, at least in California, preservationists were really called upon to see that the kinds of places and stories they had been focused on were so incomplete, and they were compelled to think about the meaning of place to different communities and about different strategies for surfacing their stories. One thing that was so prescient about the way the SHPO structured that project is that they commissioned teams of scholars and community-based historians to document sites associated with their own communities. They used race and ethnicity as their lens, looking at the five largest nonwhite groups in California at the time: Native American, Mexican American, Chinese American, African American, and Japanese American. That project was published in 1988 and continues to yield really interesting insights and questions. [4] I look at that as a missed opportunity for a field that could have been reshaped earlier in a more socially inclusive way. It has taken a long time for even an awareness of race and ethnicity—as a complicating factor in the way we think about our landmarks—to really take hold.

In the three decades that I've been involved with preservation, many people have come to understand that traditional approaches in preservation have tended to privilege the architectural and aesthetic qualities of historic resources, which tilts programs and landmarks toward high-design buildings that were generally erected by and for affluent and white populations. Listed sites that were chosen to reflect histories associated with women and people of color continue to be a very small fraction. Now there are organizations and municipalities that try to address that. I'm most familiar with ones in California where, especially in San Francisco and Los Angeles, preservation planning programs have tried to chip away at the constraints that result in their own landmark lists mainly reflecting the city's affluent, white, male cultures. Likewise, the National Park Service, some State Historic Preservation Offices, and some nonprofits are trying to expand the ways that they think about whose history should be recognized in a place.

There are obviously still a lot of barriers to a more inclusive "landscape of landmarks," for lack of a better phrase. I believe that one obstacle is the overrepresentation of architectural historians in the field. Architectural historians are crucial and obviously contribute a lot. But they often lack training in or sensitivity to the broader social histories that places contain and that are integral to a more socially diverse preservation practice. So in addition to having more diverse community voices in policy-making, we need a broader range of disciplines to be fully integrated into preservation practice.

Another issue that has held preservation back in terms of social inclusion—and that is so difficult for formal landmark programs to crack—is the insistence on physical integrity. When you require that a landmark or a potential landmark have original physical fabric (based on the assumption that a building's physical fabric conveys its significance), it presents serious obstacles to preserving places that matter to many marginalized communities. Many populations haven't had the resources to erect their own buildings, so they've inhabited places constructed by others on a temporary basis. Or if they have built buildings, they might have lacked the finances to maintain them in a way consistent with their "period of significance." Integrity can be a real barrier to designation, which obviously has implications for how socially inclusive our landmark lists can be.

The inability of many marginalized communities to control physical space is pervasive, but I've especially seen it in the community-based projects I've worked on. For example, Japanese Americans were legally barred from owning property in California. Then, in World War II, they were forcibly removed from the communities they created. And then, in many cases, as communities struggled to rebuild, they became targets for redevelopment. So the luxury of being able to own and control a site over time was very rare. Likewise, until the last couple decades, much of LGBTQ history took place in spaces on a temporary basis and in places that LGBTQ people didn't own outright, or that were programmed under the radar. Examples like these show the fallacy of thinking that all historic places can reflect a story from sixty, seventy, a hundred years ago in their physical structure, which is a difficult bar for many marginalized communities to meet.

What do the experiences of working with underrepresented communities in California bring to the broader dialogue about socially inclusive preservation policy across the United States?

As demonstrated by the "Five Views" project, many Californians recognize the complexity of our state and regional social landscape. In terms of race and ethnicity, California passed the majority-minority tipping point several years ago; nonwhite residents constitute more than half the state population. When I go to the East Coast and the South, it seems there's a default historical perspective that takes precedence, and it leads people to see United States history and the challenges of racial justice only in terms of Black and white. But there are many more kinds of people living in those regions, and so I'm baffled by the weight of that frame. For example, the National Trust recently launched an African American Cultural Heritage Action Fund that uses the tagline "Telling the nation's full story." I don't mean in any way to diminish the need for more resources for African American cultural heritage projects, I just think we've evolved past such a binary frame. I believe that we are ready to imagine an expanded preservation field that is more complex than that and that is more accurate in reflecting American history and current American lives.

It's harder to look at things in terms of Black and white here in California when most communities not only have African American and white people but many Latinx people and Asian Americans from many, many nations. Native peoples across the state are making their social justice and cultural heritage claims heard more clearly now too. Cities like San Francisco and Los Angeles have tried to add complexity by framing their social diversity beyond race and ethnicity—for example, they were the first two cities to put focused attention on integrating LGBTQ history into their preservation programs.

I do think that recognition of a broader range of social diversity is more baked into our consciousness here in California. Another difference is that—because so much of our usable built environment is from the last fifty to seventy-five years—I think there's more recognition of the recent past and how it can capture people's imaginations because it sometimes feels more relevant than what happened many generations ago.

Yet we all have a long way to go to really become fluid in recognizing and honoring the diversity of experiences beyond race, ethnicity, and gender. People are starting to think about disability and preservation, but there are aspects of identity that may not have even surfaced yet in our thinking, so we should approach this with humility. To have the default be Black and white or just race/ethnicity I think impairs the way we think about what social inclusion can mean.

In San Francisco, you've been helping to develop new strategies that have been put into policy or adopted by the city in some way. What are your thoughts about how some of these questions have played out in government action?

In 2010 the historic preservation commission in San Francisco asked the preservation planning staff to describe how the preservation program in San Francisco reflected the city and where it fell short. And of course the answer was it fell very short in reflecting anything other than the experiences of affluent, white males, and so the commission formally started pushing for and funding individual landmark nominations and historic context statements to help address some of those gaps. They've supported work in one form or another on Japanese American, Chinese American, Latinx, African American, and LGBTQ history.

Recently activists, city agencies, and the lead local advocacy group, San Francisco Heritage, have pushed to make preservation planning in the city a more diverse process. When the second wave of tech wealth started to very clearly push many, many of the city's historically marginalized communities (as well as many other people) out of San Francisco, advocates started recognizing that we're losing history and culture as we lose these people, and asking, how might we use the tools of preservation to keep people in place and push back against displacement?

San Francisco prides itself on diversity, on nonconformity, and, to some degree, it's a living embodiment of social inclusion. As that character is being radically and quickly undermined, there's a lot of anxiety in the city, and people are casting about for ways to stem this tsunami. That led San Francisco community advocates to pick up on a conversation that had already taken place in San Francisco's Japantown over ten years ago. At that time, I was part of a team hired by the city to create the very first San Francisco neighborhood plan that used cultural history as its basis rather than geographic boundaries or urban typologies.

We were creating a Japantown "Better Neighborhood Plan" in response to Japantown advocates who were worried about the last vestiges of the neighborhood, which had suffered assault after assault and had limited traces of its historic character and vitality left. So the planners and I worked with community members and came up with a plan, but what we found was that the preservation tools available to us were really not important to the community advocates. They didn't want to designate anything and were only mildly interested in urban design guidelines. What they really wanted were tools that would help them keep their legacy institutions, whether they were community organizations or businesses or annual events that brought people together from the diaspora of Japanese Americans in the broader Bay Area. And at that point, the planning staff couldn't envision how our planning tools, including preservation tools, could help them. They came up with a pretty standard plan that had a different name, "Japanese Cultural Heritage and Economic Sustainability Strategy." It still relied on quite typical tools of preservation and community development, but took some modest steps toward addressing the goals that the community had laid out.

Within a few years the conversation about displacement in San Francisco became so heated that San Francisco Heritage and community advocates pushed preservation planning staff into recognizing that we had to do something. One of the instances that brought this crisis to a head was what happened with Marcus Books, the oldest continuously operating African American bookstore west of the Mississippi. It was in the Japantown-Fillmore neighborhood—the building had been a Japanese-owned establishment before World War II, and then it was an iconic nightclub, Jimbo's Bop City. In 1980 it became Marcus Books. In 2014 a new owner bought the building and raised the rent substantially and ultimately evicted the bookstore, even though city staff and advocates had scrambled to get the building designated as a city landmark.

The demise of Marcus Books was a clear demonstration that the designation tools preservation planners rely on were not going to protect living culture and the historical memories associated with it. It helped people think about how we might incorporate what the field of preservation calls "intangible heritage" into our planning. At this point, I applaud the city and the communities for trying out new strategies, but I also have deep questions and hesitations about the way these approaches are evolving.

The Legacy Business Program was the first preservation tool developed for countering displacement. San Francisco Heritage started an honorific program for "Legacy Bars and Businesses" that evolved into a formal, city-sponsored program with allocated resources. The registry lists businesses and nonprofits if they are at least thirty years old and have contributed to the history and identity of a neighborhood or community. A business or nonprofit can nominate itself, but a member of the Board of Supervisors must forward their nomination, and they must commit to maintaining their name and their craft. It's designed to support businesses and nonprofits with a special status that is not related to brick and mortar, location, or architecture, but is based on its function and use. After the registry was accepted by the Board of Supervisors, a funding measure went to voters in the 2017 election and was overwhelmingly approved. That means that City of San Francisco dollars are helping to close the gap between market-rate rents, which have spiraled so out of reach for many businesses and nonprofits, and their ability to pay.

There are currently approximately 175 establishments listed in the Legacy Business Program. They're spread out over the city and are quite varied in the kinds of uses and communities they represent. I think the program has the potential to address social inclusion in a different way than we have imagined preservation could. But there's not yet any body formed to think comprehensively about what this program is accomplishing and what it should do. A broader perspective on how the program is developing, who it's serving, and whether the funding is actually meeting the identified needs is really critical.

The next major strategy that San Francisco has pioneered is creating cultural districts. As planners know, the term "cultural district" has been used for decades now in urban economic development and usually describes an area that has some sort of cultural and arts institutions; a city will target funding there to support economic revitalization based on the arts. This is not the model for San Francisco, where these districts support cultural heritage and marginalized communities at risk of being displaced. Two years ago, the city created a formal ordinance that describes target areas as being "distinguished by unique social and historical associations and living traditions." Right now there are five formal districts and one on the way. There's Japantown; the Filipino cultural heritage district, called SOMA Pilipinas; the Leather and LGBTQ cultural district, in the same South of Market neighborhood; the Calle 24 Latino cultural district, in the Mission District; and Compton's Transgender district, in the Tenderloin. Approval of a Castro LGBTQ cultural district is imminent.

I think it's notable that half of these districts reflect some aspect of historical and contemporary queer life in San Francisco, which is a testament to the strength of LGBTQ cultural awareness and political organizing. In terms of preservation, a designation like the Leather and LGBTQ district is interesting for how it broadens our consideration of what qualifies as intangible cultural heritage. As UNESCO describes it, intangible cultural heritage is passed down from our ancestors, and then we pass it down to our descendants. For LGBTQ people, really important aspects of cultural identity and expression don't come from traditional familial arenas. They're built by connections created with other queer people. Foregrounding queer identity and sexual practices as legitimate aspects of culture really pushes the boundaries of preservation and what heritage means. *FIG. 3*

FIG. 3: March to Remember Queer Space, San Francisco, 2018. The Citywide LGBTQ Historic Context helped to inspire a community-led procession to remember queer historic sites and to visit current LGBTQ spaces threatened by gentrification in March 2018. Photograph by Donna Graves.

One of the shortfalls I see is that these districts have not come about by any sort of broad process of community consultation or systematic evaluation of need. Instead, it's been a very political process where, in most cases, people who are connected to elected figures get a cultural district proposal developed and approved. Another fundamental problem comes from the mistaken idea that only one type of community resides in a given neighborhood, which misses a lot of what makes San

Francisco and other cities so important and historically vital. There are very few neighborhoods in San Francisco where you can draw a line and say there's just one type of person here for any of the metrics that we use for understanding social identity. Most neighborhoods are really mixed, and most individuals understand more complex dimensions of their own social identity. The new cultural districts draw a line around an area and identify a group of people based on a single aspect of identity, naming them as the group of people who are deemed to have the most needs and to whom the city is going to devote funds. I think this approach comes partially out of an overreliance on the precedence of National Register historic districts or city historic districts, where you draw a line around an area and say these are the "contributors" and these are the "noncontributors." The danger I see is that when that filter is applied to groups of people, especially members of other vulnerable communities, it can be in conflict with what motivates social justice.

There's still an important impulse behind these designations; what they're trying to foreground is the through line between an ongoing legacy of historic discrimination and contemporary injustice. That through line makes certain kinds of people more vulnerable to economic forces. I just think that the way San Francisco's cultural district is framed and the way its antidisplacement strategy is understood could use a broader lens to recognize the variety of groups who have suffered from those legacies and are vulnerable today. FIG. 4

FIG. 4: The Women's Building, San Francisco, 2018. For forty years, the Women's Building has illustrated an intersectional model of community organizing among women, LGBTQ people, immigrants, workers, people with disabilities, and others. With support from the National Park Service, Donna Graves nominated it to the National Register of Historic Places in 2017. Photograph by Bruce Reinhart.

5
Donna Graves and
Gail Dubrow, "Taking
Intersectionality
Seriously: Learning
from LGBTQ Heritage
Initiatives for Historic
Preservation," *Public
Historian* 41, no. 2
(May 2019): 290–316.

What do you see as some of the promising directions for the cultural heritage enterprise as we think more about inclusion? How can preservation be a more effective tool in confronting the legacies of injustice in the built environment?

I have thought a lot and done some writing about this with friends and colleagues. There are many avenues toward this goal; two of the arenas where I've seen great promise are intangible heritage and interpretation. As a category of experience and meaning that isn't based on property ownership, intangible heritage offers a lot that we can learn from. Preservation planning has been so captive to the logic of the real estate market and to property ownership that it's led us to rely on quantitative measures of success, such as financial investments, physical improvement, et cetera. But if we use intangible cultural heritage as a lens, I think we can learn how to recognize, define, and plan for the more imperceptible qualities that heritage brings, and we can influence policy-making. I don't have any specifics yet, but I think it's promising.

The other critical path I see toward social inclusion in the preservation field is for practitioners to become more conversant and committed to seeing interpretation as part of our toolbox. Historic preservationists have these three foundational tools they rely on: identify a resource, document it, and give it a landmark designation. But I find that rarely achieves our goals in full. We've done a portion of it with identification and physical protection, but we miss another really important piece. In my experience, most sites associated with communities that have been previously marginalized have rich stories, but the buildings that hold them often aren't visually compelling, and they don't convey their importance through their physical form. For that reason, it's critical to develop powerful and sustained interpretation and educational programs that can make these sites more widely known and relevant. Without these, protection is only a partial measure and may not inspire ongoing stewardship.

The other thing interpretation can do is acknowledge that there are often multiple stories attached to historic sites and that a place may actually be significant to a number of communities who all have a real claim to its history and its meaning. Negotiating that story in public places can allow us to better understand aspects of our histories that still shape our social landscape. One policy I would recommend is requiring interpretive strategies as part of cultural resource studies and landmark designations. Still, making interpretive strategies a component of cultural research documents—whether it's a landmark nomination for a site or a district, or a broader historic context statement—is just a first step. We need to forge partnerships and advocate for funding to make interpretive and educational elements a reality. But I believe that it is valuable for practitioners to think about how the histories they've documented can reach a broader group of people.

The last thing I've been thinking about that deals with social inclusion really directly is related to intersectionality and historic preservation planning. [5] It is important that we are conscious of the way we narrow down aspects of community identity, and how that leaves us telling incomplete and even inaccurate stories about our past. I think that we risk misrepresenting places that often have layered histories and, by doing that, we foreclose possibilities for political mobilization across identity lines—whether it's mobilizing in the interest of fostering greater social cohesion or of fighting displacement. I think that it's useful to think about multiple narratives in place or to think of intersectional places. It might be that cities prioritize public investments in places that have historical significance to multiple communities with the goal of developing a planning process that brings those communities together and hopefully builds bridges among stakeholders, or at least surfaces a more complete historic narrative.

In cities across the world, especially US coastal cities like San Francisco, the question of social equity is inextricably linked to the challenges posed by climate change and related phenomena, like sea-level rise. How do you see that intersectionality and the role of preservation?

For me, personally, I'm really invested now in making sure that a significant amount of my time that's devoted to heritage conservation and public history addresses climate change. I've been watching the work of, and talking with, colleagues around the globe who have been researching and communicating about the threats climate change poses to historic buildings and landscapes. But what I'm interested in is how our connections to history and those stories that are embedded in place can give us tools to move past the ostrich position—head in the sand—toward recognizing that our only real choice is to face this climate crisis and mobilize.

I'm currently developing programming at Rosie the Riveter World War II Home Front National Historical Park that uses the story of "total mobilization" during World War II to ask questions about what mobilization would look like now. We reorganized society at all levels back then—talk about social inclusion—and it required everybody: federal, state, and local governments, business, industry, neighborhoods, households, and individuals. I'm working with artists, a youth organization, the local art center, and NPS staff on a project exploring how we can use that history in Richmond to foster public conversations in places that are connected to that story and to help us save the future.

An interview with Claudia Guerra

Shifting Policy Toward Inclusion

ERICA AVRAMI
As San Antonio's first cultural historian, what is your role in the Office of Historic Preservation, and how is it changing the dynamics of preservation in San Antonio?

CLAUDIA GUERRA
The position was created in late 2013 in response to the demolition of the building where Univision was originally headquartered. As the birthplace of Spanish-language broadcasting in the United States, the building was meaningful to the community. The building itself had not been landmarked, but it was located in a district where new construction required review by the Historic Design Review Commission. The new construction was approved, which led to demolition of the existing structure. There was significant community outcry over loss of the building.

After the Univision building came down, community input led to the creation of the cultural historian position in the Office of Historic Preservation. The point of the position was to focus on cultural preservation, not only architecture. So my job is to make sure the next "Univision" is never demolished, whatever that "Univision" might be.

To be honest, I don't consider myself a cultural historian. I think I'm a cultural translator. I work to translate community needs to policy-makers and policy-makers' questions back to the community—they're not speaking the same language most of the time. What I try to do, really, is to interpret and to proactively identify cultural properties before they become vulnerable to demolition.

Many of the criteria guiding designation in the United States are largely influenced by architectural history, formal aesthetics, and material integrity. How does this approach complicate the inclusion of different perspectives about preservation and the ways that multiple publics might ascribe value to the built environment, as in the Univision case?

Three hundred years of colonialism has had an effect on preservation. There's a very present Eurocentric thinking that needs to label, to categorize, to provide data, and to document. We give heritage a very material and tangible focus. What we don't do is think about how the intangible is manifested in the tangible. Maybe there are materials that are not being maintained in a way that meets "preservation standards," but, even if deteriorated or altered, a place has a story—it says something about the community in which it's situated. And the very fact that we're talking about a property versus a tree or another spatial object is also an issue that we have to tackle in preservation because sometimes it's not about the building itself for communities or about how the building looks, it's the use that it serves. On a municipal level, preservation in San Antonio is not contingent on use. We do not even consider use. So that's one of the hurdles that we're trying to overcome. How do we think about a place beyond material terms? One such case was the Malt House, a traditional carhop kind of restaurant. They served malts, fried chicken, and hamburgers, and everyone from a certain community might go there after a football game, or for birthday parties, or simply to hang out in their car. It was just a fun gathering place.

It was also where our local chapter of the League of United Latin American Citizens often met. So a lot of people connected to the Malt House as an important gathering place. The Malt House was designated as a landmark in 2012 through San Antonio's West Side Cultural Resource Survey. Traditional survey methods look at architectural style, the form, massing, and setbacks. But what the Office of Historic Preservation found is that this didn't necessarily lead to an understanding of certain neighborhoods or places. The West Side is the traditionally Latino part of San Antonio. The survey looked to the community as the expert and had the community come forward to tell which places were important to them. The Malt House was one of them, so it was landmarked.

It was a large corner property. You could dine in or dine out. There were canopies where people could park their cars, and an area in the back where diners could park and picnic. And then there was the building itself, which was actually kind of small compared to the rest of the property. It really was just a concrete masonry building, a basic square form, with several modifications including brick veneer and replacement windows. Three years ago, 7-Eleven offered to purchase the property on the condition that they could demolish the Malt House and build a new structure. People objected to the idea that 7-Eleven would take over the Malt House. They wanted a small business owner to be able to continue to operate there. Some even felt that it would be fine to demolish the building and start anew—everyone understood there were code issues with the building—as long as it stayed a locally owned small business. Our current preservation purview, as in most cities, doesn't include considerations of use. We are limited to design review, including demolition and replacement plans.

Because the Malt House property was landmarked, the owner had to prove that it was financially infeasible to rehabilitate the building or demonstrate its loss of significance in order to demolish it. So when the case came to the Historic Design Review Commission, we evaluated the spatiality to really understand the physical nature of why it became such a popular gathering place. We couldn't look at it merely as an architectural space because there were many components to the property. It had a connection to the community because of its walkability, because of the kind of communal spaces that the building's canopies created. We found that you could remove two walls of the structure itself, still keep its orientation to the street, and improve the building in a way that would not sacrifice what made it important to the neighborhood and what encouraged people to gather there.

However, the real issue was that the business itself was failing. The property owner could no longer afford to keep it going. People had stopped eating there as often. Some said the quality of the food had declined. When the property owner came to make the case for demolition to the Historic Design Review Commission, the community came out in droves. It was a packed hearing room. Over three hours of testimony, person after person talked about the importance of the Malt House and why it shouldn't be demolished. But the turning point was that after the public spoke, the property owner went up and addressed the commissioners: "Well, I'm glad to hear all of these people want the Malt House to stay," he said. Then he turned around and said to the community members, "Where were you when I needed you? Where were you when you could have been eating lunch or dinner there? That's what I needed. I needed you to not come to say how important it is or was to you, I needed you to come eat there." It was very emotional, but he was able to produce the financial information documenting that he could not afford to continue operating there. The commission granted him the ability to demolish the building, and he was able to sell the property to 7-Eleven.

So it is no longer the Malt House as the community knew it. The 7-Eleven is currently under construction and probably close to being finished. They had to come back to the Historic Design Review Commission about four times before the commission approved the design because, despite the demolition, the property itself is still a landmark, which means that any modifications still have to come to the commission for review. The commissioners kept in mind the idea of a gathering space. The final design included picnic tables where originally there had been some. It included some homage to the Malt House, including preexisting signage, and it incorporated some of the canopies. It wasn't perfect, but the understanding of how the intangible was manifested in the tangible did influence the final design.

However, now the community wants to de-designate because they don't feel a 7-Eleven should be a landmark, ever. This is where some communities might see landmarking as having a different meaning than others. We've been trying to convince them that it's worth keeping the designation because then any future modifications have to be approved. It won't always be a 7-Eleven; someday it could change and become a Malt House kind of place again. Keeping the property landmarked is a way of managing the design of the neighborhood. That's our technical understanding. The community, however, sees it as an honorary distinction and, to them, there is nothing honorary about a 7-Eleven in their neighborhood.

How do you navigate these differing perspectives, especially when they extend beyond the question of translation and speak to how communities seek to self-determine their spatial conditions?

There is a process of explaining to the community what designation means to Office of Historic Preservation staff, which is really about managing change and design for neighborhoods. What we've been talking to them about is, rather than de-designating this one property, why not designate more of the West Side? Currently there are several landmarks on the West Side but no historic districts. We're talking to them about the importance of historic districts and about being able to manage change more effectively. At the neighborhood scale, it's challenging if you have a landmark in one place and you have to go blocks before you can find another one. In designating an entire geographic area, they might see the benefits of complementary design going forward.

However, this feeds into the fear of gentrification because West Side properties are still affordable. In many community members' eyes, the neighborhoods in San Antonio that are historic districts are gentrified neighborhoods. We try to point out that they were gentrified before they became historic districts. In San Antonio, historically, we have seen some older neighborhoods gentrified, properties rehabilitated, and then the new property owners want designation. So we're trying to convince communities that if they become a historic district now, we can create design standards that fit their neighborhood now—not design standards to suit a neighborhood after it has been gentrified.

It's partly an education process and partly a translation process: translating policies to constituents and translating constituents' fears to policy-makers, then trying to find that middle ground. We're at the very beginning of those conversations, so I can't say where it will end up. But I do see a lot of community members coming around to the idea and understanding that it could actually be useful—that designation can be honorary, but that it can also be a tool for preserving their neighborhoods, especially for keeping people and businesses in the neighborhood.

We have a lot of residences that don't necessarily conform to our standard historic district guidelines—that is, the basic standards applied citywide; the guidelines don't always align with how residents understand them or see their neighborhood. However, when a case comes to the design review staff, they try to understand it in its context. We have a case in another neighborhood that is actually very similar to the West Side. These are smaller, modest homes in the Missions Historic District, which is adjacent to the San Antonio Missions National Historical Park, part of a UNESCO World Heritage site listing. There is a very modest home that has been in the family for generations. It's recently been deeded over to the next generation, and they want to expand the house because now they have the wealth for that. They've been back several times with different designs to ensure that the materials, the feel of the building, and the massing of the building are in line with the neighborhood. We're lucky, and I think this is true of many of these communities, that the owner is committed to staying in the neighborhood. One of the reasons for inscribing the missions as a World Heritage site was the persistence of a unique culture created by the interweaving of Spanish and indigenous cultures; many descendants of the missions' original inhabitants continue to live in the surrounding communities and neighborhoods. If the people leave, then we're losing part of that "outstanding universal value." So design review staff has been working with the family to create a design that will fit within the neighborhood but also fit their needs. It's a process. I don't think there is a neat and clean answer, but the process allows for solutions to come through.

And sometimes that process of negotiating and translating isn't just between policy-makers and the community. Sometimes it's within communities themselves.

In all of the touristy magazines about San Antonio, you see young women dancing in Mexican outfits with flowers in their hair and young men in their mariachi costumes and hats. There are many dance troupes here that are considered elite and are internationally famous. They were put on the map because of a dance program that the city initiated in the 1930s. A famous studio where these dancers train is in a building in a city park. It was originally built in 1949 as an anglers' club alongside a beautiful casting pond. The building was eventually altered and became home to one of the elite dance troupes. Berta Almaguer was a famous teacher of these dancers and, after her death in the 1970s, the building was renamed in her honor. It was not a great place to teach dance because it had a concrete floor. About ten years ago, a good dance floor was installed, but the facility still had limitations as a teaching studio.

A bond was passed two years ago that allowed for a community center to be built in the vicinity of the studio. It was determined that the Almaguer studio should be the location for this new building, which would house a community center as well as the dance studio. But during the public review process earlier this year, the community was extremely upset. As the studio had been landmarked already, additional community engagement was necessary.

The process slowed down to accommodate community concerns. Through various discussions with the dancers and teachers, compromises were made. They agreed that they all wanted better facilities—beyond better dance studios, they didn't even have a working bathroom. But the community that had grown up with that building was against demolition. Probably an equal number of community members came out in support of demolition and a new facility as came out opposed to demolition. It was also clearly generational: Those who were against demolition were of an earlier generation, and those who were for demolition and a new studio tended to be very young. They were the student dancers along with their parents and educators.

The case recently came to the commission. The project architects articulated special issues with the building that made it financially infeasible to incorporate the existing building in the new design, a possible solution that had been floated. The building was approved for demolition, and a replacement plan was conceptually approved. In the end, the intangible heritage that is manifested in that place—the ongoing tradition of dance— trumped the material significance of that particular building.

Speaking from the municipal point of view, having that community engagement and the required public hearing allows us to weigh all sides. It slows down the process until everyone can speak and there is enough information to really weigh the different issues and solutions.

Beyond public hearings, can you tell us what community engagement looks like in San Antonio, particularly when it comes to identifying what communities value and what might be designated? How do you ensure inclusion in that process?

It really is dependent on the neighborhood. We have a designation team that uses traditional survey methods, if that's what we think is going to work for that community. If we think it's not going to work well, we use a process based on the Burra Charter that seeks to identify the aesthetic, historic, scientific, social, and spiritual values that stakeholders associate with a place. [1]

If we are considering designating an entire district, San Antonio preservation code requires support from the owners of 51 percent of the properties. Because this requirement involves so many property owners, we avoid the problem of only "the usual suspects" coming out for public meetings, which many municipal preservation agencies confront. When it comes to actual landmarking, the property owners have to be engaged.

[1] The Burra Charter was adopted in 1979 by the Australian chapter of the International Council on Monuments and Sites. The charter recognizes cultural heritage as encompassing more than just the architecture of the built environment.

Otherwise, the process can't go through. The community has to engage, whether it's through the traditional designation process or the kind of work that we try to do in our Living Heritage division.

Another approach is to hold what is called a *plática* in Spanish. It's a kitchen table kind of talk where people come together and talk about whatever it is they feel; they drive the conversation. Often, in areas where we're thinking of finding landmarks or making a district, conversations are about fears because a lot of people just fear what designation is. They fear city government; they don't trust the city. So usually those first couple of *pláticas* are all about voicing fears and building trust.

Once we're able to get over the fears and the mistrust, people open up and tell stories. We do a lot of oral history. We ask people to map out the places that are important to them. We might do a windshield survey because we need to get a sense of the neighborhood, but we look at it through their eyes first.

For a while, we had a pilot program, an app where the community could upload places of significance for them. Of course, the problem is that you have to have a smartphone. A lot of the communities that we work with don't necessarily have access to that technology. Going forward, I think it will continue to be a combination of crowdsourcing through technology and group and one-on-one conversations. We have one assistant city manager who loves to say, "Claudia will actually go to your house!" And it's true! I have a growing list of elders I need to visit to collect their stories. I wish I could do more of this because it isn't easy for some people to come to a public hearing.

From all the maps and all the stories, we're able to analyze and understand what the different values are for that area, or in some cases for just the building being designated, and have a better sense of why it's important to the community. We find that when people have a chance to explain why something is or isn't important to them, there's a lot more buy-in and trust. We take all of this information, combined with historical research, and create a cultural significance report. These reports are a way of talking to policy-makers in a language that they understand. A community may communicate orally, but putting it in a document and making it official has so much more weight for the way municipalities work. Now we have a report that can be referenced. That has become very useful.

Working in a municipal agency, how do you see these different kinds of data and different ways of knowing changing how the historic built environment is managed?

In one case, where the community was not ready for designation but was seeking some kind of distinction and asserting their voices, we enacted what we call a cultural heritage district. This is not something that is regulated by the city's Unified Development Code, but it is a departmental policy.

In the corridor we call Historic Highway 90, we identified what we have now defined as "legacy businesses" up and down the corridor. There are no big-box stores. It still very much has a small community feel. The community's fear is that as land values increase, they're going to be pushed out. They want to make sure that big-box stores don't come in. While we

103

don't have the regulatory framework to stop the sale of properties and development of big-box stores, the recognition of a cultural heritage district has allowed us to increase the amount of time that we can spend on community discussions should a change be planned.

For example, there was a recent bond project to build infrastructure along the corridor. The city team that works on bonds doesn't usually talk to the Office of Historic Preservation, unless it's a landmarked district. But because of the cultural significance report we produced, they met with us and with the community. As a result, they developed infrastructure designs that were much more in keeping with the identity and the physical environment of the neighborhood than was originally planned. So, even though we haven't gotten to a place where this is something we can actually regulate, it has heightened awareness, and we're starting to see the positive impact.

The other way we've used stories is simply to put them in an archive. We're working on a website where people can access stories they might want to hear. We're also creating an online map where people can find spaces that are related to stories, intangible heritage, or legacy businesses. We hope to grow that map. It will help everyone understand that there is an intangible heritage that is in place—literally in a tangible place—and we hope that will eventually lead to policies. It can be a slow process to work in the municipality, but these are a couple of ways we've begun to manage better and respond to citizens.

> *Related to your earlier discussion of use and honorary distinctions, San Antonio has implemented a legacy business program. Can you tell us more about that?*

Our legacy business initiative is largely honorary, though we have developed a toolkit to assist small businesses. There is a grant pilot program currently available in neighborhoods around the World Heritage missions. The grant program is still very focused on buildings as tangible places. We're hoping that this pilot program will be successful enough that we can expand it, so it can deal with things that are non-property related and will help businesses stay in operation.

Right now part of the toolkit that we offer is access to courses at one of the local universities, as well as several opportunities affiliated with our economic development department. They teach small business owners how to create a financial plan, legal plans, and structures for employees to have benefits. Those are opportunities that people don't necessarily know exist, so part of the legacy business program is to help connect businesses to the resources they need. We're hoping to get some funding to enable grants to legacy businesses. The program is still in its infancy, but it is making its way to toddlerhood this year; we were able to attract many more legacy businesses and gain recognition for them. We're hoping to also learn from San Francisco, which has a legacy business program. There are some things that haven't worked well with their grant process, so we want to make sure that we figure out the local answer for San Antonio.

Much of the interest in legacy businesses started with the Malt House we discussed earlier. During that hearing, several things bubbled up. One of them was how we protect living heritage. If we had had a legacy business policy in place, we could have helped that business owner. Some of the issues that the business owner discussed included the inability to understand how to create a business plan, how to create financial models, and how to improve a building that he had no money to improve. So our first goal was to create an educational toolkit where a business owner, like the Malt House owner, could say, "Hey, I need help understanding and learning to do this," and get help at no cost to them. Our second goal was to have some funding in place so that he could have brought his building up to code, because part of the issue was that the building did not meet the health code—they were getting shut down. If he had had a little bit of money, he could have addressed some of those problems.

To be a legacy business, we do have some criteria. They have to have existed for twenty years, and they have to represent San Antonio's culture. We're up to about twenty-two legacy businesses. We're working with the economic development department to establish metrics of success for the program. But the number one metric is that we don't lose all of our mom-and-pop businesses.

As San Antonio's Office of Historic Preservation expands into these areas of use and intangible heritage, and fostering equity and inclusion through heritage, what challenges and opportunities are you confronting within the broader policy infrastructure of the city?

At a municipal level, we have to abide by local laws and policies. For instance, when we talk about use, another city department—Development Services—has use in their purview. One of the things that we're trying to work on is, when we look at use—like legacy businesses—how are we able to inform that from the preservation perspective?

Again, looking at San Francisco as a model, the first thing we have to consider is whether "special use" is legal in our locality. In San Francisco it's legal, they can do that. But California has different laws from Texas. And so we worked with our development service department and their zoning team to understand whether this was a tool that would be legal here. It turns out that San Antonio already has special use districts. But because we're a military city, they're all for military use or zones. So what that opened up, at least for San Antonio and other Texas cities, is that we could be working with another city department to lay the groundwork for eventually expanding special use districts to include cultural heritage districts, if a community wants that.

It is a layered approach, again because of the kind of structures that cities have. I'm not sure that there's an alternative, at least not if we want to make change now—which is what we're all striving for. It's a long process within the city. And by the time you've created that process, it could be out of date, and you have to start all over again—simply because of the structures of municipalities. It's not an impediment, but we have to really understand how each of these layers is integrated in order to create a cohesive policy—not just any policy, but a good policy.

For policy-making, everything is data driven. But that's not how a lot of our communities work. It's not about data for them, right? It's about what they know, what they feel, what they've experienced. But that is how we communicate with the policy-makers. So a study will help us understand some of those metrics we need to look at. We're going through a large master planning process right now, and we are doing a lot of studies to try and get metrics so that we understand what's on the ground now. We realized we're not even sure we can get data on what currently exists in a way that's meaningful, that can help inform where we need to be and what we should be measuring going forward.

San Antonio is on a mission to bring equity to the city. First, we're looking internally to make sure that there's equity in how we treat employees within our city departments, because that will then affect how city employees deal with equity in the greater city. This is a huge initiative that the city started thinking about two years ago; this year it's been taken on in force. I'm one of the city employees that's been asked to be an equity trainer; there are about thirty of us. In those discussions, we've realized we've made more collaborative efforts, and we've talked about how, in order to make this work, we really do have to have integration. We have to have collaboration. We have to be inclusive within our own city, not just in terms of individuals' gender and race but in terms of the work and the equity lens that we bring to the work we do.

Doing some of the work we know needs to be done in social inclusion for preservation is going to require a greater effort that changes culture at a bigger level, not just within the Office of Historic Preservation. For example, the city developed a new department called Neighborhood and Housing Services to address citizens' concerns for neighborhood and housing stability. People are afraid that affordable housing is disappearing. That is something we've heard community-wide, and we can see it. We see demolitions, and we see luxury apartments coming up. The community is very afraid; they already feel like they're being pushed out of certain areas. They want to make sure they get to stay in other areas. So currently one of the ways the Office of Historic Preservation is approaching this is through a study analyzing affordable housing in relation to historic and older properties—anything that was built before a certain year. What will it show us about density? What will it show us about diversity? What will it show us about potential for keeping people in place? So the Office of Historic Preservation is collaborating with the Department of Neighborhood and Housing Services on affordable housing, because often that's how it works in the city: you have to tackle something by taking a piece of it instead of the entire thing.

The End of Bootstraps and Good Masters: Fostering Social Inclusion by Creating Counternarratives

Andrea Roberts

Challenging and Redefining Narratives

Although I grew up in Missouri City, Texas, I had never been to the Freedom Tree tucked away in the subdivision of Lake Olympia. *FIG. 1* But one day, accompanied by my friend Ayanna and her son, Zahir, I decided to see the tree for myself. I was taken by its giant extended branches. I read the historical marker, which tells the story of Palmer Plantation, founded in 1860 by Edward Palmer, one of Stephen F. Austin's "Old Three Hundred"—that is, one of Texas's original Anglo settlers. [1] The next event on the marker is Emancipation, on June 19, 1865, or Juneteenth. General Gordon Granger arrived in Galveston on that date to announce the end of slavery in Texas. The marker refers to General Granger's proclamation as the "basis for what are the annual 'Juneteenth' festivities." One enslaved man, Ed Gibbs, called "a leader of the slaves" on the Palmer Plantation, "gathered all of the workers together under the branches of this tree to explain that they were free." He also said they could stay and sharecrop. The end of the story is telling: "It is in this light that slavery ended on the Palmer land beneath the spreading boughs of 'The Freedom Tree' and may it stand ever proudly as a symbol of our freedoms as Americans."

[1] Lester G. Bugbee, "The Old Three Hundred: A List of Settlers in Austin's First Colony," *Quarterly of the Texas State Historical Association* 1, no. 2 (1897): 108–117.

[2] Erica Avrami, Cherie-Nicole Leo, and Alberto Sanchez Sanchez, "Confronting Exclusion: Redefining the Intended Outcomes of Historic Preservation," *Change Over Time* 8, no. 1 (Spring 2018): 102–120.

FIG. 1: *Freedom Tree historical marker, December 28, 2018. The historical marker, located in front of the Freedom Tree in Missouri City, Texas, explains the significance of the tree to Fort Bend County history. While the marker celebrates the announcement of emancipation, it centers the benevolence of plantation owners. Photographs by the author.*

FIG. 2: *Tension rods in the Freedom Tree, December 28, 2018. While the tension rods are barely visible, their presence is evidence of the strain on the old tree and its vulnerability. A story of tension is also embedded in the narrative surrounding the tree, as its public history espouses white benevolence and Black exceptionalism while disremembering Black agency. The tension in plain sight is barely visible or perceptible. Photograph by the author.*

3
Leonie Sandercock, "Out of the Closet: The Importance of Stories and Storytelling in Planning Practice," *Planning Theory and Practice* 4, no. 1 (2003): 11–28; Dolores Hayden, *The Power of Place: Urban Landscapes as Public History* (Cambridge, MA: MIT Press, 1995); Andrea R. Roberts, "Performance as Place Preservation: The Role of Storytelling in the Formation of Shankleville Community's Black Counterpublics," *Journal of Community Archaeology and Heritage* 5, no. 3 (2018): 146–165.

4
Laurajane Smith, "A Critical Heritage Studies," *International Journal of Heritage Studies* 18, no. 6 (2012): 533–540.

5
Alexis P. Gumbs, *Spill: Scenes of Black Feminist Fugitivity* (Durham, NC: Duke University Press, 2016); Jessica M. Johnson and André Brock, keynote conversation at "Intentionally Digital, Intentionally Black" conference (University of Maryland, October 20, 2018), https://youtu.be/6Dt5QL7ZXM4.

6
Paul Connerton, "Seven Types of Forgetting," *Memory Studies* 1, no. 1 (2008): 59–71; Laura Gillman, "Storytelling as Embodied Knowledge," in *Unassimilable Feminisms: Reappraising Feminist, Womanist, and Mestiza Identity Politics* (New York: Palgrave Macmillan, 2010); Angel D. Nieves, *We Shall Independent Be: African American Place Making and the Struggle to Claim Space in the United States* (Boulder: University of Colorado Press, 2008); Roberts, "Performance as Place Preservation."

Like any young boy, Zahir's instinct was to run and climb the tree. However, after his mother warned him not to climb, he looked at the tree more closely. It looked like a healthy tree—that is, until he noticed the tension rods. *FIG. 2* From far away, the rods are inconspicuous, but they keep this tree together. Like the historical marker, the rods exemplify a supportive white benevolence, keeping the tree erect. The truth of the tree's condition, of enslavement, of liberation, is all obscured by the seemingly smooth transition from slavery to emancipation depicted on the historical marker.

In this sublime park space, amid a master-planned landscape of Houston bedroom communities, a child sees a large tree, forgets how old it is, assumes it can hold his weight, and contemplates climbing it. This is how "forgetting as annulment" becomes child's play. Signage and his mother tell him to be careful, but nothing in the landscape or on the marker acknowledges what is missing from the narrative. Even local news articles that engage descendants of Ed Gibbs indicate little about the positionality of this particular slave and his family with respect to others on the plantation. While visitors are welcome in a public park, can these absences in the public narrative be processed and substantively engaged? How do we foreground the critical enslaved voice, which has become a "null value" of missing information?

— THE CASE FOR COUNTERNARRATIVES

Preservation is alternately blamed for spatial inequality or gentrification and lauded for the ways it can catalyze social inclusion. 2 Planning and preservation scholars point to the possibilities for increased participation through activities such as storytelling and public remembrance. 3 While support for safeguarding Black (African American) historic sites has increased in recent years, "authorized heritage discourse" inhibits identification, interpretation, and commemoration of difficult Black history. 4 Local governments struggle with how to interpret or manage fraught public histories or sites of conscience involving slavery and convict leasing. However, stories of Black agency in these contexts are often similarly repressed or overshadowed by places and sites with conciliatory or uncomplicated versions of Blackness. Within the context of public history and heritage conservation, representing Black agency demands a comprehensive portrayal of Black identity and heritage, including manifestations of fugitivity, subversion, and resistance in the past and the present. 5 Forgetting as annulment and disremembering—that is, reckless omission from public memory—of Black agency in Texas's public history and cultural landscapes must be met with counternarratives in historic Black settlements or embodied by the descendants of enslaved Black Texans. 6

Complex stories of resistance and self-making are essential to creating truly inclusive preservation practice and public history. Fissures can be identified in authorized heritage discourse where these counternarratives can interrupt or complicate foundational stories of settlement and origination. Foundational stories, Leonie Sandercock explains, involve "telling and re-telling the story" in a way that causes people to repro-duce behaviors and their identities. These stories give "communities and nations" "meaning to their collective life" and are the hinge of any society's culture. Stories define culture, Sandercock maintains, because they "bond us with a common language, imagery, metaphors, all of which create shared meaning." [7]

Structured as critical reflections on field notes, this essay describes and analyzes encounters with forgetting and remembering while record-ing Black community origin stories told by deep East Texas freedom colony descendants. These field notes explicate the ways groups in these contexts obscure community origin stories rooted in Black agency while centering narratives rooted in settlerism, white benevolence (the "good master" myth), and "bootstraps" ideologies. I pay specific attention to the ways that freedom colony descendants in one community leverage a fugitive slave narrative to center Black agency in local public history. Later, in another context, my own positionality changes as I go from being an inductive observer to a partial and then a full participant—encountering, documenting, and embodying counternarratives.

— A FRAMEWORK FOR CURATING PLACE-MAKING
   AS FREEDOM-SEEKING

Curation of a space, place, or landscape should be a process of investigating the absences—what Jacob Gaboury refers to as the "null value." Gaboury employs Edgar Codd's definition of the null value as a way to represent "missing information and inapplicable information in a systematic way, independent of data type." [8] Digital humanities scholar and historian Jessica Marie Johnson posits that this null value is actually the fugitivity of enslaved women in the archive. [9] How then does the curator become the willing accomplice of fugitivity? That is, how does the public historian or the preservationist explicitly seek out and foreground attempts to seek freedom from sociospatial constraints in racialized landscapes? [10]

The null value of the critical enslaved voice is central to recognizing place-making as African American freedom-seeking. How do we hear the omitted, the annulled, and the deliberately forgotten? Rendering these places—and other spaces of Black agency and place-making in states of bondage, fugitivity, or recent freedom—visible and geographic requires creating spaces for cocreation with those holding evidence of resistance and freedom-seeking. In my work researching freedom colonies from 2014 through 2016, I had to explore new ways to listen for and document the null value. Further, I endeavored to share power with the grassroots place-keepers and preservationists engaged in stewardship, interpretation, and advocacy in places rendered ungeographic by prevailing definitions of place in historic preservation and urban planning. The dominant white sociolegal constructions of place (and the public history that reinforces their power) negate Black epistemologies of planning and preservation, and they obscure hidden Black agency in past and current descendant communities. [11]

7
Sandercock, "Out of the Closet," 16.

8
Jacob Gaboury, "Becoming NULL: Queer Relations in the Excluded Middle," Women and Performance: A Journal of Feminist Theory 28, no. 2 (2018): 152; Edgar F. Codd, "Is Your DBMS Really Relational?" ComputerWorld, October 14, 1985, 596.

9
Johnson and Brock, keynote conversation at "Intentionally Digital, Intentionally Black."

10
Richard H. Schein, "Normative Dimensions of Landscape," in Everyday America: Cultural Landscape Studies after J. B. Jackson, ed. Chris Wilson and Paul Groth (Berkeley: University of California Press, 2003), 199–218; George Lipsitz, "The Racialization of Space and the Spatialization of Race: Theorizing the Hidden Architecture of Landscape," Landscape Journal 26, no. 1 (2007): 10–23.

11
Katherine McKittrick and Clyde Woods, Black Geographies and the Politics of Place (Cambridge, MA: South End, 2007); Katherine McKittrick, Demonic Grounds: Black Women and the Cartographies of Struggle (Minneapolis: University of Minnesota Press, 2006).

12
Loren Schweninger,
Black Property Owners in the South, 1790–1915 (Urbana and Chicago: University of Illinois Press, 1997).

13
Thad Sitton and James H. Conrad, *Freedom Colonies: Independent Black Texans in the Time of Jim Crow* (Austin: University of Texas Press, 2005).

14
Sitton and Conrad, *Freedom Colonies*, 2.

15
Patricia Davis, "Memoryscapes in Transition: Black History Museums, New South Narratives, and Urban Regeneration," *Southern Communication Journal* 78, no. 2 (2013): 120–127.

16
Arjun Sabharwal, *Digital Curation in the Digital Humanities: Preserving and Promoting Archival and Special Collections* (Amsterdam: Chandos Publishing, 2015).

Where are the narratives depicting these processes of becoming free, in which the recently freed sought out earth welcoming enough to start new, safe communities after Juneteenth?

— FREEDOM COLONIES: TRACES OF BLACK AGENCY IN THE LANDSCAPE

To understand the settlement of Texas and not just the popular Anglo settler narrative, it is essential to understand the interconnectedness of enslavement, property, and westward expansion. Tales of white settlers attaining, taming, and defending the land are the cornerstone of Texan identity. Texas grew quickly due to the availability of Spanish land grants. Further, for every enslaved person Anglo settlers brought with them, they were afforded another eighty acres. This incentivized settlers' sense of entitlement to land, expansion, and slavery. By the time African Americans were emancipated, Black Codes inhibited their access to publicly available land, which limited their ability to accumulate land. Nevertheless, African Americans acquired land through adverse possession, also known as squatting, and sometimes through outright purchase. In other cases, Anglo men who fathered interracial children willed property to their progeny. Through a combination of these methods, African Americans went from owning 2 percent of all farmland in Texas in 1870 to owning 31 percent by 1910. 12 These clusters of landowners engaged in intentional building of communities anchored by the cemeteries, churches, and schools they built near the railroads and mills in The Bottoms.

In this essay, I use "curation" to describe a process in which narratives renounce their complicity with disremembering and instead work to make visible the null value, the obscured contestations of places and landscape meanings embedded in these places called freedom colonies. 13 An umbrella term for places, settlements, and cultural landscapes in which landowning African Americans created communities based upon economic self-determination, self-definition (identity), and security, freedom colonies are both historical landscapes and the site of memory for dispersed, diasporic social geographies. Similar historic Black settlements were founded between 1865 and 1920 throughout the United States; they include Rosewood, Florida (1870); Nicodemus, Kansas (1877); Eatonville, Florida (1887); and Allensworth, California (1908). In Texas such settlements were known as "freedom colonies."

Thad Sitton and James H. Conrad, in their book *Freedom Colonies: Independent Black Texans in the Time of Jim Crow*, describe the communities as dispersed settlements "unplatted and unincorporated, individually unified only by church and school and residents' collective belief that a community existed."14 Freedom colonies, as historical and contemporary cultural landscapes, challenge conventional wisdom around national histories of Black migration and settlement. Instead of sharecropping, much of freedom colony history is filled with tales of cunning and tactical place-making on abandoned land. 15 In freedom colonies, annual commemorative events have become opportunities for the cultural and knowledge reproduction necessary to preserve these now sparsely populated places and their endangered buildings. 16

113

But what happened to the populations of these communities? Several factors contributed to their decline, including the Great Migration, population shifts toward more urban areas within Texas, and a constant threat of violence. Migration, desegregation, growth, and natural disasters all made Black settlements vulnerable. African Americans who accumulated land were frequent targets of white vigilantes. Even as the idea of self-sufficiency was defended and promoted among African Americans, this same ethic attracted the wrath of resentful, racist Anglos. With the expansion of cities, farm-to-market roads, and interstates came infrastructure projects that ran straight through freedom colonies: Interstate 45 eviscerated the Fourth Ward of Houston, Texas, also known as Freedman's Town. Jobs in industrial factories in the large cities of Texas and California drew people away from family properties that became secondary to more pressing concerns in their new homes.

In the absence of population, the character of structures and settlement patterns, demolition by neglect, and deferred maintenance made many freedom colonies ineligible for the preservation protections afforded to other local historic districts. Local districting, one of the most effective mechanisms for slowing down or halting demolition, was largely out of reach for residents of historic Black settlements, especially in formerly redlined urban areas ineligible for the home improvement loans that would enable these families to address deferred maintenance needs. The increasing invisibility of these communities means that these settlement patterns have become the stuff of intangible heritage, such as oral traditions and memory.

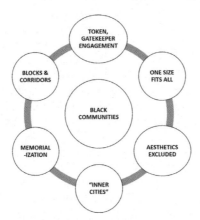

FIG. 3: Diagram of normative planning in Black communities (2018). Each circle contains one dimension of normative planning's assumptions about Black communities, which, I assert, minimize practitioners' inclusion of multivocality and spatial diversity when engaging Black places and spaces. Figure content and design by the author.

Recognition for the 557 freedom colonies we know existed (357 of which have been mapped) is obstructed by normative planning and preservation practices' operating assumptions about African American communities. These assumptions inhibit the visibility, voices, and vulnerabilities of freedom colonies from being brought to the center of planning education and practice. FIG. 3 Currently, most memorialization

17
Tim Hashaw,
Children of Perdition: Melungeons and the Struggle of Mixed America (Macon, GA: Mercer University Press, 2018).

18
Frederick L. Olmsted, *A Journey through Texas, or, A Saddle-Trip on the Southwestern Frontier: With a Statistical Appendix* (New York and London: Dix, Edwards & Co., S. Low & Co.: 1857).

of the past and engagement in the present is limited to those representatives of African American life who reflect traditional notions of success and legitimacy based on leadership in mainstream organizations; those who achieved famous firsts; or those of middle to upper income who espoused respectability politics. The aesthetics of preservation elude African Americans because their presence is interpreted as new and non-historic and integrity of their spaces and structures has often been compromised by additions and modifications. The result of imposing a one-size-fits-all authorized heritage discourse is that African Americans' spatial values and aesthetics fail to measure up to standards. National Register of Historic Places criteria center on property ownership and documentation from traditionally recognized archives in universities and libraries, creating a *preservation apartheid* in which African American spaces are disproportionately excluded from legal protections and, as a consequence, are disproportionately subject to demolition. Too often, little physical evidence or archival materials is preserved among African American families, let alone made part of these official archives.

— DEEP EAST TEXAS FREEDOM COLONIES: CONTEXT

Several waves of mixed-race or triracial peoples came to Texas in the early 1820s. One group, called the Melungeons, or "Red Bones," was originally descended from enslaved Africans in Jamestown, Virginia, who intermarried with English settlers and Native Americans. The Melungeons, more commonly associated with Appalachian mountain people, were often landholding, were free, and sometimes passed for white. They congregated in the Cumberland Gap and in the mountains, especially hidden places that were hard to access and that afforded them some isolation. They migrated from Virginia and South Carolina to Louisiana. [17] By the 1830s, Melungeons had left Louisiana and settled in the swamplands of Newton County, Texas, in an area known as No Man's Land or the Neutral Strip.

This unique mixed heritage and borderland culture along the Sabine River (between Texas and Louisiana), coupled with murky documentation of land-granting practices, destabilized land possession at the same time that it sparked the formation of freedom colonies. African Americans, mulattos, and mixed-race couples all came from the Tidewater states to Texas, believing they would be afforded equal rights and safety under Mexican governance. These settlers sought freedom as well as land. In the 1850s, Frederick Law Olmsted witnessed a Texas that belies the common story of Anglo settlement: "This county has been lately the scene of events, which prove that it must have contained a much larger number of free negroes and persons of mixed blood than we were informed on the spot, despite the very severe statute forbidding their introduction… Banded together, they have been able to resist the power, not only of the legal authorities but of a local Vigilance Committee… on the banks of the Sabine…"[18] Coexisting with mixed-race people and African Americans passing as white slaveholders were also fugitive enslaved peoples. In 1860, 25 percent of "white" residents in Newton County owned ten or more enslaved people, and there were 1,013 enslaved people in total.

19
Roberts, "Performance
as Place Preservation,"
147–148.

Shankleville, located in Newton County, about fifteen miles from
the Louisiana border and the Sabine River, is one of many historic Black
settlements founded after emancipation. What is notable about this
particular community is the role of storytelling, not just as a pastime or
entertainment but as a way to sustain descendants' attachment to this
sparsely populated and remote community in the woods. The story begins
with two enslaved Africans in Mississippi: Winnie, who was sold away
to Texas, and Jim Shankle, who ran after her. The fugitive man crossed
three great rivers for his love, whom he finally found at a spring less than
a quarter mile from the Odom Homestead, which is listed in the National
Register of Historic Places. This story in many ways sustains the sense of
place that (in part) justifies recognition and preservation of the historic
homestead and cemeteries. I heard the story again at an event I hosted.
Harold Odom begins his story by describing the sale of his ancestors:

> You have a decision made by one slave owner in Mississippi that a
> slave is going to be sold, either because she was profitable or valu-
> able with the children. Moreover, someone made the decision to
> buy her, and they broke the family apart and sold Winnie and the
> children. Heartbroken, Jim ran away and swam 400 miles, across
> three rivers, "all because of the love of Winnie and the children." He
> went from plantation to plantation, asking the enslaved people he
> encountered if they had seen Winnie and the children. Jim would
> then describe Winnie by height and appearance. He continued his
> quest until he found the plantation where Winnie and the children
> were enslaved, adjacent to present-day Shankleville.
>
> Jim found her under a magnolia tree, at the spring. It was not
> called Shankleville back then, but there ended up being a spring
> down the lane, where Winnie would go to get water and to deposit
> milk, butter, and perishables in the cold spring box down there for
> him. Jim remained hidden at the spring, and Winnie brought him
> food from the plantation kitchen. He even devised a system for secret
> communication: a special whistle that only Winnie recognized.
> Unfortunately, Jim was discovered.

Harold concluded that Winnie had to tell her master, as the "deliv-
eries got heavier, got a little more frequent, and a little longer." [19] She
convinced the slave master to buy Jim, and the two were publicly reunited.

This seemingly fantastical story has catalyzed youth engagement in
preservation and descendants' return to the settlement. A descendant of
Jim Shankle, Harold Odom leads the rehabilitation of the homestead and
is the keeper of the spring where Jim and Winnie reunited; he teaches
younger children to retell the story, and they drink from the spring in
something much like an African libation ceremony. They reenact and
retell fugitive-centered narratives at events such as their annual homecoming celebration, when people return from all over to a community
that—by way of a church or a blood or social kinship—they call home.

Homecoming events emerged during the 1930s and 1940s as a result of the Great Migration. These annual events were a means by which members of the diaspora could reenact their commitment to place preservation. During the two-day event in Shankleville, a church service is held along with an evening music program. Representatives from nearby settlements announce their homecoming events and contribute to the offerings, which support the event as well as maintenance of Shankleville's historic cemeteries. The same practice is reciprocated at other freedom colony homecomings in the area over the next several months.

In 2015 I was asked to be one of the co-planners of Shankleville's freedom colony symposium. The symposium was led by descendants of the settlement's founders and included exchanges with experts, government agencies, and white county historical commission leaders. Still, the event centered on freedom colony information-sharing. Self-reliance, land-based heritage, and the bodily and physical sovereignty experienced in freedom colonies came up repeatedly over the day. As participants told stories passed down through generations, they co-counseled each other on approaches to conservation, managing tax liabilities, and the ways sovereignty operates on both an individual and a mass scale.

Soon after the event, I accompanied descendants (who may or may not live full-time in the freedom colonies) on walking tours through unmapped, no longer populated freedom colonies that contained cemeteries with fresh burials and recently replaced flowers. I recorded stories and distributed a paper survey. At other times, I was simply a guest in people's homes. The stories I encountered perfectly

FIG. 4: Huff Creek Community, July 14, 2015. This photo was taken on a walking tour of Jasper County freedom colonies. The former Rosenwald School (now a chapel) is across from a community cemetery on Huff Creek Road, where James Byrd Jr. was murdered in 1998. Huff Creek Community once had an ample Black population, according to freedom colony descendants. Anglos and Latinos now sparsely populate it. Photograph by the author.

exemplified the coexistence of fugitivity and repression of the local heritage of freedom-seeking through place-making.

Most of my research took place in the neighboring counties of Newton and Jasper. Huff Creek Community, in Jasper County, is one of many freedom colonies whose foundational stories were buried under racial violence or overshadowed by the commemoration of Confederate veterans' history. 20 In particular, Huff Creek Memorial Chapel is an example of the coexistence of Black agency and anti-Blackness in Texas's cultural landscape. Formerly the Rosenwald School for African Americans, the chapel is in an area that served as an informal border crossing between Newton and Jasper Counties. FIG. 4 Jasper County is best known today, however, for the dragging death of James Byrd Jr. in 1998. Many believe the incident happened in the city of Jasper. However, Byrd was actually dragged behind a pickup truck down Huff Creek Road—which is not just a road but also the site of a freedom colony—to the foot of the Huff Creek Memorial Chapel sign; that's where pieces of his body were found. Yet that is not the story of the place that people share. Instead, the people I spoke to told the story of how students came to the school from each county, how they later married and even founded more freedom colonies. But still, in the public imagination, the story of white violence suppresses this story of ongoing place-making through social interaction.

20
Jeffry A. Owens, "Placelessness and the Rationale for Historic Preservation: National Contexts and East Texas Examples," East Texas Historical Journal 43, no. 2 (2005): 3–31.

21
Gregg Cantrell and Elizabeth H. Turner, eds., Lone Star Pasts: Memory and History in Texas (College Station: Texas A&M Press, 2006); Theodore R. Fehrenbach, Lone Star: A History of Texas and the Texans (New York: Da Capo Press, 2000).

22
Terry Fitzwater, "Gonzales Moving Forward on Freedom Colonies Project," Gonzales Inquirer, August 9, 2018, http://gonzalesinquirer.com/stories/gonzales-moving-forward-on-freedom-colonies-project,25507.

— CO-CURATING BLACK AGENCY IN THE BODY

Gonzales County, Texas, home of the "come and take it" cannon, is a great place to contemplate the connection between Texas public history and implicit bias. 21 In Texas, the story of this cannon is an example of the romanticization of white settlerism as it represents Anglos' tenacity in their formation of a republic. Considered the "Lexington and Concord" of Texas independence, Anglo settlers fighting for independence defended the cannon given to them by the Mexican government—thus the saying "come and take it." Absent from the story is the centrality of the right to enslave, which is what precipitated tensions between the Mexican government and what would become the Republic of Texas. Daring the Mexican government to retrieve its cannon was a proxy for Texans' conflict over their right to own slaves. The cannon is now housed in a large art deco building that serves as a mini-museum. Less than a mile away in Gonzales's town square stands a Confederate monument.

I was invited to Gonzales to participate in a workshop organized by the Gonzales County Historical Commission in partnership with the Texas Historical Commission's certified local government (CLG) program. As part of the workshop, held August 1, 2018, I provided training on addressing implicit bias and including more freedom colonies in survey processes. 22 The workshop took place in the historic Providence Missionary Baptist Church in a freedom colony in Gonzales. The training included a storytelling activity, but rather than having only freedom colony descendants share, I invited all attendees to share their stories and to make relevant connections between their core stories and the foundational stories of the State of Texas.

23
Walter L. Buenger,
"'The Story of Texas'?
The Texas State
History Museum
and Forgetting and
Remembering the
Past," *Southwestern
Historical Quarterly*
105, no. 3 (January
2002): 480–493; Gregg
Cantrell, "The Bones
of Stephen F. Austin,"
in Cantrell and Turner,
Lone Star Pasts.

Centering freedom colonies was a foundational shift for the county commissioner, county historical commissioners, and other leaders present. Predominantly women, these lay preservationists are the quasi-governmental bodies through which consultation, CLG funding for surveys, and other public monies pass. They are mostly white, and many of them can trace their origins back to the Republic of Texas, including the "Old Three Hundred," those first recipients of land grants in Texas. 23 Foundational to the workshop was not only self-assessment but also an introduction to freedom colony preservation and to the Texas Freedom Colonies Project Atlas, an online mapping tool create by my research team, which participants were invited to use to collect and store data about newly identified Black settlements. During the storytelling exercise, this exchange with an older white woman attending the training took place:

> *Andrea Roberts:* As you were going through this, how did you see your home-place story as the story of Texas, what was the relationship? Did you make any connection?
>
> *Participant:* I grew up on a thousand-acre original land grant from the Republic of Texas. [The land grant was] through a great-great-grandfather for his service during the Indian wars. They couldn't pay him, so they gave him a thousand-acre land grant.
>
> *AR:* Who are "they"?
>
> *Participant:* The Republic of Texas. It was a republic before it was a state. So the government gave that land to my third or fourth grandfather. He went to Austin and helped form the first legislature and everything… It is woven throughout my family on both sides. It doesn't get any farther back, going back to the Republic of Texas before it was even a state. That's a long history.
>
> *AR:* I identify with that a lot. So, anyone here familiar with the Old Three Hundred? I have an ancestor named Julia. My ancestor Julia was born in Sumter, Tennessee, in 1821, and she was eventually sold to the Kuykendalls (one of the Old Three Hundred) and specifically to Joseph Kuykendall in Fort Bend County. So I have been here since then too. And so when I think about the story of Texas, I very much think about the Republic of Texas, and I very much think about those land grants, and I very much think about how much land they were afforded by virtue of bringing Julia here. These are multidimensional stories, are they not? It is not one story at all—that's what I want us to think about today, and that I see you thinking about here in Gonzales.

The woman's story—which centers war, land as reward, and intergenerational claims to the state's true origin story—is an explicit example of the disremembering that is pervasive among leaders of Texas's 180-plus county historical commissions. This workshop attendee understood her core story, which she surmised was also the story of Texas, to begin with her fourth great-grandfather's heroic struggle against Native Americans in the Indian wars, and with his acquisition of a land grant as one of the Old Three Hundred because Texas welcomed slave owners and those who wanted to get a fresh start or escape debt.

The next stage of the workshop was a deeper examination of bias and how it manifests itself in local preservation planning and surveying. To mark the transition to this stage, I quoted a poem by Lucille Clifton called "why some people be mad at me sometimes": "They ask me to remember / but they want me to remember / their memories / and I keep on remembering / mine."[24] This poem bridged our conversation from the past to the present and to the recognition of the human impulse to be heard and understood while confronting the biases that inhibit inclusive public histories. I then asked attendees to suggest ways they could engage in inclusive storytelling on a local level. Glenda Gordon, chair of the Gonzales County Historical Commission and our host,

24
Lucille Clifton, *The Collected Poems of Lucille Clifton, 1965-2010* (New York: BOA Editions, 2015), 262.

FIG. 5: *A descendant of freedom colony residents shares memories of life in Gonzales County at CLG public training, August 1, 2018. Image by Texas Historical Commission Staff, Public Information and Education Division.*

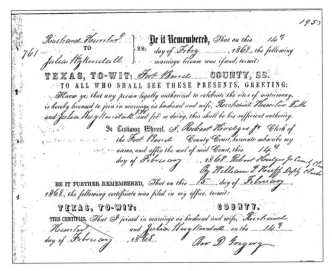

FIG. 6: *Julia Kuykendall and Richard Hunter's marriage certificate in Fort Bend County, Texas, February 14, 1868. My ancestor Julia was born in Sumter, Tennessee, in 1821. She was eventually sold to Joseph Kuykendall (one of the Old Three Hundred) in Fort Bend County. I referenced Julia's story when I asked workshop participants to make a connection between individual stories and popular public narratives. The exercise revealed the dominance of Anglo settler narratives in Texas public history and showed how collaborative counternarrative work is essential to diversifying both public history and local preservation leadership.*

25
Richard Roberts,
"History and Memory:
The Power of
Statist Narratives,"
*International Journal
of African Historical
Studies* 33, no. 3
(2000): 513–522;
Andrea R. Roberts,
"Interpretations &
Imaginaries: Toward
an Instrumental Black
Planning History,"
*Planning Theory and
Practice* 19, no. 2
(2018): 254–288.

responded, cautiously illuminating the bias toward a particular narrative about Gonzales: "There were so many important things happening during the Texas Revolution and that is our claim to fame. And it's very difficult to include other ethnicities… It's been our goal for the last five or six years to expand past that time period and to tell all stories that want to be told, and to expand into other times. Texas public history clashes with county historical commission outreach and anti-bias training."

Regardless of how they are obscured or disremembered, Texas's origins are inextricably linked to human bondage. *FIG. 5* How then do we move past insular story-sharing or shocking confrontations with the ghosts of ancestors past? How do we decenter settler narratives and trouble the systems that keep those who tell these stories in charge of public history in Texas? By creating spaces in which the null, the fugitive, can be given a chance to articulate itself through memory, story, and confrontation with forgetting as annulment. *FIG. 6*

— INTERRUPTING ANNULMENT, ATTENDING TO THE NULL

CLG workshops like the one in Gonzales that I participated in can serve as a model for how county historical commissions can diversify their leadership and surveying processes. When tensions among attendees arise, there must be room to analyze the latent collusion with dominant narratives that overshadows more diverse narratives. The implications of these exercises occurring in state-led processes are consequential. For example, states can require participation in similar trainings or exercises to access funding for surveying and listing new sites on the National Register of Historic Places. In Texas, as well as in many other states, county historical commissions are particularly good spaces for fostering these values because they are also the interested parties that are consulted during Section 106 review processes. If unaware of the diverse people and places impacted by a federally funded project yet undocumented in the historical record, county historical commissions become complicit in the erasure of endangered places. Leveraging culturally situated and state-led social curation work spaces enables us to examine the ways that biases perpetuate certain constructions of state identity and statist narratives, constructions that undermine stories of Black self-making and the creative, insurgent survivalism manifested in stories of African American place-making. 25

Preserving LGBT Places:
The NYC LGBT Historic Sites Project

Andrew S. Dolkart

Challenging and Redefining Narratives

As I write this essay, the celebration of the fiftieth anniversary of the Stonewall riot has just concluded in New York City, with several million people from across the United States and all over the world visiting to take part in a parade, an alternative march, parties, concerts, and many other events. Stonewall, of course, has become a touchstone of the burgeoning movement for LGBT liberation and equality in the United States. 1 FIG. 1 But it is important to remember that there was a great deal of political activism within the LGBT community before Stonewall and that LGBT people played a significant role in American society, albeit often anonymously, since the founding of the nation (and, even before Europeans arrived in North America, in native communities). In many ways, LGBT history is American history. Preservation has an important role to play in identifying and interpreting the history of LGBT people as part of the diverse experiences that contribute to the richness of America. But due to discrimination, most LGBT people were, until recently, forced to live closeted lives, thus creating a formidable challenge for preserving LGBT-related sites and including LGBT narratives in preservation discourse. The NYC LGBT Historic Sites Project, which I founded with two colleagues in 2015, seeks to make this invisible history visible by identifying, interpreting, and, where appropriate, seeking official recognition and preservation of sites of significance to LGBT history and, by extension, to American history in general.

1
In this essay, I have chosen to use the term "LGBT" rather than "LGBTQ." As my colleagues and I developed what became the NYC LGBT Historic Sites Project, we debated whether to use LGBT or LGBTQ but settled on the former since the word "queer" historically had a negative meaning and most of the sites identified date from the period before the 1990s, when groups such as Queer Nation started to reclaim the word. I do use the word "queer" to discuss more contemporary issues in the community.

2
George Chauncey, Gay New York: Gender, Urban Culture, and the Makings of a Gay Male World, 1890–1940 (New York: Basic Books, 1994).

3
For the role of gay men in preservation, see Will Fellows, A Passion to Preserve: Gay Men as Keepers of Culture (Madison: University of Wisconsin Press, 2004).

4
Megan E. Springate, ed., LGBTQ America: A Theme Study of Lesbian, Gay, Bisexual, Transgender, and Queer History, 2 vols. (Washington, DC: National Park Foundation and National Park Service, 2016), www.nps.gov/ subjects/telling allamericansstories/ lgbtqthemestudy.htm.

5
In both San Francisco and Los Angeles, the city commissioned a context statement for LGBT site-based history, while in New York, the study was completed by the NYC LGBT Historic Sites Project, with funding from the National Park Service, through the New York State Historic Preservation Office. For more on San Francisco, see Donna J. Graves and Shayne E. Watson, Citywide Historic Context Statement

FIG. 1: Stonewall participants standing in front of the Stonewall Inn, June 29, 1969. Photograph by Fred W. McDarragh/Getty Images.

for LGBTQ History in San Francisco (City and County of San Francisco, 2016), http://default. sfplanning.org// Preservation/lgbt_ HCS/FinalLGBTQ_ HCS_March2016. pdf; for Los Angeles, see GPA Consulting, SurveyLA LGBT Historic Context Statement (City of Los Angeles Department of City Planning Office of Historic Resources, 2014), http://www. preservation.lacity. org/files/LGBT%20 Historic%20 Context%209-14.pdf; and for New York, see NYC LGBT Historic Sites Project, Historic Context Statement for LGBT History in New York City, Jay Shockley, lead author (2018), http:// www.nyclgbtsites. org/wp-content/ uploads/2018/11/ NYC_LGBT_ Sites_Context_ Statement_102618_ web-compressed1. pdf.

6
Catherine Fosl et al., Kentucky LGBTQ Historic Context Narrative (Louisville: University of Louisville, Anne Braden Institute for Social Justice Research, 2016), https://www. nps.gov/articles/ kentucky-statewide- lgbtq-historic-context- narrative.htm.

7
The amended National Register nominations are the Whiskey Row Historic District and the Elks Athletic Club (the location of the Beaux Arts Cocktail Lounge).

8
Thanks to Catherine Fosl, lead author of the study, for providing information about its reception.

9
For the Los Angeles Conservancy micro- site, see https://www. laconservancy.org/ lgbtq.

In the fifty years since Stonewall, there have been great, if uneven, strides in LGBT rights in the United States. Political advances—such as federal recognition of same-sex marriage—would have been unthinkable even a decade ago, but in many states, there are still no laws protecting LGBT people from being dismissed from their jobs or evicted from housing because of who they are. Throughout the country, violence and sexual assault against trans individuals is a growing problem. And it is always important to remember that there are many countries in the world where same-sex relationships are still illegal, and several where they are punishable by death.

— PRESERVATION AND LGBT HISTORY

Since the publication of George Chauncey's *Gay New York* in 1994, there has been a steady stream of books examining LGBT history in specific cities or regions of the United States. [2] However, the historic preservation community has been slow to recognize the importance of America's LGBT history and the contributions of LGBT individuals to American history and culture. Even though attempts to connect historic preservation and LGBT history began in the early 1990s, only in the past few years has the move to identify, interpret, and preserve sites of significance to LGBT contributions to American history gained traction. It is particularly ironic that LGBT-related sites have received so little attention from the preservation community until recently since there have been so many gay and lesbian professionals in the historic preservation field. [3]

The most expansive preservation tool relating to LGBT issues has been the enormous, two-volume study published by the National Park Foundation and the National Park Service in 2016, which investigates the LGBTQ history of various places and among diverse social communities. [4] A handful of more specific LGBT context statements have been completed for specific cities, including San Francisco, Los Angeles, and New York, which have large, vocal LGBT communities. [5] What is especially heartening is that efforts to identify LGBT sites and recognize their local significance have also taken root in places that might surprise some activists. One especially notable effort is the 126-page *LGBTQ Historic Context Narrative* completed for the state of Kentucky in 2016. [6] As a result of this report, two National Register listings were officially amended to include their significance to the LGBT community. [7] But progress made under such studies can be tenuous. The Kentucky study was completed soon after the state elected a conservative governor, and, although the new administration allowed the project to proceed unimpeded, the change in political climate meant that the planned publicity for the report was shelved and related projects have been slow to take shape. [8]

Besides the theme studies (which take a great deal of time to produce and depend on a long-term funding commitment), smaller scale identification, interpretation, and preservation projects have taken hold in a variety of communities, sponsored by both city governments and private groups. In Los Angeles, the private Los Angeles Conservancy has posted a "microsite" that identifies about three dozen LGBT-related sites. [9]

In Boston and Cambridge, volunteers at the History Project created a Stonewall 50 project, hanging banners and posters from local buildings important to LGBTQ history. *FIG. 2* These sites are also interpreted through an interactive map. 10 And in Chicago, the city's official tourism marketing group has created "Exploring Gay Chicago in History: LGBTQ Landmarks Tour," highlighting eight LGBT-related sites. 11

In several cities where historic markers are a major component of preservation efforts, various sites have recently been recognized for their importance to the LGBT community. Philadelphia pioneered such efforts in 2005 with a plaque recognizing the Independence Hall Annual Reminder Days demonstrations, when gay and lesbian activists picketed Independence Hall on July 4 each year from 1965 through 1969, conservatively dressed in business attire and holding rather polite signs such as "discrimination against homosexuals is immoral" and "homosexuals should be judged as individuals." *FIG. 3* The final demonstration took place only a few days after Stonewall. 12 By 2019 historic markers celebrating specifically LGBT places and events could be found in cities as varied as Nashville, Tennessee; Kansas City, Missouri; Dallas, Texas; Cleveland and Dayton, Ohio; and Roanoke, Virginia.

10
For the Stonewall 50 project, see https://uploads.knightlab.com/storymapjs/72526841f2384b2f30c3b514a37d4887/boston-stonewall-50-commemoration-locations/index.html.

11
For the Chicago tour, see https://www.vamonde.com/adventure/explore-gay-chicago-history-lgbtq-landmarks-tour/360.

12
The Reminder Days are discussed in Lillian Faderman, *The Gay Revolution: The Story of the Struggle* (New York: Simon & Schuster, 2015), 188–189.

FIG. 2: *Banner installed for Stonewall 50 at Old West Church, Boston, by the History Project, 2019. Photograph by the author.*

FIG. 3: *Independence Hall, Reminder Days plaque, Philadelphia, 2019. Photograph by the author.*

House museums, like marker programs, are a traditional yet vital part of the larger preservation movement and have also recently begun interpreting the LGBT history of their owners and residents. Guides in these museums have always imparted detailed information about the heterosexual inhabitants of houses but, until recently, never discussed gay relationships—perhaps to avoid controversy or because the guides or the museum curators were uncomfortable with such subject matter. In recent years, however, houses as diverse as Henry Sleeper's Beauport, in Gloucester, Massachusetts, and the Sarah Orne Jewett House, in South Berwick, Maine, both operated by Historic New England; the Gibson House, in Boston (which inaugurated its "Charlie Tour," named for museum founder Charles Gibson, during Stonewall 50); Jane Addams's

13
For the issue of LGBT lives and house museums, see Susan Ferentinos, *Interpreting LGBT History at Museums and Historic Sites* (Lanham, MD: Rowman & Littlefield, 2015). For resistance to recognizing and interpreting LGBT people at house museums, see Tatum Alana Taylor, "Concealed Certainty and Undeniable Conjecture: Interpreting Marginalized Heritage" (master's thesis, Columbia University Graduate School of Architecture, Planning, and Preservation, 2012).

Hull-House, in Chicago; the Alice Austen House, on Staten Island, New York (now often referred to as the Alice Austen and Gertrude Tate House); and Pendarvis, a Cornish immigrant community in Mineral Point, Wisconsin, restored by partners Robert Neal and Edgar Hellum, recognize their LGBT history. FIG. 4 And, in October 2019, Connecticut Landmarks opened the early nineteenth-century Palmer Warner House, in East Haddem, to the public, with an interpretation that focuses on its mid-twentieth-century occupants, partners Frederic Palmer and Howard Meztger. Yet, while the National Trust for Historic Preservation puts Philip Johnson's relationship with David Whitney at the center of interpretation at its Glass House in New Canaan, Connecticut, the gay ownership of two of its other house museums, Shadows-on-the-Teche in New Iberia, Louisiana, and Villa Finale in San Antonio, Texas, is still not part of the story that is told at these sites. And the more famous a person is, the more difficult it is for museum stewards to acknowledge LGBT issues as a central feature of significance, as is evident at sites relating to Walt Whitman and Eleanor Roosevelt. 13

FIG. 4: *Life-size cutout of Robert Neal and Edgar Hellum, founders of Pendarvis, Mineral Point, Wisconsin, 2012. Photograph by the author.*

But there is still a long way to go even in more progressive places, with few designated sites specifically related to LGBT history. Of the 94,668 sites listed on the National Register in June 2019, only a few dozen even tangentially mention LGBT issues, with fewer focused on LGBT people and events. A few cities have designated individual properties as landmarks, protected under their local preservation ordinances. For example, three buildings in San Francisco are official city landmarks, four in Los Angeles, one in Chicago, and, until June 2019, only one building—the Stonewall Inn itself—was a landmark designated for its LGBT significance in New York. 14 Additional official landmarks in these and other cities are associated with LGBT stories, but their LGBT history was not called out as part of their designations—Jane Addams's Hull-House and the Lorraine Hansberry House in Chicago are two examples of this all too prevalent problem.

— LEARNING FROM THE NEW YORK CITY EXPERIENCE

My colleagues Ken Lustbader and Jay Shockley and I have been advocates for the recognition of LGBT sites in New York City for more than twenty-five years. In the 1990s we sometimes undertook subtle interventions that changed the focus of historic sites—adding the discussion of two LGBT sites to the New York City Landmarks Preservation Commission's *Guide to New York City Landmarks* in 1992 and incorporating LGBT themes into the commission's designation reports. 15 Meanwhile, in 1993 Lustbader wrote his master's thesis on preserving gay and lesbian sites in Greenwich Village. 16

The first major public project on the significance of LGBT sites was completed for the twenty-fifth anniversary of Stonewall in 1994, when we were on the preservation subcommittee of OLGAD, the Organization of Lesbian and Gay Architects and Designers. In celebration of the anniversary, we (along with other colleagues) compiled and published *A Guide to*

14
The landmarks in San Francisco are Castro Camera and the Harvey Milk Residence (designated in 2000), Jose Theater/NAMES Project (2004), and Twin Peaks Tavern (2013); the Los Angeles landmarks are the Black Cat (2008), Margaret and Harry Hay Residence (2014), the Tom of Finland House (2016), and the Standard Oil Company Sales Department Building/Woman's Building (2018); and in Chicago the Henry Gerber House (2001) is an official landmark.

15
Andrew S. Dolkart, *Guide to New York City Landmarks* (Washington, DC: Preservation Press, 1992); the two sites discussed are Stonewall and the 171 West 12th Street Apartments, home to several lesbian couples in the circle of Eleanor Roosevelt. For designation reports, see New York City Landmarks Preservation Commission, "F. W. I. L. Lundy Brothers Restaurant Building," report prepared by Gale Harris (Landmarks Preservation Commission, 1992), 11n38 (the first designation report to make any reference to an LGBT individual); "Louis N. Jaffe Theater (Yiddish Art Theater)," report prepared by Jay Shockley (1993), 10 (the first report to use the word "gay"); "East 17th Street/Irving Place Historic District," report prepared by Gale Harris and Jay Shockley (1998), 54–55, 61 (the first report to use the word "lesbian").

16
Ken Lustbader, "Landscape and Liberation: Preserving Gay and Lesbian History in Greenwich Village" (master's thesis, Columbia University Graduate School of Architecture, Planning, and Preservation, 1993).

FIG. 5: A Guide to Lesbian & Gay New York Historical Landmarks, *prepared by the preservation subcommittee of OLGAD, the Organization of Lesbian and Gay Architects and Designers, for Stonewall 25, 1994. Collection of the author.*

17
OLGAD, *A Guide to Lesbian & Gay New York Historical Landmarks* (1994).

18
"Stonewall National Register Nomination," report prepared by David Carter, Andrew Scott Dolkart, Gale Harris, and Jay Shockley (2002).

19
New York City Landmarks Preservation Commission, "Stonewall Inn," designation report prepared by Christopher D. Brazee, Corinne Engelbert, and Gale Harris (2015).

20
NYC LGBT Historic Sites Project, *Historic Context Study for LGBT History in New York City*, Jay Shockley, lead author (2018); the new National Register listings are Julius', a bar in Greenwich Village that was the site of a "sip in," where, in 1966, activists challenged the New York State Liquor Authority's rule that it was illegal for a bar to serve a known homosexual; Caffe Cino, the birthplace of Off-Off-Broadway and gay theater, in Greenwich Village; Columbia University's Earl Hall, where the Student Homophile League, the first collegiate gay group in America, was founded and the site of early monthly gay and lesbian dances; and the James Baldwin House on West 71st Street, home to the famed gay African-American writer and activist. The nomination for the Alice Austen House on Staten Island was amended to recognize Austen's relationship with Gertrude Tate of over fifty years. Another amended listing is pending: the Church of the Holy Apostles in Chelsea, recognizing its importance as a site for meetings by many early, post-Stonewall political and religious groups.

Lesbian & Gay New York Historical Landmarks. 17 FIG. 5 This brochure consisted of a map with the location of important sites in Greenwich Village, Midtown, and Harlem (plus a few major sites elsewhere in the city), and brief descriptions of why each site was significant. We believe that this was the first published guide to lesbian and gay historic sites in the United States.

A few years later, in 1999, we spearheaded the listing of Stonewall on the National Register, the first site ever listed for LGBT significance. FIG. 6 The National Register listing includes not only the Stonewall Inn building but also the small park across the street (Christopher Park) and the adjacent streets where the 1969 riot took place. 18 A year later, Stonewall became a National Historic Landmark, one of only a small number of historic sites with this designation. Surprisingly, it was not until 2015 that the New York City Landmarks Preservation Commission finally designated the Stonewall Inn as a landmark, again making it the city's first designation for LGBT significance. 19 This took place a year before President Barack Obama established Stonewall National Monument specifically to commemorate LGBT history, a history not previously recognized by the National Park Service.

FIG. 6: *The former Stonewall Inn, 2016. Photograph by Christopher D. Brazee/ NYC LGBT Historic Sites Project.*

Stonewall was an obvious landmark, and our other actions have been relatively small in comparison to the impact that LGBT people have had on New York City. More needed to be done to recognize LGBT-related sites. This realization led to our successful grant application to the National Park Service's Underrepresented Communities Grant Program. With this grant, in 2015 we launched the NYC LGBT Historic Sites Project, a citywide survey of extant LGBT sites dating from the establishment of New Amsterdam in the early seventeenth century to the year 2000. The project has completed a theme study for LGBT sites in New York City and successfully prepared several new and amended National Register nominations, but our central focus is a growing, interactive website (www. nyclgbtsites.org) with detailed entries, archival images, ephemera, and multimedia.[20] Our complimentary activities include lectures, tours, and classroom presentations at New York City public schools.

Why are we doing this? We see the NYC LGBT Historic Sites Project as a pioneering cultural heritage initiative and educational resource that is comprehensively identifying and interpreting sites connected to LGBT history and culture in New York City. This is the first such comprehensive survey of LGBT sites ever undertaken in the United States. Our aim is "to make an invisible history visible" and to bring to the fore the contributions that LGBT people have made to both local and national history and culture. The NYC LGBT Historic Sites Project includes, but goes far beyond, the more obvious sites like Stonewall, or gay and lesbian bars, or places of sexual encounter, or locations of political activism to include sites related to LGBT individuals and their accomplishments, thus accentuating the central place that LGBT people and communities have had on America. As part of this effort, we specifically call out places related to architecture, dance, literature, music, theater, and visual arts. For example, the Winter Garden Theatre is recognized as the site of the premiere of *West Side Story*, a masterpiece that was almost entirely the work of gay men and lesbians—notably composer Leonard Bernstein, choreographer and director Jerome Robbins, lyricist Stephen Sondheim, librettist Arthur Laurents, set designer Oliver Smith, costume designer

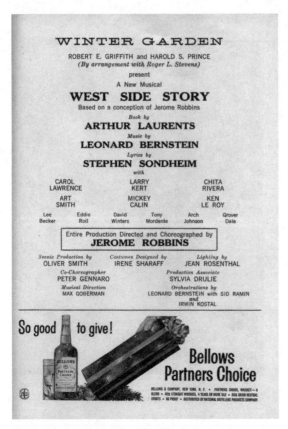

FIG. 7: West Side Story, *Playbill title page, 1957.*

Irene Sharaff, lighting designer Jean Rosenthal, lead actor Larry Kert, and other members of the original cast. *FIG. 7*

A key aspect of the NYC LGBT Historic Sites Project is to shed light on an aspect of American history that is largely overlooked, ignored, or, especially in the past, discussed in a negative light. Many people believe that gay history began with Stonewall. At the announcement of the National Park Service's LGBTQ theme study in May 2014, LGBT philanthropist Tim Gill of the Gill Foundation, lead funder of the study, stood in front of Stonewall and stated that the gay community had only a brief history, and one that began there. While demonstrably false, this idea is widely believed as LGBT people often have had to hide their identities or have had their histories erased and, therefore, their accomplishments as LGBT people have not been acknowledged. This ignorance makes it of paramount importance to document and recognize significant LGBT sites.

FIG. 8: Ken Lustbader, codirector of the NYC LGBT Historic Sites Project, planting a rainbow flag at the Green-Wood Cemetery grave of composer/conductor Leonard Bernstein, 2018. Photograph by Amanda Davis/NYC LGBT Historic Sites Project.

The NYC LGBT Historic Sites Project is also a social justice initiative. In spite of the enormous advances of LGBT rights over the last fifty years, there are still threats to these rights and to queer people across America—evident, for example, in Trump-administration actions against the transgender community and its opposition, before the Supreme Court, to including sexual orientation and gender identity in anti-discrimination protections. The interpretation of extant sites where individuals or groups made a mark on our history can be a powerful tool for instilling pride in members of a community and in educating the public about those contributions. This effort to identify and interpret LGBT sites parallels efforts in the African American and other communities to use historic sites as a means to explore issues of identity and the complexities of American history. Many people who have attended our walking tours have commented on how moved they have been to see the sites where LGBT people fought for their rights or simply lived their lives. People have been particularly excited as we place rainbow flags at the burial sites of LGBT individuals at Green-Wood and Woodlawn cemeteries. *FIG. 8*

21
Andrew Dolkart,
"Designating New
York City Landmarks,"
in *Saving Place: 50
Years of New York
City Landmarks*, ed.
Donald Albrecht and
Andrew Dolkart (New
York: Monacelli Press,
2015), 80.

FIG. 9: *Patrons of Brooklyn's Starlite Lounge, "The Oldest Black-Owned,
Non-Discrimination Club," protesting its closing, ca. 2010, film still from* We
Came to Sweat, *directed by Kate Kunath, 2014.*

The project also attempts to explore and celebrate diversity within
the LGBT community, not only because LGBT people can be found in
every facet of American life, but also because there is a history of lack of
inclusion within the LGBT community itself. Thus, the project has entries
associated with lesbians, gay men, bisexuals, transgender people, African
Americans, Latinos, Asian Americans, Protestants, Catholics, Jews, senior
citizens, youth, and other communities. *FIG. 9*

— CHALLENGING PRESERVATION POLICY AND PRACTICE

Identifying, interpreting, and preserving sites of LGBT history is
not always an easy task. As previously noted, many of the places where
important events occurred or where LGBT people met and interacted in
the past are simply not known since discriminatory laws and generalized
homophobia meant that they could not be publicized. Other sites were
transient, such as the private apartments where African American men
met when they were excluded from commercial gay bars or similar set-
tings where lesbians held potluck dinners because they had few public
places in which to safely socialize. Even in contemporary New York City,
homophobia can still be an issue, as we discovered when the owner of
the house in Flushing, Queens, that was the childhood home of early gay
activist Morty Manford and the place where his parents founded PFLAG
(Parents and Friends of Lesbians and Gays) rebuffed our request to list the
house on the National Register, stating that she did not want her house
known as the "gay house on the block."

Beyond simply identifying sites, a most pressing issue is how the
preservation community deals with sites that are significant for their historic and cultural value as opposed to their architectural qualities. When
the modern preservation movement developed in the 1960s, architectural
value was paramount, even as the movement paid lip service to history
and culture. This bias is a result of the fact that most of those who lobbied for preservation laws and established landmark commissions were
architectural historians or had, in some way, been trained in architecture.

22
"It's About Time,"
announcement
of Corduroy Club
opening, in West Side
Discussion Group,
Newsletter, July 1967,
Foster Gunnison, Jr.
Papers, Archives &
Special Collections
at the Thomas J.
Dodd Research
Center, University of
Connecticut Libraries.

Thus, vernacular buildings were generally ignored unless they were very old or associated with a founding father or other figure of national historic significance. 21 By the time Stonewall 50 was celebrated, the NYC LGBT Historic Sites Project had fully documented more than 200 sites with significant LGBT history; more than 350 others had been identified but needed additional research. Most of these sites are historically and culturally significant but may be of only limited architectural interest.

How can we rally the preservation community around a building that is not architecturally distinguished and where the history is hidden, as it is with so many LGBT sites? Take 240 West 38th Street, for example, a modest four-story loft in the Garment District dating from 1925. *FIG. 10* Unknown to most of those who walk by is the fact that from March 1967 through 1971, this was home to the Corduroy Club, a private social club that offered a largely older lesbian and gay community an alternative to the bar scene, with dances, card parties, plays, movie nights, and dinners. It was a significant effort by the pre-Stonewall LGBT community in New York to have a social space that was outside the control of the Mafia, New York State Liquor Authority regulations, and police arrests and entrapment. It was seen at the time as "the only true private club in the US operated by members of a homophile organization for all homosexuals." 22

FIG. 10: *240 West 38th Street, home to the Corduroy Club from 1967 to 1971, 2016. Photograph by Christopher D. Brazee/NYC LGBT Historic Sites Project.*

And what about a site of historical or cultural value that has been altered? This is an especially pressing issue since many vernacular buildings, including those of cultural value, have evolved over time, with re-sided facades and altered interior layouts. With its emphasis on integrity, including the integrity of interior spaces that the public never sees, many important sites are not eligible for National Register listing, threatening their survival. This issue, of course, goes beyond just LGBT sites. Perhaps no site in New York has been more controversial than the Walt Whitman House, at 99 Ryerson Street in the Wallabout neighborhood of Brooklyn, which was not granted a public hearing by the New York City Landmarks Preservation Commission and was rejected by the State Historic Preservation Office as a potential National Register listing. *FIG. 11* Whitman led a peripatetic life: between 1823 and 1862 he lived at more than thirty addresses in Manhattan and Brooklyn. The Ryerson Street house is the only one that survives. Whitman lived there from May 1855 to May 1856, just when *Leaves of Grass* was being published and where Ralph Waldo Emerson came to visit having read and admired the poem. The site has clearly been altered; it now has another story and is entirely clad in synthetic siding. But should we judge the site through an architectural lens, or by looking at relevant cultural interest and meaning? Shouldn't this house be saved now, protected from demolition, and, over

FIG. 11: *Walt Whitman House, 99 Ryerson Street, Brooklyn, 2016. Photograph by Christopher D. Brazee/NYC LGBT Historic Sites Project.*

FIG. 12: *69 West 14th Street, home to Alt U and the headquarters of the Gay Liberation Front in 1969–1970 (demolished), 2016. Photograph by Christopher D. Brazee/NYC LGBT Historic Sites Project.*

23
"Gay Liberation Front at Alternate U.," NYC LGBT Historic Sites Project, http://www.nyclgbtsites.org/site/gay-liberation-front-at-alternate-u.

24
The six sites are Caffe Cino in Greenwich Village; the Gay Activists Alliance Firehouse in SoHo, home to an early LGBT social and political group; the New York Lesbian, Gay, Bisexual & Transgender Community Center in Greenwich Village, since 1983 the major LGBT facility in New York; the Women's Liberation Center in Chelsea, once home to several important early lesbian rights groups; and the homes of African American writers and activists Audre Lorde on Staten Island and James Baldwin on the Upper West Side.

25
"The Problem with Limitless Landmarking," New York Post, May 18, 2019.

time, returned to a state that might be more recognizable to Whitman? It is time that we reassess how culturally significant sites are evaluated and regulated at both the local and the national levels so that extant sites with compromised architectural integrity can still be recognized and preserved.

As a result of the lack of awareness of LGBT history and LGBT-related places, buildings of historical importance are being lost. A prime example is 69 West 14th Street, on the corner of Sixth Avenue, a modest, four-story commercial building erected in 1909. FIG. 12 For many years, this building was the home of Alternate U. (or Alt U.), a politically radical, counterculture school where the Gay Liberation Front (GLF) met from July 1969 to December 1970. GLF was the first political group founded after Stonewall, with its inaugural meeting held only a few days after the riot. GLF held its meetings and weekly dances in this building. It was here that the group organized protests, including one against the progressive weekly newspaper the *Village Voice*, which had until then refused to use the word "gay." They also sponsored meetings of allied groups including Street Transvestites Action Revolutionaries (STAR) and Gay Youth. 23 Demolition began on the building in spring 2019.

Public history is one way to recognize sites and make people aware of their significance, and the NYC LGBT Historic Sites Project has harnessed new technologies to add to the ways in which historic sites can be identified and their significance communicated to the public. But if at least some of these sites are going to be preserved, some sort of governmental recognition is often needed. The hesitancy of landmark commissions to designate buildings for their LGBT significance is beginning to change, at least in New York. As part of the celebration of Stonewall 50, the New York City Landmarks Preservation Commission designated six culturally significant sites in June 2019, all of which had been suggested by the NYC LGBT Historic Sites Project in consultation with the commission. 24 There was extensive support for these designations, and they occurred despite the *New York Post*'s editorial that accused the commission of "pandering to special interests." 25 Official designation is certainly not the answer for all sites relating to LGBT history, and such designations are still not possible in many places. But the actions of the New York City Landmarks Preservation Commission, the slow increase in LGBT-related National Register nominations, the outpouring of interest in LGBT issues generated by Stonewall 50, and the support that the NYC LGBT Historic Sites Project has garnered leave me guardedly optimistic that, despite opposition, we can continue to make progress in the identification, interpretation, and preservation of historic sites that represent the influence of LGBT people and, with this, we can expand the reach of historic preservation in an increasingly inclusive manner.

I would like to acknowledge the assistance of my colleagues at the NYC LGBT Historic Sites Project: Ken Lustbader, Jay Shockley, and project director Amanda Davis.

BlackSpaces: Brownsville
Codesigning Black Neighborhood Heritage Conservation

Emma Osore

Brownsville is a 1.163-square-mile residential neighborhood in eastern Brooklyn, New York. In the 1930s the demographics of the population began the pivot from a Jewish majority toward an African American and Latinx majority, with Black people primarily coming as migrants (and refugees) from the Jim Crow-era South. 1 In 1940 Black residents made up 6 percent of Brownsville's population. By 1950 there were double that number, and white flight ensued. 2 As of the 2010 census, 76 percent of Brownsville's population of 86,377 identifies as Black. 3

Since the 1960s Brownsville and neighboring Ocean Hill-Brownsville have had a rich legacy of radical neighborhood activism. The Black Panthers had a headquarters in Brownsville, and parents and community members demanded community-control of their local schools. 4 At BlackSpace, we have learned from many of the neighborhood's Black residents about the numerous other heroes and organizers who demanded and created better public services while the government disinvested and crime increased in the ensuing decades.

Despite consistently ranking as an area with one of the highest crime rates in the city, we learned that Brownsville has been a haven for people escaping everything from the Jim Crow South to the modern-day shelter system. Its diverse population includes Black entrepreneurs and creatives, as well as the elderly and Brownsville-born millennial returnees. While Brownsville has one of the country's highest concentrations of public housing (intentionally designed as a repository for the displaced and designated for the "colored" in the 1950s by white urban planner Robert Moses), it is, by some accounts, buffering the ravaging effects of the gentrification sweeping Brooklyn. 5 Since 2010 the resurgence in public investment in Brownsville has made residents wary of gentrification, with recent studies confirming this fear. 6

BlackSpace is not a Brownsville-based or -focused organization, however: it is a collective of Black professionals working in the disciplines or interested in the impact of urban planning and design, architecture, real estate, culture and heritage, and economic development in Black communities and environments. BlackSpace leverages our collective network to strengthen support for Black professionals in fields that influence the built environment in addition to working with communities to promote and protect Black neighborhood agency. 7

As a collective, we demand a present and a future in which Black people, Black spaces, and Black culture matter and thrive. When the collective was founded in New York City in 2015, we could not help but be overwhelmed by the rapid and violent effects of gentrification on the city's historically Black neighborhoods. As an urban planning-based group, we have a strong understanding of the complex economic underpinnings of gentrification that begin long before that gentrification becomes physically noticeable. We openly acknowledge that the racial stratification of US neighborhoods is due to legacies of racial discrimination in place-based policies that continue to be made in and by the institutions many of us work for today.

We were less knowledgeable about how to tackle these multi-issue problems and how to confront the cultural erasure we were experiencing daily with just the tools of our independent professions. So, in 2018, BlackSpace took an opportunity to put inquiry into action. With the support

1
Kay S. Hymowitz, *The New Brooklyn: What It Takes to Bring a City Back* (Lanham, MD: Rowman & Littlefield, 2017).

2
Wendell E. Pritchett, *Brownsville, Brooklyn: Blacks, Jews, and the Changing Face of the Ghetto* (Chicago: University of Chicago Press, 2002).

3
US Census Bureau Population Estimates, 2013, adapted from "Brooklyn Community District 16: Brownsville [New York City]," https://www1.nyc.gov/assets/doh/downloads/pdf/data/2015chp-bk16.pdf.

4
University of Washington, Civil Rights and Labor History Consortium "Mapping the Black Panther Party in Key Cities," Mapping American Social Movements, https://depts.washington.edu/moves/BPP_mapcities.shtml; Mike Stivers, "Ocean Hill-Brownsville, Fifty Years Later," *Jacobin*, September 12, 2018, https://jacobinmag.com/2018/09/ocean-hill-brownsville-strikes-1968-united-federation-teachers.

5
Ginia Bellafante, "Resurrecting Brownsville," *Nation*, April 17, 2013, https://www.thenation.com/article/resurrecting-brownsville.

6
Andrea Leonhardt, "Study: Brownsville Could Be Next to Face Gentrification," *BK Reader*, March 22, 2019, https://www.bkreader.com/2019/03/22/study-brownsville-could-be-next-to-face-gentrification.

7
To access the playbook and BlackSpace's core principles, visit www.blackspace.org.

8
"BlackSpace
Manifesto,"
BlackSpace Urbanist
Collective, http://
www.blackspace.org/
manifesto.

of the J. M. Kaplan Fund, we began a yearlong multidisciplinary heritage conservation effort in Brownsville. While none of us were trained heritage professionals, the reality of Black cultural loss/erasure in the surrounding neighborhoods was so great that we became heritage conservationists according to our own definition. As Black urbanists, we sought to save and understand cultural touchstones unique to Black people, in a Black enclave like Brownsville, to gain a fuller historical context than was being presented in the academic and professional literature.

Over the course of a year, BlackSpace worked with community members to document neighborhood memories on maps, identify neighborhood cultural assets and heritage values, and create space for local heritage conservationists to connect and build platforms for sharing Black neighborhood history and culture. We developed a deliberately nonlinear and reflective process to codesign neighborhood heritage conservation efforts.

— BLACK HERITAGE CONSERVATION

As we had suspected, and despite the dearth of literature, Black-led neighborhood heritage conservation has been going on for a long time in Brownsville. As an organization primarily of outsiders (to both the neighborhood and professional historic preservation), we hoped to acknowledge and strengthen the work already happening in Brownsville and add a fresh perspective to preservation as a field. We established a working umbrella term, "heritage conservation," based on what we learned in Brownsville and drawing from our multidisciplinary fields. We define heritage conservation as *the act of protecting and enlivening culturally significant markers, both nonphysical and physical, to understand a place and to value the past, present, and future of its people.*

While we do not generally agree that culture and heritage alone can solve problems like gentrification or economic disinvestment, we do agree that heritage conservation can be a radical act that strengthens Black agency in place-making, place-keeping, and place-saving. From our perspective, heritage conservation acknowledges intangible heritage as assets equal to built ones, advances neighborhood-level narratives that are collectively determined, inspires local advocates, affirms people's rights to their places, resists cultural erasure and racism, fortifies social networks, and deepens a sense of and investment in community, among other benefits. That means heritage conservationists can be those rooted in or making the shared values or culture of a community ("cultural producers"); those who keep and share neighborhood history and culture, informally or formally, including those who might not recognize their work as heritage conservation; and local and nonlocal practitioners in collaboration, using an antiracist, codesigning, and skill-sharing model to advance neighborhood heritage.

In addition to more expansive definitions that seek to be more inclusive of the kinds of heritage we aim to conserve, we have also developed fourteen principles to guide our work and hold us accountable to one another, our partners, and the public. 8 We drafted them based on our research, design experience, and yearlong engagement in Brownsville, and we invite others to incorporate principles from the manifesto into their work.

These interdisciplinary and Black-centric principles are grounded in thinking beyond established heritage conservation practices toward a more holistic view of the future. To be socially inclusive, especially of the Black experience in America, future neighborhoods must be spaces that both acknowledge the triumphs *and* the oppressions of their people, must manifest people's aspirations *and* challenges.

— INTENTIONS AND OUTCOMES

Beginning any efforts in any neighborhood—and especially those that are historically Black and/or societally and economically marginalized—requires insisting on justice for its natural resources and its people and assuming that the people and places are already gems descended from rich and nuanced histories.

A more nuanced, people-centered heritage conservation demands that participants *learn, listen, and activate; reflect and synthesize; codevelop; and cocreate and link.* Each of these is a phase whose subtext includes "magic moments" or eye-opening experiences, lessons learned, and actionable tools and directives that can help novices and professionals document, conserve, and amplify cultural assets in historically Black neighborhoods. We hope sharing "Codesigning Black Neighborhood Heritage Conservation" guides practitioners to expand their understanding of heritage conservation and to enact socially inclusive practices that restore people as well as buildings and artifacts.

Still, this is just one pathway to heritage conservation practice that centers equity and justice for people. We hope that practitioners, both local and nonlocal, will strive to collaborate with their communities to document, conserve, and amplify Black neighborhood cultures. We are experts in our experience but not in any one process—this is a record of our journey.

More than thirty people shared their stories and memories with us, and we are thankful for the generosity of the many residents of Brownsville, the past and present heritage conservationists we did not meet but who have been keeping the culture of the neighborhood alive, and members of the BlackSpace collective, for their numerous contributions to making this experience possible.

— PHASE 1: LEARN, LISTEN, ACTIVATE

As a first step, it was critical for us to learn about the cultural landscape of the place where we were working and to determine how our team would work together. We assumed there would be existing heritage and cultural practice and conservation activity, so we took the following steps:

- Conducted preliminary research online and with local sources to find the appropriate spaces to learn more about Black cultures in the neighborhood.
- Intentionally developed relationships with people and their spaces based on our existing informal connections.

9
Anonymous father and resident, "Tenth Annual Pitkin Avenue Easter Parade and Brownsville Easter Egg Hunt Listening Session 1," interview by Kenyatta T. McLean, March 31, 2018.

- Geolocated and documented tangible and intangible cultural assets on a shared map (as closely as we could and as much as we could), based on the stories Black Brownsvillians shared.
- Attended cultural events and talked to the people there. We set a goal of attending at least seven kinds of events, including the major heritage events as well as event-specific groups. These included a writer's workshop, a homecoming festival, a parade, a youth creative workshop, and an event at a heritage center.
- Leveraged prewritten questions to build a conversation around the stories that community members wanted to share, rather than rigidly sticking to the script; we took the time to listen.
- Probed lightly for spatial locations hidden in responses to questions, and recorded information on our phones or took notes. Over the course of many conversations, we gained a rich understanding of the geographic layout of events, places, buildings, and people significant to the neighborhood. By being humble learners who practiced deep listening, we found that Brownsville's Black history and culture began to emerge to us.
- Supplemented in-person learning with Internet and social media artifacts about Brownsville (and added links to content in the online map).
- Respected people's anonymity, requested permission before capturing any images or recordings, and followed up with those who were interested in ongoing participation in the project—especially cultural producers and neighborhood heritage conservationists.
- Learned and adjusted to the different levels of sensitivity required in visiting intimate heritage spaces.

MAGIC MOMENT

Community members continued to remind us of the importance of everyday experiences and that we should not assume there were "right" ways to answer our questions.

Interviewer
What are your favorite cultural experiences in Brownsville?

Interviewee
Ah, the bodegas, of course—to me, they're close to my heart.

The interviewee went on to describe how he loved the daily ritual of getting the news and building connections with regulars at the bodegas in the neighborhood. 9

- Sought people who might traditionally be overlooked for input on neighborhood issues—like young people and artists. We found it crucial to consider race, age, gender, sexuality, class, education, ability, and relationship to the neighborhood (and the intersections of these qualities) to better recognize places of cultural significance for groups that might not typically be asked.

141

Next, because we recognized the importance of a deliberate and iterative process, we established times to regularly reflect on what we had learned and to plan upcoming engagements. We transcribed each story by breaking it down, laying it out horizontally, and then, as a team, identifying patterns, themes, and inspirations. Afterward, we identified outstanding questions to be explored next. Each time, we distilled the stories we heard, and we refined those insights in public, at other events and gatherings. We rehearsed this process with a wide variety of neighborhood stakeholders multiple times in many ways, all in service of learning and getting closer to the next step, rather than in service of designing some sort of object.

Over time, the summaries and syntheses of our listenings and learnings resulted in a set of major cultural heritage themes that reflected some of the values of the Black heritage of the neighborhood. As part of the process, we also did the following:

- Built in reflection time to not only share the stories we collected but also refine our process of engagement, realize mistakes, highlight successes, and unlearn traditional and often limiting methods and strategies we had learned in our schools or workplaces.
- Set clear goals for each engagement, so the time spent was intentional, transparent, and in service of insightful conversations.
- Wore branded T-shirts and gear at outdoor events (although not in intimate/indoor groups where it would have felt imposing) to identify ourselves as part of a coordinated effort, as well as to encourage curiosity and build trust. Distributing branded items to respondents also helped foster a practice of exchange rather than extraction.
- Incorporated "microdesigns" into activations—that is, low-cost and workable heritage conservation solutions that we could deploy in real time. One example was teens using spray chalk and stencil letters to mark the sidewalk at notable places around the neighborhood.
- Prototyped a set of heritage solutions at community events to gain feedback. We found that these prototypes also made us more approachable for people of all ages and contributed to the vibrancy of existing public events.
- Returned to reflection and synthesis to determine whether we needed to learn more or to move to the next phase.
- Offered opportunities for the BlackSpace members to learn and grow dynamically as a group of design professionals. With every public interaction, there were tough moments where our motives were questioned and our biases were revealed, as well as moments of catharsis and healing from acknowledging, affirming, and amplifying Black spaces as Black people.
- Debriefed each neighborhood interaction in a group. These discussions opened major opportunities for us to adjust our processes and clarify our values.
- Created connections and relationships with many kinds of people who had strong connections to and cared deeply about spaces and places in their neighborhood.

- Wove Brownsville young people into our work. By hiring them to record our engagements and reflection sessions in photography and video, we created entry points for them to meaningfully engage in the process. Working alongside them had a residual benefit of enhancing (read: correcting) our interpretations of local insights while also providing opportunities for positive interaction in the neighborhood and building their knowledge of cultural production, design-based careers and tools, and neighborhood cultural heritage alongside people who looked like them.

— PHASE 3: CODEVELOP

We distilled all the listening and synthesis down to six themes, more than fifty heritage assets we could map, and a list of twenty-seven cross-disciplinary cultural producers. It was time to convene the cultural producers and heritage conservationists we identified in the community to guide the culminating collaborative project or "heritage happening."

At our first planning meeting for the happening, we shared our project motivations, the iterative design process, microdesign concepts and results, and major heritage themes and values distilled. This way, collaborators had a framework for dialogue about fortifying Brownsville's neighborhood heritage. We gathered for a family-style dinner and asked each participant to share a current or a future project they were working on and the human, financial, and spatial resources required. On a large piece of butcher paper with prepared categories, each participant listed their projects and indicated which of the five working heritage values were most closely aligned to their projects (celebrates resilience, connects history to present and future, amplifies green space and physical beauty, opens space for collective storytelling, facilitates connections across generations). This process helped the group communicate their work and visualize how their projects aligned toward the goal of heritage conservation and cultural production. While participants shared information and resources, we guided a discussion about what we might do in the immediate and longer terms to fortify the heritage of the neighborhood. We also did the following:

- Cocreated alongside a subset of the groups we had met throughout the process. Of all the people we met throughout the "listen, learn, activate" phase, the best group to codevelop and cocreate with were the people already producing and conserving culture distinct to the neighborhood.
- Decided that the design, making, and installation should involve community members; such involvement is essential to a heritage conservation effort that aligns with the real needs, capacities, and ideas of a neighborhood and its people. It would have been easy for BlackSpace to research the neighborhood, design a solution behind closed doors, and independently fabricate a project, but that would have been counter to our values and goals.
- Made spaces flexible to allow for the unexpected moments that ultimately defined this work. Despite the many time and logistical

constraints, it was critical that we also sometimes freed our pre-developed agendas/activities to be responsive to the moment, to follow community members' best judgments, or to honor requests or critiques made beyond the terms of the project.

— PHASE 4: COCREATE, LINK

Cultural producers and conservationists who expressed interest in collaborating were invited to a planning meeting to cocreate heritage happenings based on our shared visions. BlackSpace acted as a convener and coproducer for the ideas that the local cultural producers generated. BlackSpace members organized WhatsApp groups, arranged space and food for meetings, ordered necessary supplies, offered prompts and frameworks to help move the group forward, and helped set up and execute each heritage happening.

For example, we coproduced a pop-up neighborhood storytelling tour called the Brownsville Sankofa Trail at the annual October Harvest Festival sponsored by the Pitkin Avenue Business Improvement District. Based on an idea generated by local conservationists to combine several skill sets (storytelling, visual arts, event production) into one new event, a visual artist built six interactive storytelling "environments" inspired by African and Black American visual/neighborhood cultures: inside each were women storytellers, or griots, who shared short stories important to them and their neighborhood.

More than sixty families moved from station to station collecting passport stamps at each one. At the end of the storytelling trail, each person drew their own stamp symbols representing the neighborhood and received Halloween treats sponsored by a local car club and civic group, Trucked Out. This ephemeral celebration of intangible neighborhood heritage not only acknowledged, affirmed, and amplified Black cultural assets, it embodied the Brownsville Black neighborhood heritage values that we identified. After the event, we heard from participants that strengthening Black cultural assets also strengthened Black agency in place-making, place-keeping, and place-saving processes.

MAGIC MOMENT

"This event has inspired me to finish my book on the history of Brownsville."—*Cathie, griot and former resident*

"It's surreal to be back here. My dad grew up here and was told to leave and do better for himself, and now I'm back here by my own choosing."—*Cara, BlackSpace member*

"Our youth creative team got really excited and wants to make a local Black neighborhood history board game."
—*Steven, Made in Brownsville employee*

"Wow—it feels great to return to the old neighborhood—I have fond memories of this place."
—*Clariesa, former Brownsville resident*

10
Betsy Head Pool, a WPA-era facility and a part of Betsy Head Park, is one of two historically designated buildings in Brownsville and was last renovated in 1983. The one-hundred-year-old pool is a cultural and public asset that many Brownsvillians mentioned as an important part of the neighborhood and a safe, programmed space for youth. While the pool is alluded to in the announcements of the recent 2016 $30 million Betsy Head Park renovation, the pool is not included in the actual capital project plan (only "reconstruction of pool piping hangers" is). It is unclear whether the pool's historic designation (and potential for added costs as a result) may have blocked it from receiving part of the $30 million investment in this important local asset.

11
This refers to Octavia Butler's fictional religion, Earthseed, from her book *Parable of the Sower:* "All you touch, you change. All you change, changes you. The only lasting truth is change. God is change" (New York: Warner Books, 1995), 1.

BlackSpace continues to connect existing groups under the umbrella of heritage conservation for projects like online maps, toolkits, storytelling events, publications, and exhibitions that cultural producers and conservationists can use to further amplify and fortify their individual and collective place-based work. These platforms are also a mechanism to imagine new and future ways to work together to enliven the history of the neighborhood in the present day. We also accomplished the following things:

- Coproduced a one-of-a kind heritage happening customized by/for Brownsvillians by connecting in-person and online with neighborhood storytellers like griots, event producers, writers, mural artists, dance company owners, documentarians, fashion designers, and others. We deeply valued community leaders committed to producing place-based experiences that celebrate local Black leaders, culture, and spaces.
- Made neighborhood visioning and future-making a main goal of conservation. We deliberately limited the word "gentrification" and instead made a present-day experience and co-envisioned a future that supported the expression of neighborhood cultural heritage. We cocreated moments that would include elements of joy. Reckoning with history can be frustrating and painful, so we always met in environments that were approachable, welcoming, colorful, and organized. We often shared our own personal projects, and we laughed a lot over hearty, family-style meals from Brownsville's Black-owned catering companies. We took the time to welcome in neighborhood celebrities, passersby, and characters and to offer each other loving feedback. These steps brought joy and warmth to the spaces in which we worked and helped us to build trust and get to know each other as we worked.

— POST-PROJECT REFLECTIONS

Allowing the fundamental values of historic preservation to rise to the top and focusing on practices that center people and justice can be healing not only for disinvested cultural assets but also for neighbors and professionals. A deliberately nonlinear path toward restoration, repair, and justice is an underexplored way to leverage the past to create the future. Below are some of our reflections on this way of working.

BlackSpace's work begins to break open what is professionally possible. In a place like Brownsville, the work of built-environment professionals is complicated, especially because stories of neighborhood injustice and resistance implicated our traditional practices in the situation of Brownsville today. [10]

Allowing the process to change us as we changed it was liberating. [11] Even as many of us were non-native to Brownsville, BlackSpace members also experienced feelings of restoration and repair as Black people and as professional practitioners. Working together to deconstruct and solve problems that we care deeply about has been restorative and humbling—to prioritize core values over efficiency, to deliver on a project without knowing what it will be at the outset, to be in constant reciprocity and exchange with many kinds of people, and to move at the speed of trust. 12

Heritage conservation can be about the built environment, people, and justice. Black neighborhood histories can be rich inspiration for justice in design, and design processes can be tools of restoration and repair. At the same time, "social justice activities could ironically bring more attention from gentrifiers"—a critique we heard in our codesigner's feedback survey. Still, creating platforms together (online, ephemeral, tangible, built, or otherwise) where stories can be publicly shared makes them valued and valuable in the process.

Reflection and critique catapulted our learning forward. BlackSpace members evaluated the BlackSpaces: Brownsville process with Ideo's Lifeline Cards, a mode of critique for human-centered design processes. The facilitated critique helped us recognize how we struggled with some of the challenges of a nonlinear and evolving process. 13 These were among our missteps:

- Not always walking into a neighborhood event with a clear set of goals or intentions made some of our engagements feel interactive but not necessarily meaningful.
- Making decisions on a tight timeline meant engagements were not always the most well programmed or designed.
- Neglecting rain plans led us to change our event plans at the last minute and compromised some integrity.
- Not immediately tracking or downloading data and footage resulted in some lost information important to a fuller picture of Brownsville history.

The wider definition of heritage conservation includes people's current experiences of a place and assigns value to a broad set of historical and cultural assets. BlackSpace members are critical of the field of historic preservation and any fixed ideas that the built environment has to be saved exactly as it existed in the past. Traditional tools like historical designations are debatable in their help or harm to a place like Brownsville. It is important for heritage conservationists to invest in the present-day cultural producers, intangible assets, and tangible assets (as equal assets) as a way to conserve heritage.

In Brownsville, BlackSpace members found value not only in recording tangible and intangible heritage of the past but also in reckoning with stories of the past. That meant we had to unlearn the habits of our professions, which treat disinvested spaces as a blank slate ripe for urban development and new design ideas. Instead, we approached Brownsville with reverence, respect, and curiosity—a prerequisite to any design intervention. By leveraging history as a starting point in one Black neighborhood, we are planning for a more collaborative, magical, and just future where Black people, culture, and spaces matter and thrive.

12
"Move at the speed of trust" is a strategy put forth by adrienne maree brown in *Emergent Strategy: Shaping Change, Changing Worlds* (Oakland, CA: AK Press, 2017).

13
Ashlea Powell Sommer, "This Deck of Cards Will Change the Way You Work," Ideo blog, April 25, 2018, https://www.ideo.com/blog/this-deck-of-cards-will-change-the-way-you-work.

Equity and Social Inclusion from the Ground Up: Historic Preservation in Asian American and Pacific Islander Communities

Michelle G. Magalong

Challenging and Redefining Narratives

The histories and contributions of historically marginalized communities in the United States represent less than 8 percent of the listings on the National Register of Historic Places. Historic preservation scholars and practitioners have long acknowledged the disparities of representation in terms of landmark designations, yet there is still inadequate attention to issues of representation and participation for and by marginalized groups. [1] Asian American and Pacific Islander communities have been documenting, preserving, and protecting historic sites and cultural resources for the last fifty years, even if they have not always done so actively or according to professional standards. [2] As a result, governmental preservation agencies and mainstream preservation organizations often overlook historic sites associated with Asian Americans and Pacific Islanders or question their significance and integrity.

One of the main challenges for the inclusion of Asian American and Pacific Islander (AAPI) heritage in historic preservation is the lack of representation and participation of and by Asian Americans and Pacific Islanders in preservation agencies and organizations, in governmental funding and programs, and in culturally relevant education. For historically marginalized groups, there remains a perception that the preservation movement is not for their interests or needs. As a result, in the last decade the National Park Service has embarked on heritage initiatives to encourage better representation of Asian Americans, Native Hawaiians, and Pacific Islanders, along with African Americans, Latino Americans, Native Americans, women, and members of LGBTQ communities. [3] These initiatives seek to address long-standing barriers and challenges to rectifying this disparity. Community partnerships have been especially critical to these efforts, not only by encouraging more nominations to the National Register of Historic Places and as National Historic Landmarks, but also by developing long-term and sustainable relationships between governmental agencies and these underrepresented communities. Relationships like these create further opportunities for community engagement in historic preservation work and for education and advocacy efforts from within these communities.

Supported by a scholarship to encourage diversity, in 2007 a small number of Asian Americans and Pacific Islanders attended the annual national conference hosted by the National Trust for Historic Preservation. But these few AAPI participants could not adequately reflect the many community organizations and individuals who, for decades, had been preserving historic sites and cultural resources in AAPI communities. In the face of limited representation at the national level, they formed an affinity group within the National Trust, developed a working group of preservation scholars and practitioners in the AAPI community, and convened the first National APIA Historic Preservation Forum in 2010 in San Francisco. By 2012 this ad hoc group had formed a national volunteer-run organization, Asian and Pacific Islander Americans in Historic Preservation (APIAHiP). APIAHiP's mission and vision are as follows:

> To protect historic places and cultural resources significant to Asian and Pacific Islander Americans through historic preservation and heritage conservation by: (1) creating an information-sharing network which can provide support for established and emerging

1
Ned Kaufman, *Place, Race, and Story: Essays on the Past and Future of Historic Preservation* (New York: Routledge, 2009).

2
Franklin Odo, "Public History and Asian Americans," in *The Oxford Handbook of Asian American History*, ed. David Yoo and Eiichiro Azuma (New York: Oxford University Press, 2016), 413; Michelle G. Magalong and Dawn Bohulano Mabalon, "Cultural Preservation Policy and Asian Americans and Pacific Islanders: Reimagining Historic Preservation in Asian American and Pacific Islander Communities," *AAPI Nexus: Policy, Practice and Community* 14, no. 2 (2016): 105–116.

3
"Heritage and History Initiatives within the National Historic Landmarks Program," National Park Service, https://www.nps.gov/subjects/national historiclandmarks/heritage-and-history-initiatives.htm; Ned Kaufman, "Historic Places and the Diversity Deficit in Heritage Conservation," *CRM: The Journal of Heritage Stewardship* 1, no. 2 (2004): 68–85.

4
"Learn More about
APIAHiP," Asian
and Pacific Islander
Americans in Historic
Preservation, https://
www.apiahip.org/
about-us.

historic preservation programs, and also to define issues; (2) establishing educational programs for raising public awareness and impacting historic preservation policy on local, state, and national levels; and (3) increasing public and private resources for building historic preservation capacity. The terms "historic preservation" and "heritage conservation" are meant to include educational and community development activities involving the preservation, conservation, and protection of tangible and intangible historic and cultural resources. [4]

APIAHiP has developed a multipronged approach to address issues of representation and participation in preservation policy and practice; their work combines community engagement, education and advocacy, and capacity building and leadership development.

APIAHiP's three program areas demonstrate the need for community-driven engagement, participation, and representation to address issues of social inclusion and disparity in historic preservation. APIAHiP plays a critical role as an intermediary between AAPI communities and preservationists, particularly in terms of navigating preservation policy and planning and in advocating for better representation (of sites) and more participation in decision-making (by people). While APIAHiP is a national nonprofit organization, it represents diverse communities through its mission and programming. At a national level, APIAHiP represents more than 20 million Asian Americans and Pacific Islanders across the nation to mainstream preservation entities. On local and state levels, APIAHiP provides a national voice on historic preservation. In the last decade, APIAHiP has grown in size and scope and has expanded through initiatives like the National APIA Historic Preservation Forum, a biennial gathering; East at Main Street, an online crowdsourced mapping project; and Preservation in Action, an education and advocacy toolkit. As a national organization representing diverse AAPI populations across the nation, its mission and strategies can inform the next generation of preservation policy and practice.

— BROADENING THE TERMS OF PRESERVATION FROM THE GROUND UP

The three cofounders of APIAHiP, Michael Makio, Joseph Quinata, and Bill Watanabe, met at the National Trust conference. Makio and Quinata represented Guam Preservation Trust and had more than twenty-five years of experience in preservation work in Guam and on surrounding islands; Watanabe had worked for more than thirty-five years at Little Tokyo Service Center, a social services center in Los Angeles. Together, they identified the need to create a national network of Asian Americans and Pacific Islanders doing preservation work in historic AAPI neighborhoods and sites, and they developed a working group to create a national convening of community preservationists and traditional preservation entities. The National APIA Historic Preservation Forum is a biennial gathering that convenes practitioners and scholars working on and within APIA communities. Attendees travel from areas as diverse as Lowell, Massachusetts, and Pagat, Guam, to the National Forum, which highlights historic sites and cultural resources in the host city through educational panel discussions, walking tours, and networking opportunities. Forums have been held in San Francisco in 2010 and 2018; Los Angeles in 2012; Washington, DC, in 2014; and Stockton, California, in 2016.

At the first National Forum in 2010, attendees represented APIA community organizations, historical societies, students, preservation organizations, scholars, and governmental agencies. For many APIA community organizations, it was their first time meeting staff from the National Park Service, National Trust for Historic Preservation, and other historic preservation agencies. The National Park Service provided scholarships to encourage college and graduate students interested in historic preservation and Asian American studies to participate. Education programming included technical assistance (e.g., informational sessions on the Section 106 review process of the National Historic Preservation Act, historic preservation tax incentives, federal grants) and community-led discussions (e.g., ethnic affinity meetings, community-based projects). Technical assistance workshops were developed so mainstream preservation agencies and partners could introduce various preservation tools and resources to those AAPI individuals and community organizations with limited knowledge of historic preservation; sessions covered topics such as federal technical assistance grants, preparation of nomination applications, federal policies on historic preservation, and federal or state agency programs. Walking tours and community-led workshops on AAPI historic sites and resources highlighted local organizations, projects, and sites and covered topics like community economic development, museum and archival projects, intangible heritage, and community planning. This community-led programming was intended both to inform mainstream historic preservation partners about AAPI historic sites and cultural resources and to share resources (e.g., best practices, funding opportunities, technical assistance) with other AAPI partners.

At the first forum, attendees also developed a definition of historic preservation that is inclusive and relevant to the APIA historic preservation community:

> Historic preservation in the United States is an evolving movement that, for much of its history, focused primarily on buildings and sites reflecting events and people associated with wealth and power. More recently, definitions of historic significance have been expanded to include a broader and more inclusive narrative of American culture and heritage, thus opening the door for Asian and Pacific Islander American (APIA) communities to define what historic preservation means and to change the very face of preservation.
>
> In APIA ethnic communities, historic preservation includes a broad scope of efforts that seek to protect buildings, landscapes, and places of historical significance to this diverse group of peoples. As well, preservation efforts must seek to understand and conserve related tangible and intangible cultural resources, such as the contributions, values and beliefs of a people. It incorporates the various cultural art

5
"2010 National APIA
Historic Preservation
Forum," Asian and
Pacific Islander
Americans in Historic
Preservation, https://
www.apiahip.
org/2010-forum.

6
Christina Illarmo,
"US Military Plans
Mega-Base for Guam
(Guahan)," *Peace and
Freedom* 70, no. 2
(2010): 4.

7
Eduardo Rojas,
"Social Actors in
Urban Heritage
Conservation: Do We
Know Enough?" in
*Preservation and the
New Data Landscape*,
ed. Erica Avrami
(New York: Columbia
Books on Architecture
and the City, 2019),
169–174; Janet Hansen
and Sara Delgadillo
Cruz, "Big City, Big
Data: Los Angeles's
Historic Resources" in
*Preservation and the
New Data Landscape*,
ed. Avrami, 21–36.

8
"East at Main Street:
APIA Mapping
Project," Asian and
Pacific Islander
Americans in Historic
Preservation, https://
www.apiahip.org/
apia-mapping.

forms, traditions, language, associations, businesses, stories, food, festivals, and all the other activities that help to define these place-based ethnic communities.

For some APIA communities, historic preservation may mean working to preserve ethnic identity for neighborhoods dealing with demographic changes or the forces of gentrification. It also encompasses discovering and protecting places whose historic meaning for APIA communities has been veiled by time but can be revealed by new efforts to document and educate about our heritage and contributions. For newer APIA communities, historic preservation may mean the recognition and awareness that places where significant events occurred, or businesses and cultural institutions have been established, may someday achieve significance which needs to be shared with the nation and remembered by succeeding generations. [5]

This perspective on historic preservation reflected the needs and interests of the forum's constituents and served to frame the organization's work. APIAHiP has continued to host the National Forum biennially to elevate local projects and issues to a national level. For example, in 2010, APIAHiP opposed the US Department of Defense's plans to use a historic sacred site in Pagat, Guam, for a military firing range. [6] This resolution, along with letters of opposition by community groups and organizations from across the nation, supplemented and supported efforts of the Guam Preservation Trust. The resolution was brought to the attention of President Barack Obama and his administration, and the Department of Defense withdrew its plans for Pagat. These efforts inspired additional partnerships, such as with the National Trust for Historic Preservation, which provided legal and advocacy support for the Guam Preservation Trust for this campaign—including listing it on its annual list of America's Most Endangered Historic Places in 2010.

— INCLUSION THROUGH COMMUNITY PARTICIPATION

Data on historic sites and cultural resources are critical to the process of nominating places to the National Register of Historic Places and its state and municipal counterparts, particularly in providing access to historically marginalized communities. [7] While mainstream preservation organizations may struggle to identify and recognize historic sites and cultural resources important to AAPI communities, AAPI individuals and community organizations have already been identifying, documenting, and preserving historic places. To bridge this gap, APIAHiP developed East at Main Street, a crowdsourced online map that documents and tells the stories of people, places, and events associated with Asian Americans and Pacific Islanders. [8] The map intersects with a series of workshops and a curriculum of place-based and people-based histories utilizing digital archives, oral histories, and historic preservation. This project helps address the "diversity gap" by informing both preservation agencies and the general public about AAPI historic resources and making historic sites and preservation more accessible. As a digital platform, East at Main Street maps culturally and historically significant places associated with Asian Americans and Pacific Islanders (whether designated or not) through public participation, community-based archiving, and information-sharing.

In terms of participants, process, and product, East at Main Street demonstrates the importance of community engagement in making preservation more democratic and inclusive. In collaboration with community groups, nonprofit organizations, archives, and individuals, the project collects materials (e.g., photographs, newspaper clippings, historic maps) and stories (e.g., oral histories or talk story, written narratives) connected to a specific location or place (e.g., Angel Island Immigration Station in San Francisco Bay). 9 Community workshops are conducted online and in person to instruct users about the platform as well as about the fundamental concepts of historic preservation. Users can even interact with other contributors online.

The aims of East at Main Street are twofold: to engage a broader audience in sharing archival materials related to site-specific places or locations; and to encourage the public and preservationists to identify potential sites for further documentation, preservation, and/or landmark designation. However, there have been challenges in terms of outreach and information-sharing, as well as for project management and funding. 10 The project is intended to democratize historic resource surveying; however, lack of education and awareness about historic preservation and hesitance to share information about archival materials have become barriers to participation. For instance, targeted participants may lack knowledge about historic preservation or believe it irrelevant to their interests, and some participants are hesitant to share their archival material online due to risk of copyright infringement or misuse of the data. In-person informational workshops in partnership with local community organizations have helped address these issues and inform participants about the project's impact and uses. The workshops have also provided examples of archival materials that participants may think are "ordinary" or insignificant to the public (e.g., a program booklet from an annual community event) but that are, in fact, rich in information (e.g., a list of businesses inside the booklet that includes addresses and other relevant information) that could be geolocated and added to East at Main Street. In other words, providing culturally appropriate educational resources on the importance of historic preservation and digital humanities can potentially improve public awareness within the AAPI community.

Both the National Park Service and the City of Los Angeles have used East at Main Street for their projects associated with AAPI history and preservation. Through the National APIA Historic Preservation Forum, APIAHiP developed a relationship with the National Park Service to support programming and funding for APIA-related projects. The NPS Asian American Heritage Initiative and Theme Study was launched in 2013 with an advisory panel of scholars and practitioners that included members of APIAHiP. 11 *Finding a Path Forward: Asian American Pacific Islander National Historic Landmarks Theme Study* was completed in 2018; APIAHiP provided workshops and presentations on the importance of the theme study and helped disseminate it at the 2018 National Forum.

The National Park Service AAPI Heritage Initiative and Theme Study

9
"Talk story" is an expression used in Hawaiian culture to describe the tradition of passing down stories, songs, and customs directly from generation to generation.

10
Greg Donofrio, "Preservation and Digital Humanities: A Conversation with Donna Graves and Gail Dubrow," *Preservation Education & Research* 10 (2018): 115–118.

11
Franklin Odo, ed., *Finding a Path Forward: Asian American Pacific Islander National Historic Landmarks Theme Study* (Washington, DC: National Park Service, 2018).

12
See Hansen and
Delgadillo Cruz, "Big
City, Big Data."

13
Hansen and Delgadillo
Cruz, "Big City, Big
Data," 29.

14
Ken Bernstein
and Janet Hansen,
"SurveyLA: Linking
Historic Resources
Surveys to Local
Planning," *Journal of
the American Planning
Association* 82, no. 2
(2016): 88–91.

has been used as a resource both for public audiences and for project staff and partners. The National Park Service hosted a webinar featuring East at Main Street to provide examples of historic sites and cultural resources in AAPI communities, to raise public awareness, and to serve as a resource for scholars contributing to the theme study. Sites from the federal initiative are featured on East at Main Street, and, in turn, the project is a resource for information and for the identification of potential sites for further documentation, preservation, and/or landmark designation.

East at Main Street's framework for community outreach, participation, and data collection was modeled after MyHistoricLA, part of SurveyLA: The Los Angeles Historic Resources Survey, which identified significant historic resources through community input and participation in Los Angeles. [12] SurveyLA was a citywide survey of historic resources, innovative for its methodology in collecting data and in engaging with diverse communities in the city, particularly through MyHistoricLA, which incorporated community outreach through public activities, interviews, and property-based data gathering. MyHistoricLA and SurveyLA also invited the public to collect a wide range of historic information and submit it online or on a paper form. This crowdsourced platform allowed participants to "take ownership of and manage their own contributions to SurveyLA." [13] APIAHiP worked with SurveyLA in its outreach and data collection efforts in historic Asian American neighborhoods in Los Angeles. [14] Following the completion of SurveyLA, APIAHiP continued to partner with the city's Office of Historic Resources when the city secured a two-year National Park Service Underrepresented Communities Grant to produce citywide historic context statements for Asian American communities. Completed in 2018, the Asian Americans in Los Angeles Historic Context Statements identified important themes to guide the identification and designation of sites associated with Chinese, Filipino, Japanese, Korean, and Thai American communities in Los Angeles from 1850 to 1980. Leaders in Asian American communities (including members of APIAHiP), representing a wide range of organizations and institutions, and Asian American history scholars were invited to form an advisory committee. Using data from SurveyLA, the committee identified significant locations, recommended research sources, and reviewed draft context statements. The city also held community meetings for members of the public to provide input and to identify additional significant sites or places. This research resulted in a National Register of Historic Places Multiple Property Documentation form titled "Asian Americans in Los Angeles 1850–1980" and an accompanying individual National Register nomination for the Filipino Disciples Christian Church (also known as Filipino Christian Church) in Historic Filipinotown. Both were listed in the National Register of Historic Places in 2019.

— ADVANCING PRESERVATION EDUCATION AND ADVOCACY

Throughout the National Forums, education and advocacy have been ongoing elements in APIAHiP's programming. Within the AAPI communities, this education has focused on historic preservation and on the role of advocacy in preserving threatened sites or elevating potential sites for landmark designation. With APIAHiP's mainstream preservation partners, education initiatives have emphasized the complexities in the AAPI community in terms of ethnicities, histories, languages, religions, and customs. APIAHiP acts as an intermediary, bridging the distance between and within AAPI communities and with preservation entities. While it is important to increase the numbers of landmark designations associated with Asian Americans and Pacific Islanders, it is more imperative to frame inclusion and relevancy in preservation through culturally appropriate approaches.

15
See Magalong and Mabalon, "Cultural Preservation Policy."

From opposing the potential military use of Pagat Village in Guam to supporting federal programs associated with Asian Americans and Pacific Islanders, public education and advocacy remain central to creating and sustaining community participation. For APIAHiP, education and advocacy work are often done when a historic site is either being threatened or being considered for potential landmark designation—both require increasing awareness about such sites and their significance to Asian Americans and Pacific Islanders. With increased engagement online and in person, the aim is to elevate the importance of saving both tangible and intangible resources.

Locals, both individuals and organizations, turn to APIAHiP for help navigating governmental policies and programs or for advocacy support to help preserve or protect a site, particularly in elevating the campaign onto a national level. APIAHiP can recommend educational resources (e.g., the NPS AAPI Theme Study or other related publications) and provide technical support, which may involve legal or planning assistance. [15] Advocacy involves providing letters of support for nominations or letters of opposition in cases of potential demolition. In effect, APIAHiP has developed a toolkit of resources, techniques, and ideas that can help preserve or protect a historic site or a cultural resource. The toolkit includes an introduction to conducting research on a neighborhood or an individual building, as well as basic information about historic preservation and funding opportunities. It suggests forms of advocacy that include lobbying for governmental policies or funding; tracking plans and policies of local, state, and national actors and how their actions affect historic preservation; and attending and speaking at meetings of local or state preservation commissions.

In Los Angeles, APIAHiP has provided educational resources and advocacy support for three historic sites—the Japanese Hospital, in Boyle Heights; the Filipino Christian Church, in Historic Filipinotown; and Tokio Florist, in Silverlake—each of which was nominated for landmark designation. The Japanese Hospital was designated a Historic-Cultural Monument by the City of Los Angeles in 2016 and nominated to the National Register in 2019. The Filipino Christian Church was designated a Historic-Cultural Monument by the City of Los Angeles in 1998 and listed on the National Register in 2019. Tokio Florist is currently under review by the city as a Historic-Cultural Monument nomination. Only Tokio Florist was deemed as potentially under threat of demolition; the other two simply requested advocacy support for their respective nominations. For all three sites, widespread education within AAPI communities has been critical. While each had AAPI preservationists involved in the process, public education on the potential impacts, opportunities, and challenges of historic preservation played a critical role in garnering community support. With the Japanese

Hospital, community support was huge, but one crucial person opposed the designation—the owner. APIAHiP attempted to facilitate dialogue between the nominating organization, Little Tokyo Historical Society, and the property owner, a Filipino American. This effort involved inviting city staff, including Tagalog-speaking Filipino Americans, into discussions and providing information about the potential benefits and limitations of the designation. With Tokio Florist, APIAHiP assisted a group of historians and preservationists who were preparing the nomination with identifying city staff to help with the process. Yet a few key individuals who were unlikely to support the Historic-Cultural Monument designation shaped the owner's public stance—they argued that landmark designation would be potentially restrictive for future use and might negatively affect the sale of the property. In contrast, the Filipino Christian Church had full support from key stakeholders and community members, including the property owners and congregation members. APIAHiP coached city officials and property owners throughout the process, including development of a public event to demonstrate the importance of the nomination.

In addition to education and elevation of local preservation efforts, advocacy efforts for more inclusive preservation are shaped by policy and funding. With the NPS AAPI Heritage Initiative and Theme Study's aims to increase representation of AAPI sites on the federal level, preservation policies and funding have shifted to address disparities in representation. Even compared to other historically marginalized groups, Asian Americans, Pacific Islanders, and Latinos have received little to no funding or programming support. [16] Currently, the National Park Service has three grant programs to address this lack of support: the Underrepresented Communities Grant Program (under the Historic Preservation Fund), the Japanese American Confinement Sites (JACS) Grant, and the Native American Graves Protection and Repatriation Act (NAGPRA). JACS and NAGPRA are specific to programs for Japanese Americans and Native Hawaiians, respectively, while the Underrepresented Communities Grant Program is more broadly accessible and works toward diversifying the nominations submitted to the National Register of Historic Places. Projects include surveys and inventories of properties associated with communities underrepresented in the National Register, as well as development of nominations to the National Register for specific sites. While the aim of these grants is to address issues of representation, funding is nevertheless limited, and there are barriers to accessing that funding. Eligible applicants for these grants are limited to State Historic Preservation Offices, federally recognized tribes, Alaska Natives, Native Hawaiian organizations, and certified local governments—entities that most community-based organizations do not have access to. Furthermore, in recent years, funding allocations for these grant programs have been minimal: only $500,000 for the Underrepresented Communities Grant Program; $2,845,000 for the JACS Grant; and $2,331,000 for NAGPRA was allocated in 2019. While minimal in monetary support, these grant programs are critical to preservation work.

Asian Americans and Pacific Islanders represent less than 1 percent of listings on the National Register and receive little federal funding, but APIAHiP has acted as a national leader in advocating for federal funding and programs, particularly at times when these federal grant programs have been most at risk. Other national preservation groups, like Latinos in Heritage Conservation and Rainbow Heritage, have also emerged and worked in collaboration to advocate for more inclusive and relevant preservation planning and policy. APIAHiP has worked with these groups, as well as with groups like the Japanese Americans Citizens League, to oppose proposed funding cuts and to support federal policies and programs in their attempt to be more inclusive through sign-on letters and statements, lobbying members of Congress, public education, and media campaigns.

— MOVING FORWARD: OPPORTUNITIES, LIMITATIONS, AND IMPLICATIONS

In recent years, the historic preservation field has made significant progress in being more inclusive of AAPI stories and places. As historic preservation seeks to be more inclusive and relevant to diverse peoples and histories, preservation planning and policy must be informed by these diverse communities in terms of representation, participation, and decision-making. It is imperative to be informed from the bottom up through community organizations like APIAHiP in order to be more reflective and more relevant. Community participation is crucial in the development of preservation policies and practices, as well as in building trust and rapport with these communities. While national preservation groups like the National Trust for Historic Preservation and governmental agencies like the National Park Service are attempting to address the disparities of social inclusion, it is critical to have organizations like APIAHiP to challenge the traditional practices and standards in the field that have created and perpetuated the underrepresentation of historically marginalized groups. While it is important to have more and better representation of these groups in preservation policies and planning, APIAHiP also challenges the ways in which preservationists think and function with regard to what historic preservation is and how places are preserved. APIAHiP provides a framework for centering community engagement in preservation policies and practices through education and advocacy, informing the field from the ground up and from the margins, and improving standards and practices to be more robust and accountable in terms of social inclusion.

In this attempt to be more inclusive and to work beyond the traditional realms of historic preservation, APIAHiP provides an example of how to work across disciplines (e.g., ethnic studies, museum and information sciences, public policy and urban planning), sectors (e.g., AAPI community development nonprofit organizations, museums, historical societies), and in partnerships (e.g., with preservation organizations, governmental agencies, other historically marginalized groups). At the same time, APIAHiP offers a framework for how preservation can be more inclusive and relevant to the communities and places that they are trying to preserve and protect. In order for preservation policy and practice to be more socially inclusive, organizations like APIAHiP will be critical to shaping and informing representation and participation for the next generation of preservation planning and policy.

The Community Foundations of Allyship in Preservation: Learning from West Mount Airy, Philadelphia

Fallon Samuels Aidoo

Challenging and Redefining Narratives

In 1959 neighbors in West Mount Airy, Philadelphia, began pooling their financial and social capital to fight interconnected economic threats and environmental hazards to their community's acclaimed racial, economic, and ecological diversity. [1] Their work—in effect, a preservation practice—initially focused on the neighborhood's array of private property in residential use: two-family bungalows, apartment co-ops, single-family colonials, and multigenerational landscaped estates built between 1880 and 1920 within walking distance of the neighborhood's half dozen commuter rail stations. FIG. 1 This stewardship of historic homes soon after extended to railroad "station-houses"—two-story, wood, brick, and stone structures designed by esteemed Victorian architects like Frank Furness for a mixture of uses: to shelter rail commuters, to host community activities, but, most of all, to house railroad employees and concessionaires, such as the building's superintendents and ticket attendants. In the process, West Mount Airy homeowners revived an old practice of cultural landscape preservation, that is, community aid to station-house tenants, attendants, and superintendents in the form of monetary donations, in-kind contributions, and voluntary service. [2]

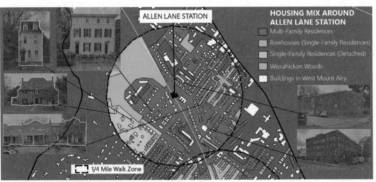

FIG. 1: The building typologies of West Mount Airy—from apartment co-ops and single-family dwellings to historic estates—that can be found in walking distance of Allen Lane Station. Map courtesy of the author.

West Mount Airy Neighbors, Inc. (WMAN), incorporated in 1959, is one among dozens of community foundations that have confronted the repeated loss and recovery of historically inclusive architecture in "railroad suburbs." [3] According to the US Department of Transportation and the National Endowment for the Arts, these philanthropic facilitators of architectural restoration had rehabilitated more than three hundred railroad stations in the United States for community reuse and market-oriented redevelopment by 1975. [4] WMAN and its counterparts built knowledge of how buildings and landscapes weather fiscal crises and environmental threats from hands-on preservation work; West Mount Airy neighbors in particular developed preservation workforces that challenge prevailing assumptions about whose aid and what kind of aid are needed to restore a historic neighborhood. Station revitalization in West Mount Airy illuminates the "preservationist mentality of fixing things" among not only West Mount Airy's philanthropists but also the foundations, financial

1
On racial change and liberalism in Philadelphia's West Mount Airy neighborhood, see Abigail Perkiss, Making Good Neighbors: Civil Rights, Liberalism, and Integration in Postwar Philadelphia (Ithaca, NY: Cornell University Press, 2014).

2
John R. Stilgoe, "The Railroad Beautiful: Landscape Architecture and the Railroad Gardening Movement, 1867–1930," Landscape Journal 1, no. 2 (1982): 57–66.

3
Railroad suburbs, long neglected, are now the focus of writings on suburban diversity such as Christopher Niedt, ed., Social Justice in Diverse Suburbs: History, Politics, and Prospects (Philadelphia: Temple University Press, 2013); Kenneth T. Jackson, Crabgrass Frontier: Suburbanization of the American Frontier (New York: Oxford University Press, 1987) nonetheless remains the definitive text on railroad architecture in suburbia.

4
Preservation and Reuse of Railway Stations of Historic or Architectural Merit: Hearing Before the Committee on Commerce, US Senate, 49th Cong., 1st session, S. 2056 (July 10, 1975), 10; National Endowment for the Arts (NEA), Reusing Railroad Stations, vols. 1 and 2 (New York: Educational Facilities Laboratories, 1974, 1975).

5
Randall Mason, "Fixing Historic Preservation: A Constructive Critique of Significance," Places 16, no. 1 (2004): 65. Herein Mason reflects on the epistemic boundaries of restoration architects, whom he defines as those licensed and steered to practice preservation of historic architecture and other built environments rather than intangible heritage and cultural landscapes.

6
Claire Dunning, "New careers for the Poor: Human Services and the Post-industrial City," *Journal of Urban History* 44, no. 4 (2018): 669–690.

7
As the urban crisis waned, the contraction of public services and closure of public spaces actually accelerated. See Kevin Fox Graham and Miriam Greenberg, *Crisis Cities: Disaster and Redevelopment in New York and New Orleans* (Oxford: Oxford University Press, 2004), 24–57; Suleiman Osman, *The Invention of Brownstone Brooklyn* (Oxford: Oxford University Press, 2011), 233–269.

8
Douglass R. Appler, "The Future of Fair Housing in a Diverse Suburb," in *Social Justice in Diverse Suburbs*, ed. Niedt, 213–238.

9
Perkiss, "Finding Capital in Diversity: Making Racialized Space," in *Making Good Neighbors*, 31–55.

10
The same two commuter rail and trolley lines that created the ethnically diverse population of Mount Airy in the early twentieth century and later kept "white" families of Polish, Italian, and Irish descent from moving to car-centric suburbs were necessary to obtain and sustain the investment of upwardly mobile professionals across the racial spectrum. Single-family Capes, two-family Victorian houses, and luxury apartment buildings surrounding Upsal, Carpenter, and Allen Lane stations gained occupants of color and property value in the 1960s. Perkiss, *Making Good Neighbors*, 40–60.

institutions, and governmental agencies developing workforces to restore station tenancy and improve attendance elsewhere. 5

In the case of West Mount Airy, "support" for preservation was both fiscal and figurative. Two decades after WMAN became racially and religiously integrated, middle-class Black and Jewish households found that their small community foundation needed additional financial assistance to render aid to station tenants, superintendents, and attendants that performed and supervised building and landscape preservation. More established and endowed foundations, namely the William Penn Foundation and the Philadelphia Partnership, stepped in to provide financial and operational support for station restoration projects and supported workers for those projects. Differences in philanthropists' missions, capital, and approaches to preservation—the focus of this chapter and an understudied area of scholarship—are crucial to understanding architectural reconstruction amid the environmental and economic restructuring of the 1970s and decades thereafter.

Endowed foundations rendered financial aid and operational assistance to WMAN directly and indirectly via their workforce development grants. At the behest of its fiscal sponsors, West Mount Airy's restoration architects developed alliances with unemployed, unhoused, and ununionized tradesmen from outside their neighborhood. 6 Such allyship, albeit enduring, limited architectural restoration to the space and time in which rail stations served as houses and its tenants provided services to homeowners (for example postal, banking, and retail services, plus community policing). Unfortunately, by the end of the "decade of the neighborhood," as urban historian Suleiman Osman aptly describes the 1970s, urban transportation authorities began closing station-houses to residential and community use in favor of corporate use or closure. 7

— THE (RAIL)ROAD TO PRESERVATION

Commonly referred to today as "fair housing," West Mount Airy's city blocks of multifamily and single-family houses made it ripe for a "slow disaster" of white flight and working-class concentration in the 1960s. 8 To prevent "panic selling" among landed white elites and middle-class immigrant families, the Real Estate Committee of WMAN began in 1952 to match the aging housing stock owned by elderly Catholic, Protestant, and Jewish residents with Black home buyers capable of improving them. 9 In a testament to the committee's interfaith strategy and interpersonal tactics, historian Abigail Perkiss found that about forty-five Black professionals, including presidential advisors Sadie Alexander and William T. Coleman, had taken up the political, social, and financial costs of "intentional integration" with white Mount Airy neighbors by 1955.

West Mount Airy's newest African American neighbors reoriented WMAN to address disinvestment in the infrastructure that sustained, however tenuously, the neighborhood's diverse population and properties. 10 Contracting with the Real Estate Department of Penn Central Transportation Company, WMAN's first Black president chartered the RR Fix-Up Committee, dedicated to keeping the three stations in West

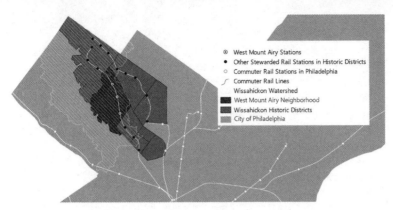

FIG. 2: *Stations under the protection of West Mount Airy Neighbors between 1964 and 1984 were surrounded, throughout that period, by stations stewarded by station tenants and neighboring property owners in other communities within the Wissahickon watershed: Chestnut Hill, Germantown, and East Mount Airy. Map courtesy of the author.*

FIG. 3: *Drawing of Allen Lane Station, by Charles Snyder, as published in the* Philadelphia Inquirer *and sold as prints in 1974 to raise funds for station preservation. Individual donations of $18 to $25 for the Allen Lane Station Restoration Project ultimately added up to $4,000 (1974 dollars or $20,880 in 2019 dollars)—double the Station Committee's fund-raising goal. Image courtesy of the Chestnut Hill Conservancy. Catalog No. 2007.2.408.7.*

Mount Airy attractive and active. *FIG. 2* The committee took on legal liabilities, accounting protocols, design standards, and labor policy for returning the railroad architecture to its former glory, full functionality, and fiscal health. Carpenter Lane station, for example, was a gabled brick gateway to West Mount Airy that had housed multiple families upstairs and small businesses downstairs since the late nineteenth century. Initially, Carpenter Lane received as much attention as Allen Lane Station, the quintessentially Victorian local landmark that later served as a centerpiece of WMAN fund-raising. *FIG. 3* The monumentality and intricacy that earned both stations inclusion in the National Register of Historic Places in 1981 exasperated Penn Central's struggles to sell and service

11
Guian A. McKee, "Blue Sky Boys, Professional Citizens, and Knights-in-Shining-Money: Philadelphia's Penn Center Project and the Constraints of Private Development," *Journal of Planning History* 6, no. 1 (2007): 48–80; T. Kizzia, "Philadelphia: Help Is on the Way and None Too Soon," *Railway Age* 181, no. 13 (July 1980): 34–39.

12
Donald C. Scott to H. H. Vaughan, Regional Manager, PRR, August 20, 1963, WMANA Acc. 737, box 4, folder 25: Correspondence, RR Stations, 1964–1966, Temple University Urban Archives (TUUA), Philadelphia, PA.

13
The author compared 1960s contracts between the Pennsylvania RR Co. (and its successors) with the West Mount Airy Neighbors association/West Mount Airy Neighbors, Inc. (hereafter WMAN), St. Martins Station Grounds Committee, Inc., and Chestnut Hill Community Association.

14
Budgets and donor registries, WMANA Acc. 737, box 4, folder 25: Correspondence, RR Stations, 1964–1966, TUUA.

15
Receipts for payment to tree planting and removal company, WMANA Acc. 737, box 4, folder 25: Correspondence, RR Stations, 1964–1966, TUUA.

16
WMAN flyer, WMANA Acc. 737, box 4, folder 25: Correspondence, RR Stations, 1964–1966, TUUA.

17
License agreement between Pennsylvania Railroad Company and West Mount Airy Neighbors Incorporated, August 20, 1963, WMANA Acc. 737, box 4, folder 25: Correspondence, RR Stations, 1964–1966, TUUA.

these distressed assets. Railroad executives (with approval of state regulators) could only lease the properties to local governments and civic groups willing to subsidize and sustain the company's operations, which is precisely where WMAN stepped in. [11]

A license to work on Penn Central's station grounds encouraged WMAN to repair the buildings and landscapes that were within its purview in spatial if not legal terms. Penn Central neither required nor incentivized WMAN to work with the Brotherhood of Maintenance of Way Employees, who managed Penn Central's "station-grounds," or with the superintendents of Penn Central's station-houses in Mount Airy. [12] In fact, Penn Central's leasing contracts with four of Philadelphia's railway conservancies left space for lessees and licensees to delegate certain work within their purview to third parties of their choice—for example, landscaping and carpentry were assigned to neighborhood watch groups and station tenants. [13]

WMAN took full advantage of its right to outsource rehabilitation and to hire nonunionized tradesmen with track records of servicing historic homes or serving homeowners of color. The RR Fix-Up Committee members first delegated care for station parkland, bridges, tunnels, and hardscapes to contractors recommended by WMAN's Real Estate Committee, which built a roster of "good neighbors" in the building trades for the benefit of their new African American neighbors and for the preservation of neighborhood integration more broadly. Carpenters, painters, landscapers, and tree surgeons that made the list conducted seasonal work supported by philanthropic neighborhood residents and other "friends" of West Mount Airy stations, such as commuter rail riders and East Mount Airy residents. [14] For larger projects, such as tree surveying, planting, and cutting, WMAN board members paid the bills of bonded contractors, whose insurance protected against damage to Penn Central assets that WMAN's own limited liability insurance did not cover. [15]

Procurement policy functioned as a way for preservationists in West Mount Airy to prioritize allyship in neighborhood integration and preservation. Flyers for community cleanup days welcomed "workers of all shapes and sizes," but contracts for conservation work went exclusively to WMAN members and non-WMAN contributors to the organization's maintenance regimes. [16] By outsourcing labor only to tradesmen willing to work on property owned by both whites and African Americans, the RR Fix-Up Committee joined WMAN's Real Estate Committee in encouraging equitably minded people into preservation while crowdsourcing conservation labor. In other words, relying on community members for restoration meant that West Mount Airy was able to make neighborhood preservation an inclusive project, and one not reliant on professional conservation experts.

WMAN's RR Fix-Up Committee and its supporters may have anticipated the outcry from the Brotherhood of Maintenance of Way members already contracted for station grounds work over the development and deployment of an alternative workforce. In 1964, when WMAN signed its first station lease agreement with Penn Central, the chairman of the company board informed WMAN president Matthew Bullock that its "license to beautify and improve the stations serve[d] to release the railroad of its responsibility to worker compensation" and its regulatory liabilities. [17]

In addition, stewards of Penn Central station grounds just outside of Mount Airy informed WMAN's RR Fix-Up Committee of their decision to support salaried, unionized workers at risk of losing work to seasonal, independent contractors. 18 WMAN, in short, broke the picket line when they created their own maintenance plan for station-houses and -grounds and hired their own workforce to execute it.

—— A LABOR OF LOVE NO MORE

Even after five years of preservation work, a combination of vigilant committee members, reliable contractors, and experienced railroad super-intendents could not keep the stations in West Mount Airy off the roster of pending "unmanned" facilities. 19 Citywide fiscal changes meant that stations throughout Philadelphia were losing their residential staff, and the stations in West Mount Airy were not exempt. Without a tenant and/or an attendant, the Allen Lane, Upsal, and Carpenter Lane stations lacked proverbial "eyes on the street" to assist WMAN with the identification of hazards to be removed and damage to be repaired. *FIG. 4* The disaster preparedness efforts that once preceded each storm and the architectural restoration after these extreme weather events would not work without tenants and attendants, WMAN's executive secretary, Ruth Steele, told the Pennsylvania Public Utility Commission in 1969. 20 She and WMAN president Douglass Gaston III insisted, nonetheless, that community foundations had a workable plan for the buildings neither private nor public transportation companies wanted to preserve.

Indeed, labor-friendly and tenant-friendly preservation plans surfaced from philanthropic friends as they assessed the damage that railroad bank-ruptcies and 1972's Hurricane Agnes had wrought on community assets. 21 The leadership of Chestnut Hill Community Fund, which supported

18
Fallon Aidoo, "Rights-of-Way: Critical Infrastructure for the Right to Work in Postwar Philadelphia," *Spatializing Politics: Essays on Power and Place*, ed. Delia Wendel and Fallon S. Aidoo (Cambridge, MA: Harvard Graduate School of Design, 2015), 152–182.

19
Fallon Samuels Aidoo, "The Other 'Philadelphia Plan': Community Philanthropy and Corporate Investment in Critical Infrastructure for Back-to-the-City Movements, 1950–1985" (PhD diss., Harvard University, 2017), 167–178.

20
Ruth Steele to Chris Van de Velde, May 29, 1969, WMANA Acc. 737, box 4, folder 25: Correspondence, RR Stations, 1964–1966, TUUA.

21
Stations that survived Hurricane Agnes in 1972 without storm-water or wind damage stayed boarded up after the storm if they were not slated for rehabilitation by their stewards or by the state. Tony Wood, "On Agnes' Anniversary, Recalling a Reign of Terror," *Philadelphia Inquirer*, June 1, 2017. See also Kizzia, "Philadelphia," 34.

FIG. 4: *Tenants of the Penn Central station house in West Mount Airy before the City of Philadelphia legalized homesteading in 1977. Image courtesy of the* Philadelphia Inquirer.

22
Steele to Van de Velde,
May 29, 1969.

23
D. Douglass Gaston to
William H. Moore, pres-
ident and CEO of Penn
Central Transportation
Company, July 20,
1972, WMANA Acc.
737, box 4, folder 27:
Correspondence, RR
Stations, 1972–1978,
TUUA.

24
Brian Goldstein, "The
Urban Homestead
in the Age of Fiscal
Crisis," in *The Roots of
Urban Renaissance:
Gentrification and the
Struggle over Harlem*
(Cambridge, MA:
Harvard University
Press, 2017), 153–196.
See also Jeffrey
Lowe, *Rebuilding
Communities
the Public Trust
Way: Community
Foundation Assistance
to CDCs, 1980–2000*
(Lanham, MD:
Lexington Books,
2006).

25
Andrew Feffer,
"Show Down in
Center City: Staging
Redevelopment
and Citizenship
in Bicentennial
Philadelphia,
1974–1977," *Journal
of Urban History* 30
(2004): 798–799.

FIG. 5: *With its windows boarded up and shingles weathered, Gravers Lane Station (built in 1883) stood vacant before the Chestnut Hill Historical Society undertook a major restoration project in the 1980s. Image courtesy of Chestnut Hill Conservancy, Philadelphia, PA. Catalog No. 1996.604.11, Nancy Hubby Collection.*

railroad station rehabilitation financially and operationally, convinced WMAN board members to join them in redesigning and reappropriating every dimension of their neighborhood stations—from station parking lots, parkland, and platforms to building technology and tenancy. 22 As WMAN president-elect Gaston envisioned in 1972, the "friends" of evicted tenants would acquire stations and then "lease back" these workplaces and homes to unemployed individuals and unhoused institutions. 23 Retaining diversity within and beyond station grounds in the railroad suburb evidently remained a priority for WMAN leadership.

A one-two punch of economic devaluation and environmental degradation—bankruptcies and stormwater—pushed a groundswell of Philadelphia community foundations into preservation planning in the early 1970s. 24 A civic body designated by the city to commemorate its founding fathers and principles, the Bicentennial Corporation of Philadelphia sponsored the surge in philanthropic preservationists in hopes of restoring railroad architecture across the region in time for the bicentennial celebration in 1976. The foundation expected thousands of visitors to travel by rail en route to events celebrating national heritage and independence—including historic districts riddled with damaged railroad tracks and stations, such as Old Germantown, Mount Airy, Chestnut Hill, and historic places farther afield. 25

The corporation's board of directors turned to established philanthropists like the William Penn Foundation to curate visitors' experience of the historic landscape of the city and the region. With William Penn's original vision of Green Olde Country Towns throughout the region as a guidepost, the private trust offered microgrants to less well-endowed community foundations capable of cofunding the restoration of historic architecture. The foundation's microgrants of $6,000, however, were still $4,000 less than the annual fee for West Mount Airy's limited liability insurance. The microgrant could fund only projects that were also supported by another sponsor. In West Mount Airy, the Philadelphia Partnership filled the gap.

Unlike the William Penn Foundation and the Bicentennial Corporation, the Philadelphia Partnership participated in disaster recovery and preparedness discussions following Hurricane Agnes. The tropical storm, the most deadly and costly to hit the Mid-Atlantic until Superstorm Sandy, detached gabled roofs across eastern Pennsylvania and pushed contaminated waters of the Delaware and Schuylkill Rivers ashore, flooding the stations and houses alongside them. 26 Debates over how and where to allocate emergency aid covered everything from national freight infrastructure to the city of Philadelphia's concentrated commuter rail architecture. To rail executives, trustees, debtors, regulators, and policy-makers, most battered railroad architecture appeared unlikely to recover physically or financially from the acute damage caused by the hurricane and chronic disrepair. 27 FIG. 5 With a workforce development plan in mind for West Mount Airy stations, the Philadelphia Partnership's executive director, Graham Finney, and the board of the Old Philadelphia Development Corporation convinced the authorities that any system worthy of public, private, and philanthropic investment must keep rail infrastructure accessible, attractive, and active. 28

WMAN's newest allies—the William Penn Foundation and the Philadelphia Partnership—did not share a common mission or even the same mission as the West Mount Airy Neighbors. For WMAN, accepting financial assistance from these two foundations meant taking on their agendas—their funders' vested interests in "professional" restoration and the training of marginalized workforces would have to take priority over WMAN's program of community-led projects. Both of the foundations wanted a workforce with experience in the restoration of deteriorated real estate, yet neither cast WMAN members—hundreds of middle-class households engaged in routine maintenance as well as dozens of tradesmen and tenants who performed periodic repairs—as disaster experts or restoration architects. The two organizations had another condition as well: all three stations in the neighborhood would have to undergo rehabilitation in partnership with a workforce development corporation. 29 The Philadelphia Partnership granted $10,000 to the Lower Kensington Environmental Services Center "to teach good work habits and to prepare hard-to-employ youths, former drug addicts, and former convicts for employment in the open labor market" but restricted $3,000 of those funds to the Allen Lane Station Restoration Project. 30 The center founded its Impact Services Corporation to manage this microgrant and a larger grant from the Manpower Development Corporation of New York.

The Impact Service Corporation met both foundations' demands for a fiscal sponsor of station restoration in West Mount Airy. Dedicated to grant management, the nonprofit was staffed exclusively "to enhance the utility of the region's heavily used commuter rail stations so they are assets to their neighborhoods." The partnership's unrestricted and restricted grants empowered these philanthropic organizations to reorient WMAN's workforce toward "use [of] supported workers and outside funds in performing this work beyond the budgetary capacity of SEPTA and the railroads." 31 The philanthropists who supported unbudgeted work and non-union workers on rail architecture preservation included not only the partnership's undisclosed donors but also, federal and state sponsors of the Southeastern Pennsylvania Transportation Authority

26
"They Called it an Act of God," Philadelphia Inquirer Magazine, August 6, 21972, 15-23; "Waterworks will spring back to life," Philadelphia Inquirer, September 2, 2001, 115.

27
"Pennsy Asks Court for $15 Million," Philadelphia Inquirer, August 1, 1972, 17.

28
Notes accompanying two separate draft copies of Final System (Washington, DC: National Railway Executives Association): Richardson Dilworth Papers, Acc: 3112, series VI: Reading Company Receivership, 1971–74, and Series II: Civic Groups and Projects, 1948–1973: Old Philadelphia Development Corporation, Historical Society of Pennsylvania.

29
John Hass, the founder of a multinational corporation (Rohm & Hass) that manufactured rail cars, served on the boards of both the Philadelphia Partnership and the William Penn Foundation and is the person who brokered the partnership with WMAN. Chris Van de Velde to John Hass, October 1, 1975, Acc. 737, WMAN Collection, series II, box 3, folder 5, TUUA.

30
Graham Finney to Chris Van de Velde, WMAN, and Fred Jackes, Impact Services Corporation, May 16, 1975, Acc. 737, box 6, folder 25: WMAN Correspondence, RR Stations, 1973–1975, TUUA.

31
Finney to Van de Velde, May 16, 1975.

32
Finney to Van de Velde, May 16, 1975.

33
Alessandro Rigolon and Jeremy Németh, "'We're Not in the Business of Housing': Environmental Gentrification and the Nonprofitization of Green Infrastructure Projects," *Cities* 81 (2018): 71–80.

34
Although the profession of architecture was highly regulated in the 1970s by schools of architecture and professional certification boards, the practice of architectural restoration was not. Individuals and organizations required only state licensure to reconstruct and rehabilitate historic architecture of any style and age in American cities. From neighborhood associations and community development corporations to urban planning firms and construction companies, preservationists with or without formal architectural training undertook wholesale restorations and facade revitalization.

(SEPTA), the public body entrusted in the early 1970s with revitalizing the Philadelphia-area assets of bankrupted railroad companies.

Allyship between organizations and individuals that make, manage, execute, and leverage philanthropy for historic preservation warrants extensive exploration—far more than a historical analysis of architectural restoration in a single city neighborhood can provide. The prescriptions of Graham Finney, the Philadelphia Partnership's executive director, at least shed light on preservationists who gather financial resources, social capital, and, sometimes, sweat equity in "a well-organized community group" that, by their account, has "already launched a program to help underwrite the repair" of significant historic structures or infrastructure. 32 Through microgrants and micromanagement of high- and low-skilled work on the station, fiscal sponsors asserted their right to rework existing systems and assembled others to further stewardship. Recently profiled in publications on green gentrification, "friend groups" such as these can endure because of or in spite of their success in preserving precarious places. 33

— COSTLY SUPPORT FOR RESTORATION ARCHITECTURE

WMAN was not the architect of record for Allen Lane Station, which underwent rehabilitation in two phases between 1974 and 1976; rather, the state licensed WMAN only to rehabilitate historic architecture. 34 WMAN earned and extended its eligibility to work on railroad property not only with the support of the William Penn Foundation and the Philadelphia Partnership but also at the request of the Southeastern Pennsylvania Transportation Authority (SEPTA). SEPTA's 1970–1976 Capital Investment Program contracted Ueland and Junker Architects

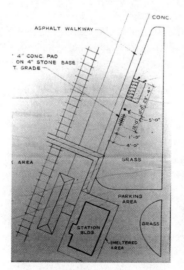

FIG. 6: *Improvements planned in 1974 for Allen Lane Station—car and bicycle parking—as drawn by City of Philadelphia engineers, based on site designs by Uekland and Junker Architects and Planners and traffic plans by Wilbur Smith and Associates. Image courtesy of the Philadelphia City Archives.*

and Planners to determine—alongside engineers, construction managers, and other so-called supportive workers—"how... the suburban stations [might] be improved." 35 FIG. 6 The station improvement program counted on support from station tenants and lessees as well as tenured tradesmen classified as unionized employees and ununionized licensees (contractors), such as WMAN and its peers. However, WMAN's contract with SEPTA, which committed the state to cover two-thirds of the costs of station restoration projects in West Mount Airy, was different from the licenses held by its peers. 36 SEPTA engineers cast the community foundation as an ally of the state, or more specifically as a preservation consultant with a philanthropic role in the design process for each station and for all station development plans. 37

Not coincidentally, the fiscal sponsors of WMAN's station restoration projects took the reins of the projects just as the US Department of Transportation began to sponsor the restoration of SEPTA's suburban stations. In 1968 SEPTA's superintendent of suburban stations sought aid from the US secretary of transportation, who supported experimental work and contingent workforces, including unlicensed workers supported by a licensed architect. 38 Graham Finney, of the Philadelphia Partnership, pledged support for SEPTA's capital program at the same time that he provided WMAN with a $10,000 grant to train "people who are job-ready yet need work experience before entering the mainstream of the economy." 39 Despite or because of this fiscal sponsorship, SEPTA trusted that WMAN—with no professional training in architecture but with extensive knowledge of real estate—could support the tradesmen and tenants within their leaseholds.

The plan for transitional and temporary employment at Allen Lane Station depended on allyship among tradesmen and trainees supported by the architectural restoration grants. In October of 1975, WMAN president Chris Van de Velde informed the Philadelphia Partnership's leading donor and board chairman that tradesmen in training could undertake only "a pilot paint up, fix-up of a commuter rail station" and wagered that their work would not "lead to a highly visible demonstration of Impact's capabilities." 40 Still, Finney insisted they could prove to SEPTA that contingent labor had a place in station preservation.

The Allen Lane Station Restoration Project proved so effective that the fiscal sponsors agreed to finance more work on WMAN's original vision: the restoration of all three stations in West Mount Airy by experienced preservationists—restoration architects, contractors, conservators, and laborers with a history of building rehabilitation. This time, however, unionized laborers successfully contested the expansion of contingent work. When the Philadelphia Partnership extended its financial support and volunteered the workers it supported, AFL-CIO leadership set out to stop SEPTA from taking on two-thirds of the cost of these station improvements. 41 The Railway Executives Association successfully claimed that the reconstruction of historic structures required a different level of expertise than the Philadelphia Partnership's tradesmen were trained to perform. Moreover, the union of station superintendents allied with trade supervisors to reinforce their right to work on restorations with fair compensation if not the right to work without fear of replacement.

35
Ueland and Junker Architects and Planners, Community Meeting Minutes—SEPTA No. 458—Task 4, July 27, 1977, series III, box 4, WMAN, TUUA.

36
SEPTA Capital Improvement Program, 1970–1976, series III, box 4, WMAN, TUUA.

37
Graham Finney, the Philadelphia Partnership, to Richard Pinkham, asst. GM, RR Division, SEPTA, December 27, 1974.

38
Reference and brief description of "SEPTA, Regional Rail Division, Application to the US Department of Transportation for an Environmental Protections Program," made in SEPTA, Capital Program, 1970–1977 (1976), Acc. 60-6: Mayor's Correspondence & Files, Administration of Frank Rizzo, 1972–1980, Philadelphia City Archives.

39
SEPTA, Capital Program, 1970–1977, Acc. 60-6 Mayor's Correspondence & Files, Philadelphia City Archives; "Application to the US Department of Transportation for an Environmental Protections Program," in SEPTA, Capital Program, 1970–1977 (1976).

40
Chris Van de Velde to John Hass, October 1, 1975, Acc. 737 WMAN, box 4, folder 27, TUUA.

41
E. H. Steel, engineer, maintenance-of-way, to Francis Herold, GM, Impact Services Corporation, Acc. 373, WMANA, October 17, 1975, box 3, folder 9, TUUA.

42
Steel to Herold,
October 17, 1975.

43
Graham Finney,
Philadelphia
Partnership, to Leon
Alexander, July 8, 1975,
Acc. 373, WMANA, box
3, folder 9, TUUA.

44
Van de Velde to Hass,
October 1, 1975.

45
Draft and Final
Agreements for
Station Renovations,
WMAN to James C.
McConnon, chairman
of the board of SEPTA,
August 2, 1977, Acc.
373, WMANA, box 3,
folder 9, TUUA; Labor
Agreement, Allen Lane
Station Restoration,
1975, WMAN series III:
box 4, TUUA.

46
Interview with Chris
van de Velde by the
author, March 30, 2014.

FIG. 7: Gordon Linton Jr. (far right), the state representative for WMAN, joins Friends of Allen Lane Station (far left) and two SEPTA officials (center) in 1992 for a celebration of the restoration of Allen Lane Station. Image courtesy of the Chestnut Hill Conservancy, Philadelphia, PA. Catalog No. 2007.2.408.12.

SEPTA discontinued preservation work on these historic railroad stations for nearly two years due to litigation. AFL-CIO railway executives accused the SEPTA-supported workers—from WMAN and the Impact Services Corporation—of reassigning trade supervisors to training work not authorized in their union contracts. 42 During that time, SEPTA assured its philanthropic partners that "obstacles presently preventing further work of this type will be resolved soon." 43 Van de Velde also assured a major donor in October 1975 that "men who have been given an opportunity to have meaningful work" would soon "be thanked by those of us who will be able to take pleasure daily in the refurbished stations." 44 To do so, WMAN (by way of the Philadelphia Partnership) paid union dues to compensate for its license to work on railroad properties during a labor shortage, strike, or extreme weather event. 45 In fall 1977, after a year of cost-sharing negotiations and bicentennial celebrations, SEPTA officials and WMAN leadership relaunched station restorations on more equitable grounds. *FIG. 7*

— THE COST OF SUPPORTIVE FRIENDS

Fiscal sponsors of station restoration in West Mount Airy invested in a diverse workforce of licensed professionals, experienced volunteers, and on-the-job trainees, but none invested directly in the philanthropic trust supporting WMAN's year-round maintenance regime and new staff. Finney offered advice, not funding, for making WMAN projects marketable to market-oriented philanthropists. 46 Notably, he and Philadelphia Partnership board members erroneously advised WMAN to count on new homesteaders in Philadelphia to direct their discretionary income and in-kind contributions (e.g. donated legal, accounting, or other professional services) toward WMAN's architectural restoration projects. Predominantly white young professionals with rehabilitation resources and little rehab experience, these new homesteaders remade vacant spaces of various types (e.g. station-houses, warehouses, and townhouses) into single-family homes in accordance with their lease terms before Philadelphia's Homesteading Ordinance of 1977 legalized and institutionalized the practice. 47

Presumably, self-identified "pioneers" would make up for longtime donors to the RR Fix-Up Committee moving away or redirecting their donations elsewhere. Solicitations sent to both constituencies simply read:

> For too long the train stations of West Mount Airy have been grossly neglected. The bankrupt Penn Central is incapable of anything but the barest minimum of maintenance, and past community efforts to improve the situation have been little more than a drop-in-the-bucket. It is in response to this situation that West Mount Airy Neighbors has organized the Friends of the Allen Lane Station Committee. It is hoped that the Committee can develop a viable on-going program of station maintenance and improvement, and that this program can serve as a model for similar programs at the Carpenter Lane and Upsal stations. 48

Failing to return older households to WMAN's donor rosters or to enroll young homesteaders in its stewardship project, WMAN leadership was left to solicit donations by mail and mass media from philanthropists across the city.

Support within WMAN for tradesmen that supported their mission of racial integration wavered as Allen Lane Station fund-raising turned sour in 1974. As WMAN membership grew less affluent, the West Mount Airy residents that had incorporated WMAN at mid-century increasingly carried the financial burden of preservation work and workforce development. To the original donors, some of whom served on the WMAN board, emergent tradespeople developing the skills to serve their historic, diverse neighborhood and others could meet WMAN's mission. 49 For different reasons, WMAN's newest African American and Jewish members—many of whom were political conservatives (who favored small government, local control, and privatization) and/or fiscal conservatives (who promoted free markets as a route to freedom and enfranchisement)—insisted upon training hard-to-employ people to replace its costly cohort of inclusive contractors. Represented by WMAN President, Chris van de Velde, these Black and Jewish leaders joined their counterparts across the country in appealing to federal and philanthropic grant makers who began to abandon racial liberalism for color-blind neoliberalism in the mid-1970s. 50

Outside aid that WMAN Presidents Douglass Gaston III and Van de Velde brokered in the 1970s triggered a backlash from West Mount Airy's proponents of neighborhood control and Black self-determination. Some, organizing as West Mount Airy Action, Inc., subjected station restoration trainees and instructors supported by WMAN's workforce development grants to a new culture of vigilance. Their oversight strategy—roving neighborhood watch groups working in partnership with police—turned legal surveillance tools and the law enforcement technique of "broken windows" policing on the Allen Lane Station restoration architects, supervisors, and workers that their donations supported. 51 Demonstrating how

47
Marisa Chapell, "The Curious Case of Urban Homesteading," Jacobin, March 13, 2017, https://www.jacobinmag.com/2017/03/jack-kemp-hud-acorn-public-housing.

48
Solicitation, Allen Lane Station Restoration Project, WMAN series III: box 4, TUUA. There is no private documentation of the Allen Lane Station restoration architects or workers that architectural restoration supported. There are only public records such as news clippings—for example, Howard Shapiro, "Old Station, New Look," Philadelphia Inquirer, November 24, 1974.

49
Perkiss, Making Good Neighbors, 137–142.

50
On the racial politics and partnerships of community developers and preservationists, see Julia Rabig, "'A Fight and a Question': Community Development Corporations, Machine Politics, and Corporate Philanthropy in the Long Urban Crisis," The Business of Black Power: Community Development, Capitalism, and Corporate Responsibility in Postwar America (Rochester, NY: Boydell & Brewer), 245–273; and Karen Ferguson, Top Down: The Ford Foundation, Black Power, and the Reinvention of Racial Liberalism (Philadelphia: University of Pennsylvania Press, 2013), 21–166.

51
Public letter from Doug Gaston III, WMAN board chairman, November 7, 1975, WMAN Acc. 737, box 10, folder 23, TUUA.

52
Thomas J. Sugrue and
Andrew P. Goodman,
"Plainfield Burning:
Black Rebellion in
the Suburban North,"
*Journal of Urban
History* 33, no. 4 (2007):
568–601.

53
"Don't be a Victim of
Scare Tactics," flyer,
April 1975.

54
West Mount Airy
Action, Inc. took on
other many issues
besides outsourcing.
See Perkiss, *Making
Good Neighbors*,
137–142.

heavy-handed oversight of WMAN's preservation practices and personnel could become, West Mount Airy Action, Inc. exhibited the distrust that both grant makers and grant seekers can develop as a portfolio of funders and workers undergoes diversification.

Black WMAN leadership protested the backlash to outside aid but their stand posed little challenge to the combined forces of fiscal and political conservatism in the 1970s. 52 "Don't be a Victim of Scare Tactics," began a flyer that WMAN board members Doug Gaston III and Ruth Steele distributed to WMAN members in response to West Mount Airy Action:

> West Mount Airy Action tells us we are in the heart of a high crime area. But are we? The Fourteenth Police District doesn't think so. WMAA claims to have an answer on April 7. But will they? Are vigilante patrols and funding of regressive programs the answer? West Mount Airy Neighbors thinks not. There are better ways to deal rationally with community concerns of all kinds. WMAN urges you to attend the meeting and counteract this negative approach to our neighborhood. 53

At the insistence of Van de Velde, Gaston and Steele issued a public apology and resigned in November 1975 for using WMAN's donor list to discredit dissent to their integrationist approach to community preservation. 54 In the wake of this leadership fallout, WMAN showed its fiscal sponsors that it had shed its longstanding commitment to community control of neighborhood preservation.

Between 1964 and 1974, WMAN developed a united workforce of contractors parallel to the railroad companies' unionized superintendents and the Brotherhood of Maintenance of Way workers. Familiarity with WMAN's network of workers—who was a member and whose privileges should be revoked—differentiated "friends" of WMAN's RR Fix-Up Committee and other "good neighbors" of rail stations from the wider population of residents and riders. Any plan to break the seal on this preservation praxis might have amounted to breaking the proverbial picket line. Not surprisingly, a preservation plan without West Mount Airy fixers triggered backlash from the first fiscal sponsors of station restoration: the now worn-out stewards of the neighborhood's washed-out structures.

— INDIVIDUAL AND INSTITUTIONAL RESTORATION

Who responds to the distinct yet interconnected disasters that affect vulnerable communities, and what remedies and resources define their restoration and recovery? This essay has offered a window onto the world of philanthropic individuals and institutions that sponsored the restoration of rail stations, distressed and gentrified alike, in Philadelphia's West Mount Airy neighborhood. Architectural restoration, conducted by philanthropic individuals and institutions, propelled Philadelphia's budding preservation community into a burgeoning field of grant-making: workforce development. Whereas present-day practitioners look to architects licensed through state accreditation boards, fiscal sponsors of various types—corporations, foundations, and governments—and their allies have previously been licensed to support disaster aid with demonstrable success.

Philanthropy in preservation is understudied relative to its outsized influence on grassroots advocacy and governmental action in support of historic resources. The future of philanthropy-supported preservation work and workers is particularly at risk, given the marginality of labor in preservation history. In West Mount Airy during the 1970s, restoration work took diverse forms of performative citizenship—such as "buy local" campaigns for home buying, "lease back" contracting with residential and commercial landlords, and workforce development. In the process, West Mount Airy Neighbors, both the organization and the wider community, built a *neighborhood-wide* network of fixers through intra-community interaction and community action, rather than documentation and survey. This network acquired the support of community foundations and government grant makers in the 1970s precisely because it depended on bonded contractors and community bonds, not architecture licenses or union membership. A half-century later, philanthropic organizations and individual philanthropists remain ad hoc and at-large members of preservation networks at every scale. The contingency of philanthropy in local, regional, national, and global communities, I argue, poses a threat to inclusive visions of preservation practice at these scales.

Though many scholars are exploring and debating the role of historical societies, preservation trusts, and other institutions that sponsor architectural restoration, individual philanthropists and the community foundations they support are not their focus. 55 In the meantime, however, the underwriters of social innovation continue to treat fiscal sponsorship as a hedge against unfavorable market conditions and uncertain market actors in the practice of preservation. Most recently, for example, the William Penn Foundation joined more than a half dozen other community and corporate foundations to assist Friends of the Rail Park in Philadelphia with planning, design, and marketing of the Reading Viaduct. An abandoned, elevated right-of-way built of stone in 1874, the structure carried Mount Airy neighbors and many others to downtown Philadelphia for nearly a century before Hurricane Agnes damaged its foundations; a state grant sponsored its rehabilitation. Such financial, political, and institutional support for preservation can enable architectural restoration to take place, but it can also extinguish philanthropic support for maintenance of problematic pasts and precarious historic places.

Neither West Mount Airy Neighbors nor its fiscal sponsors can be found in the National Endowment for the Arts 1974 report on railroad station rehabilitation, reuse, and revenue for the US Department of Transportation. 56 Their absence from this two-volume report could be accidental or intentional; the adverse impact of their absence—a lack of claims for diversity in restoration architecture in a foundational document for preservation policy-makers—is significant either way. If stories of station restoration and reuse merely reflect the narratives of restoration societies, preservationists undoubtedly will lose sight of alliances they have yet to forge and allyship they could perform.

Who survives such partnerships—and at whose expense—can be clear only if the storytellers reflect the diversity of those allied for and

55
Notable exceptions include, Scot French, "Social Preservation and Moral Capitalism in the Historic Black Township of Eatonville, Florida: A Case Study of 'Reverse Gentrification,'" *Change over Time* 8, no. 1 (Spring 2018): 54–72; Robert R. Weyeneth, *Historic Preservation for a Living City: Historic Charleston Foundation, 1947–1997* (Columbia, SC: University of South Carolina Press, 2000); and Charles B. Hosmer, "Preservation Comes of Age: From Williamsburg to the National Trust, 1926–1949," *Bulletin of the Association for Preservation Technology* 12, no. 3 (1980): 20–27.

56
NEA, *Reusing Railroad Stations*, vols. 1 and 2, 1974. NEA ordinarily provided no funding for small stations with spaces for commuters to walk-and-ride or kiss-and-ride but no parking spaces for commuter buses or other transit vehicles. Gravers Lane Station was not one of these multimodal hubs, but NEA awarded Chestnut Hill Historical Society a grant to restore the structure anyway.

against saving historic places from all hazards, including disasters of our own making. West Mount Airy neighbors rarely acted in concert with other conservancies, yet these self-styled disaster experts recognized that disinvestment would cost them more. Many preservation societies founded in the 1950s, including WMAN at its outset, counted on "friends" of their work and their leadership to donate small amounts—$10 to $100, usually—throughout the year and sweat equity on occasion for the betterment of their neighborhood and the cause of preservation more broadly. Through additional allyship with fellow fiscal sponsors, they could preserve or restore support received amid and in response to a disaster.

Not by chance, "supportive workers" are also missing from records of rail-related preservation. Restoration architects, who assemble diverse materials, labor, and finances, continue to classify amateur practitioners of preservation as foes or friends. This case study suggests, however, that support work is a form of aid—financial and intellectual aid to both disaster experts and experienced practitioners of landscape maintenance, building rehabilitation, and community preservation. Restoration architects who lead recovery from the next disaster, in other words, may come from union halls—if the rank-and-file and leadership of "friends" groups allow it.

— Examining Questions of Exclusion
— Shifting Policy Toward Inclusion
— Challenging and Redefining Narratives
— Connecting to Community Development

Historic Preservation and Community Development: Past and Future Synergies

Vicki Weiner

Connecting to Community Development

Since the passage of New York City's Landmarks Law in 1965, government agents and citizen advocates of historic preservation have traditionally refrained from engaging in the complex issues of social justice that confront many historic neighborhoods. With such a powerful regulatory tool at their disposal, preservationists have focused on designating as much historic fabric in the city as possible. Their achievement is impressive: more than 1,500 individual buildings and interiors and 149 neighborhood historic districts—comprising more than 37,000 properties altogether—currently enjoy Landmarks Preservation Commission protection. In these places, the buildings are secured. But what about everything else that makes a place historic, unique, important, and special—like the businesses and institutions housed within buildings? And what about the people who inhabit the place, who shop in the neighborhood commercial corridor, who worship as part of a congregation near their homes, who play with their kids in the park on the corner? While the physical fabric of a designated historic district may be protected from drastic alteration, if everything else in the district changes, can we say that these communities are really *preserved*?

Throughout the five decades since the passage of the Landmarks Law, the city's economy has fluctuated and, relatedly, its demographics have evolved and changed. Particularly during the recovery from the economic crash of 2008, New Yorkers of low, moderate, and middle income have found themselves with less and less choice of where to live. Many are people of color who face the extreme challenges brought about by our nation's long history of racism in housing and economic policy. These challenges are exacerbated by the presence of people of means who have the ability to choose their employment and neighborhood of residence, and who have the privilege and purchasing power to buy their own homes. The result has been the rampant displacement of families and individuals from communities they have lived in for decades, as well as growing homelessness and increasing despair. [1]

What role should preservationists play in addressing these urban problems? Traditionally, historic preservation law focuses on addressing the ways that market forces affect *buildings*, absent consideration of the gross inequity of displacement or the impact on a community when its population is driven away. On the other end of the spectrum, community development corporations (CDCs) and other community-based organizing groups stand at the forefront of addressing the injustices experienced by *people*. In partnership with grassroots activists organized around combating racial, gender, and economic inequality in the city, CDCs are working on the ground in more than a hundred neighborhoods to preserve and develop affordable housing, foster local entrepreneurship, preserve minority-owned businesses, create parent-engaged local schools, and improve community health. Their efforts to preserve community include (but go well beyond) the physical fabric of a neighborhood—they are trying to fundamentally change how the city functions to ensure that marginalized groups have equitable choices and the right to live and thrive in the neighborhoods they call home.

Historic preservation as a discipline and as a practice can contribute—and is, in discrete ways, contributing—to this effort. But as we look

1
Jen Becker, Elena Conte, and Renae Widdison, "Flawed Findings: How New York City's Approach to Measuring Displacement Risk Fails Communities," *Pratt Center for Community Development Report* (2018).

2
Alice O'Connor,
"Swimming Against the
Tide: A Brief History
of Federal Policy in
Poor Communities,"
in The Community
Development Reader,
ed. James DeFilippis
and Susan Saegert
(New York: Routledge,
2008), 18.

3
Walter Thabit, How
East New York Became
a Ghetto (New York:
NYU Press, 2003).

4
Virginia Sánchez
Korrol, "Puerto Ricans,"
in The Encyclopedia
of New York City, ed.
Kenneth T. Jackson
(New Haven, CT: Yale
University Press, 2010).

back on more than fifty years of preservation "battles" and landmark designation activities, it's tempting to conclude that the exclusive goal of historic preservation policy in New York City is to memorialize a past architecture and ignore everything else. Despite preservation efforts that take on the challenge of preserving intangible heritage, historic preservation is still, in many urbanist circles, an undesirable heading that denotes saving buildings not as a means to understanding and perpetuating the city's rich ethnic and cultural diversity, but as an end in itself.

In advancing social equity through the practice of preservation, it may be instructive to examine the modern history of historic preservation and community development. While robust research about early preservation efforts in New York City has been underway for twenty years by scholars as well as organizations such as the New York Preservation Archive Project, the relationship between historic preservation and community development in the city has not been much discussed. In fact, the synergies that can be seen during the formative years of both movements are striking. To those of us who seek to practice in the space between these fields, the past provides an important platform for us to build upon in our work today.

— URBAN DECLINE AS BACKDROP FOR
NEW CITIZEN-LED MOVEMENTS

The historic preservation and community development movements in New York City, as we understand them today, have their roots in the city's mid-twentieth-century decline. The postwar years transformed the city economically, demographically, and physically, in part because of a confluence of federal policies, deindustrialization, and migration. Federal policies at the time were distinctly anti-urban, with public subsidies supporting the development of suburbs as well as a highway system that connected suburban residents to jobs in the central city. Together, these policies encouraged middle-class white urbanites to leave urban areas, taking the city's tax base with them. [2] From 1970 to 1995, core urban counties in the New York metropolitan region lost three hundred thousand residents, while the outer suburban ring gained two million. Along with this exodus came the deindustrialization of New York City. In 1950 local manufacturers provided more than a million jobs for New Yorkers; over the decades since, a steady decline has cut that number by three-quarters, dramatically reducing employment opportunities for middle-class New Yorkers, some of whom followed the employment trail out of the city to the sprawling areas to the south and west. [3]

Just as white middle-class New Yorkers and middle-class jobs were starting to trickle out of the city, large numbers of southern Blacks and Hispanics—most notably native Puerto Ricans—were migrating in, looking for better opportunities. New York City's Puerto Rican population increased by more than thirteenfold between 1940 and 1970, and the city's Black population more than tripled. [4] Beginning in the 1930s, the government-backed policy of redlining hastened the decline of urban communities as banks and the real estate industry refused to

FIG. 1: In 1964 a group of ministers in Bedford-Stuyvesant requested technical assistance from Pratt Center for Community Improvement (now Pratt
Center for Community Development) to evaluate a city-sponsored urban
renewal plan in their community. Pratt Institute's Ron Shiffman (far right)
joins local leaders in presenting the Bedford-Stuyvesant Alternative Plan to
then-Brooklyn borough president Abe Stark (center). Shirley Chisholm, then a
New York state assemblywoman and later the first African American woman
in the US Congress, stands to Stark's left (1966). Image is property of Pratt
Center for Community Development.

FIG. 2: In 1967 community leaders brought US senator Robert F. Kennedy
and other elected officials to tour the neighborhood and attend a conference
on community development, all part of the community's campaign to receive
federal support for its plans. This event culminated in the establishment of the
Bedford-Stuyvesant Restoration Corporation as the nation's first federally-
funded community development corporation. Image is property of Pratt
Center for Community Development.

5
O'Connor, "Swimming Against the Tide," 12.

6
Rachel G. Bratt, "Community Development Corporations and Other Nonprofit Housing Organizations: Challenges Presented by the Private Housing Market," *Lincoln Institute of Land Policy Working Paper* (2006).

7
O'Connor, "Swimming Against the Tide," 18–20.

8
For more information on the early twentieth century emergence of urban renewal policy and its impacts in New York City, and on the pre-1960s history of the Historic Preservation movement, see excellent research by Rachel G. Bratt, Randall F. Mason, Alice O'Connor, and Laura Wolf-Powers, among others.

finance home purchases in the neighborhoods to which Blacks and immigrants were moving. This decline was compounded by blockbusting, whereby banks and developers purchased properties at below-market prices from frightened white homeowners and resold them at a profit to minority families. 5 In many neighborhoods, new owners with little or no expendable income rented out apartments or rooms to other low-income tenants. Despite the additional income, in many cases homeowners were unable to physically maintain their buildings. Some white middle-class homeowners refused to sell, instead relocating to the suburbs and renting out their old homes but neglecting them horribly. Arson, inadequate housing conditions, and rising crime rates followed, and the shrinking tax base did nothing to shore up the city's failing economy. As the 1970s economic crisis set in, New York City's infrastructure eroded, schools failed, retail and manufacturing businesses folded or moved elsewhere, and unemployment brought about considerable neighborhood decline.

Federal urban renewal policies that were intended to assist low- and moderate-income New Yorkers to keep their housing only worsened the decline. New development programs set up to foster public-private partnerships, with public subsidies to private for-profit developers, effectively cleared out "blighted" historic neighborhoods. 6 These urban renewal plans reorganized urban communities into high-rise complexes to house the poor, while middle-class housing subsidies were still largely geared toward suburban development in the first-ring suburbs of Westchester and Long Island. 7 The city's slum clearance approach demolished block upon block of nineteenth- and early twentieth-century residential buildings, replacing some with "tower in the park"-style housing but leaving many more blocks vacant. Meanwhile, very little was being done to provide the kinds of assets a healthy community needs—such as decent schools, shopping areas, and jobs.

— COMMUNITY DEVELOPMENT CORPORATIONS FORM IN RESPONSE

The community development (CD) and historic preservation (HP) movements emerged, in part, as a response to these conditions. While the public policies and civic engagement that epitomize both CD and HP predate the 1960s, the assault on the built fabric brought about by the city's vigorous urban renewal programs and the master planning of Robert Moses sparked grassroots action on a new scale. 8 Religious and community leaders recognized that the government was not going to address the problems in distressed low-income neighborhoods. With the help of progressive urban planners and architects from Pratt Institute in Brooklyn's Clinton Hill neighborhood, itself torn apart by urban renewal policy, they "birthed" the city's grassroots community development movement in the 1960s. These new community-governed nonprofit organizations were able to take on economic development and physical planning projects through community empowerment and strategies of self-help.

The nation's first federally-funded CDC, the Bedford-Stuyvesant Restoration Corporation, was created in 1967 with the support of Senator

Robert Kennedy, who, at the invitation of community leaders, visited Bedford-Stuyvesant in central Brooklyn and saw firsthand what disinvestment and urban renewal had done to the once thriving community. 9 *FIGs. 1, 2* Bed-Stuy Restoration sought (and still seeks) to revitalize its community through a variety of programs that blended social services, job creation, physical renovation, community building, business development, and outreach. 10 The organization was one of many such CDCs that formed in New York City and other urban centers in this early period. In pockets of the city, grassroots community rebuilding efforts reclaimed abandoned buildings to create affordable housing for residents displaced by urban renewal. Throughout the 1970s they renovated thousands of units of housing and "laid the groundwork for the renewed city, an observable truth ignored or minimized by most contemporary histories of the city." 11 The

9
Laura Wolf-Powers, "Expanding Planning's Public Sphere: STREET Magazine, Activist Planning, and Community Development in Brooklyn, New York, 1971–1975," *Journal of Planning Education and Research* 28, no. 2 (2008): 182.

10
P. Jefferson Armistead and Matthew B. Wexler, "Community Development and Youth Development: The Potential Convergence," *New Designs for Youth Development* 14 (1998): 27–33.

FIGS. 3, 4: Bedford-Stuyvesant Restoration Corporation has created or preserved more than 2,200 units of housing and restored the facades of more than 150 homes. Pictured here are "before" and "after" views of one of the corporation's housing preservation projects from the early 1980s. Images are property of Pratt Center for Community Development.

11
Roberta Brandes
Gratz, *The Battle for
Gotham: New York in
the Shadow of Robert
Moses and Jane Jacobs*
(New York: Nation
Books, 2010), 19–20.

12
Wolf-Powers,
"Expanding Planning's
Public Sphere," 182.

13
O'Connor, "Swimming
Against the Tide," 21.

CDCs focused on economic development and social services, as well as renovating neglected or substandard existing buildings, as opposed to developing new housing. By engaging community residents in civic action, CDCs brought a sense of bootstrap empowerment to communities that had felt neglected and ignored.

As philanthropic and government support emerged—from the Ford Foundation's Gray Areas program, the Housing Development Corporation, and financial intermediaries like Enterprise and Local Initiatives Support Corporation, among others—the scale of what CDCs could do began to expand. Public and private entities provided direct capital to CDCs to invest in building renovation and property development, while intermediaries like Pratt Institute Center for Community and Environmental Development (known as PICCED from 1970 to 2005, and now as Pratt Center for Community Development) provided operational support to help build and train staff members recruited from within the community, and contributed technical assistance such as urban planning and architectural services. 12 In 1977 Congress passed the Community Reinvestment Act, which required banks to meet the needs of all creditworthy customers regardless of income levels, thereby ending the official practice of redlining. In the 1990s the US Department of Housing and Urban Development joined forces with philanthropies and financial institutions to form the National Community Development Initiative, which provided hundreds of millions of dollars in grants and loans to CDCs around the nation to strengthen local communities and build new housing. 13

The focus for many of these citizen-led organizations was rehabilitating abandoned buildings and revitalizing blocks that had been decimated by the racist housing policies of the preceding decades. Through a combination of funded work and sweat equity in neighborhoods like Mott Haven in the Bronx and South Williamsburg in Brooklyn, they transformed rubble-strewn lots into thriving urban farms and rehabilitated hundreds of abandoned row houses into viable, livable housing for low-income residents. CDCs developed an impressive variety of community and social service programs to address environmental issues and community health; they also provided job training, helped residents find employment, and worked to address a variety of other social and economic issues facing their communities. By engaging community residents and other stakeholders, accessing resources to foster community self-help, and building community power, CDCs have helped restore, rehabilitate, and preserve their communities—physically, environmentally, socially, and economically. FIGs. 3, 4

— "MODERN" HISTORIC PRESERVATION EMERGES

While CDCs emerged in more than a dozen low-income communities of color in New York City to address the most debilitating social and physical urban problems, community-based historic preservation organizations evolved at around the same time in other neighborhoods. The postwar years brought the demolition of many notable historic buildings, including Pennsylvania Station, which became the poster child for the movement to protect the city's historic fabric. The significant losses prompted civic leaders to catalog the city's architectural treasures and investigate how aesthetic controls could prevent the city from losing more of its architectural heritage. [14] Organizations such as the Municipal Art Society of New York and the New York chapter of the Society of Architectural Historians began to look to historic preservation efforts outside New York City—in places such as New Orleans, Charleston, and Alexandria, Virginia—as models for a new Landmarks Law. [15] Meanwhile, several demographic shifts were emerging in New York City: as the inequality of government economic and housing policy displaced low-income immigrant tenants from many brownstone neighborhoods in Brooklyn and Manhattan, young white professionals were reoccupying and revitalizing historic neighborhoods such as Brooklyn Heights, Greenwich Village, and the Upper West Side. [16] These more affluent residents organized to fight urban renewal and redevelopment projects that threatened individual architectural treasures and historic neighborhoods. Because they were not blocked from access to capital like their Black and Hispanic neighbors, these white urban professionals were able to purchase historic buildings, and build equity and wealth as well.

Early efforts to save whole neighborhoods helped lay the groundwork for the creation of the New York City Landmarks Preservation Commission and for the 1965 passage of the city's Landmarks Law. While the language of the law cites social welfare, education, and economic prosperity among its broadest goals, preservationists' primary interest in architecture and history has led to a far more narrow application of it.

14
For a comprehensive account of the events leading up to the passage of the New York City Landmarks Law, see Anthony C. Wood's *Preserving New York: Winning the Right to Protect a City's Landmarks* (New York: Routledge, 2008).

15
Wood, *Preserving New York*, 102–107.

16
Gratz, *Battle for Gotham*, 34.

FIG. 5: *Graffiti from the early 1970s well describes the ethos of New York City's community development corporation movement and that of many early historic preservation advocates. Image is property of Pratt Center for Community Development.*

17
Wood, *Preserving New York*, 379.

18
Gratz, *Battle for Gotham*, 34.

19
Wood, *Preserving New York*, 183–185.

20
In a 1959 memoir entitled *The House on the Heights*, the writer Truman Capote referred to the young urban professionals of Brooklyn Heights as "brave pioneers" who brought "brooms and buckets of paint; urban, ambitious young couples, by and large mid-rung in their Doctor-Lawyer-Wall Street-Whatever careers, eager to restore the Heights...." Quoted in Wood, *Preserving New York*, 208.

21
Gratz, *Battle for Gotham*, 40.

22
Ronald Shiffman, interview by the author, June 5, 2010.

Primarily, the Landmarks Law has been used to safeguard historic built heritage through the designation and regulation of individual buildings and neighborhoods based on architectural merit. [17] A number of federal laws and government programs have also emerged to assist in this effort, such as the National Historic Preservation Act (1966), which protects significant buildings against the threat of publicly-funded development projects.

Most of the earliest preservation battles were fought by resident-advocates to protect their communities from institutional expansion, government-sponsored urban renewal developments, and Robert Moses's transportation initiatives—all of which threatened not just homes but entire neighborhoods of middle-income residents, artists, and working people, and sought to displace them from their communities. [18] From his plan to plow through Washington Square Park in order to connect upper and lower Fifth Avenue to his proposed Lower Manhattan Expressway, which would have eviscerated the cast-iron streetscapes of SoHo, Moses gave both longtime and new residents of historic New York City neighborhoods plenty of reason to organize and advocate for preservation. Dozens of citizen-heroes emerged during these fights, some of whom, like Jane Jacobs, became icons of the community preservation movement. [19] In approaching these struggles as matters of community survival, community advocates sought any and all opportunities to prevent the unthinkable—they were well versed in zoning and other land use policies, as well as the historic preservation tools emerging in other jurisdictions, and brought all of these to bear on their efforts. *FIG. 5*

These advocates were also willing and able to make considerable personal investments in the repair and maintenance of historic buildings. Their civic engagement, political savvy, and activism—in concert with citywide advocacy by organizations like the Municipal Art Society—kept "progress" from tearing down what is now some of the most valuable real estate in the city. Often referred to as "urban pioneers," the community preservation advocates prevented a number of neighborhoods with historic nineteenth-century row houses from falling into the decline seen in places like East New York, Brownsville, Harlem, and the South Bronx. [20] Some suggest that Mayor Robert Wagner signed the Landmarks Law in part to mollify and encourage these gentrifiers as they personally revitalized the urban core. [21] Their achievements are remarkable, but it cannot be forgotten that the opportunity to be "pioneers" in these neighborhoods came about because of the continued marginalization and displacement of low-income people of color.

— HP AND CD UNITY AND DISUNITY

Despite the racial and class differences, built environment advocates from the 1960s and 1970s recall a common sense of purpose in that period as community developers and community preservers worked to revitalize their neighborhoods by protecting building stock from the wrecking ball and insisting on their right to occupy it. [22] Their shared concern wasn't just for the history and architectural merit of the physical fabric; it took in—and took on—the wholesale evisceration of communities caused by urban renewal and the loss of community identity, character, and culture that robbed residents of their place in the city. Robert Moses was their common enemy; his city-building plans had a devastating impact for New Yorkers of all income levels. Battles against Moses's plans in Manhattan's West Village and Little Italy, as well as Brooklyn's Cobble Hill, brought newly launched community planning service providers like PICCED together with neighborhood preservationists such as Jane Jacobs to thwart the demolition of historic buildings and the displacement of their inhabitants. [23]

CDCs are rightly credited with turning around some of the city's most impoverished communities. They found success by focusing not just on housing but also on people—by insisting upon a seat at the table for their low- and moderate-income constituents, by identifying gaps in essential social services and bringing in resources to fill them, and by providing education and training to enhance their community's self-sufficiency. [24] Like their CDC counterparts, the HP activists often confronted the city over changes that were harming their neighborhoods. However, as members of a more privileged class, their ability to build political power and their capacity to access capital in order to become not just tenant-stakeholders but also property owners meant that they did not face the same struggles that their CDC counterparts were confronting on behalf of their low-income constituents.

The preservationists also had a legislative tool that gave an increasingly laser-like focus to their cause: the Landmarks Law, which empowered the city to intervene in potentially damaging private development plans by regulating changes to properties under its purview. But, of course, the law had opponents as well—it was the target of a number of significant court battles in which real estate interests challenged its constitutionality. The city's defense ultimately prevailed through the 1970s and 1980s; however, advocates both within and outside city government became increasingly wary of applying the Landmarks Law in ways that might invite charges of overreach. While the preservation activism of the 1960s and 1970s embraced the notion of holistic "community preservation," by the end of the twentieth century most preservationists had narrowed their interests to focus on built-environment history and architectural integrity, thereby limiting their scope to the regulation of aesthetics, which had been affirmed by the US Supreme Court and stood well within the comfort zone of the Landmarks Preservation Commission and its legal defenders. [25] The larger questions of community preservation—such as the fate of vulnerable populations and businesses—moved further and further outside their purview. [26] Earlier, outward-facing, "urbanistic" impulses yielded considerable ground to inward-looking "curatorial" ones. [27]

For CDCs and other community-based advocacy groups from the northwest Bronx to southernmost Brooklyn, the improvement in the economy and renewed investment by government and the private sector—which their bootstrap approach had catalyzed—were at first considered to be measures of success. [28] Recovery from the economic downturn of the late 1980s brought about an extraordinary building boom in New York City; to the CDCs, the renewed interest among bankers and real estate developers furthered the goals of equitable community development

23
Shiffman, interview.

24
Bratt, "Community Development Corporations," 9–14.

25
Erica Avrami, Cherie-Nicole Leo, and Alberto Sanchez Sanchez, "Confronting Exclusion: Redefining the Intended Outcomes of Historic Preservation," Change Over Time 8, no. 1 (Spring 2018): 107.

26
Shiffman, interview.

27
Randall F. Mason, "Theoretical and Practical Arguments for a Values-Centered Preservation," CRM: The Journal of Heritage Stewardship 3, no. 2 (Summer 2006): 25. Mason's research on early twentieth-century preservation in the United States provides an excellent and useful framework for understanding the impulses that drove preservation activity throughout the century.

28
Bratt, "Community Development Corporations," 18.

29
Shiffman, interview.

30
The author is grateful to New York City Council member Brad Lander for codeveloping this analysis during his tenure as director of the Pratt Center for Community Development.

31
Much has been written about this controversial development project, which also inspired two documentaries (see *The Battle for Brooklyn*, dir. Michael Galinsky and Suki Hawley, 2011 and *Brooklyn Matters*, dir. Isabel Hill, 2007) and is partially addressed in a third (see *My Brooklyn*, dir. Kelly Anderson, 2013). The fight was largely "won" by the developers and "lost" by the preservation advocates; the affordable housing that was promised can be said to have somewhat materialized, though the gentrification of this area and the communities adjacent to it has been extreme and is ongoing. The benefits of the project to low-income public housing residents nearby are hard to document, if present at all.

32
For insight on the racial gap in historic preservation practice, see Avrami, Leo, and Sanchez Sanchez, "Confronting Exclusion," 102–120; and Ned Kaufman, *Place, Race and Story* (New York: Routledge, 2009).

within the private sector. However, the promise of new development began to drive a wedge between CDC interests and those of historic preservationists—the former lobbying for development activity that would bring affordable housing and enhanced social services to their communities, the latter fighting against new development, fearing the damage it would do to low-density historic housing and culturally important places. 29

By the mid-1990s, the very different paths pursued by the two movements had estranged their advocates from one another. Many of the largest development projects divided community advocates into opposing camps. 30 In Brooklyn's Atlantic Yards, for example, preservationists fought against development in order to preserve low-density historic housing, despite their sensitivity to the housing affordability crisis in the area. Community development advocates supported the development project because it promised new affordable apartments, though they acknowledged that the project would significantly harm the historic character of the community. 31 It seemed that the equity sought by community development advocates and the historic "sense of place" sought by preservationists were somehow mutually exclusive; developers and their government supporters seemed all too willing to offer the community this set of zero-sum choices.

Today, New York City faces a very different set of issues than it faced in the 1960s and 1970s. Neighborhoods that struggled during the decline and underinvestment of the mid-twentieth century—with their attractive nineteenth-century housing stock—have been rapidly gentrifying, and residents are subjected to intense real estate pressure and rampant displacement. As change comes to these predominantly nonwhite neighborhoods, there is increasing interest in utilizing the Landmarks Law to safeguard the historic fabric. Several communities of color have advocated for designation as part of their community preservation efforts, though creating a historic district does not address many of the threats to longtime moderate-income renters. In neighborhoods such as Bedford-Stuyvesant, in Brooklyn—the community that birthed the community development movement—the discourse around historic designation points to a perception among Black residents that preservation is a tool of gentrification: that it is complicit with displacement, that its goal is to curate buildings and save the neighborhood for wealthier newcomers, while the housing struggles of longtime residents go unaddressed. 32 The desirability of using the most powerful tool in the city's preservation toolkit is, in communities of color, a subject of considerable debate.

— FINDING A MIDDLE GROUND

Advocates of historic preservation and community development share the goal of preserving community—in the form of people, places, and the businesses and institutions that support them both. A growing number of practitioners from both disciplines are seeking a middle ground. Many community development groups have turned to historic preservation tools as they create new community facilities and housing—for example, the Gibb Mansion in Brooklyn and Morrisania Hospital in the Bronx, both award-winning adaptive reuse projects that transformed neglected historic resources into assets for low-income communities. 33 Historic preservation organizations have also broadened their activities and skill sets to effect community preservation that is not limited to architecture: many, like the Upper West Side's Landmark West!, have initiated efforts to preserve local businesses, moving past physical fabric issues to support the preservation of community economic resources.

So what can be done to better integrate economic and social equity goals with those of historic preservation in New York City? One strategy is to use a values-based approach that considers the ways diverse stakeholders see the importance and value of place. Values-based preservation planning recognizes that *places*—buildings and other spaces made culturally meaningful by use and users—are important to different constituents for different reasons. 34 In order to fully understand the meaning of a place and its potential for the future, one must examine the various values constituents attach to it. It is also crucial to acknowledge that meaning and value change over time. This approach requires looking at both past and present values and considering the many different narratives that diverse constituents recall, reflect upon, and identify with. At its core, a values-based approach is as much—if not more—about people as it is about physical fabric. It requires respecting the points of view of those who have attachment to a place even if their ideas challenge long-held narratives and beliefs, or if they are place-users that are not typically consulted. And it calls for a great deal of mediation between the needs of contemporary stakeholders and the traditional physical fabric-oriented goals of historic preservation, which can result in outcomes that look very different from the "win" of landmark designation and architecturally appropriate building stewardship.

— FULTON STREET AND MOTT HAVEN: MERGING AGENDAS

Working with colleagues at Pratt Institute, I've been involved in a number of efforts to integrate historic preservation approaches and tools with those of community development. 35 Our work has explored how preservation can be used to address issues of social equity, identifying and enhancing community assets while meeting community needs. The ambitions of our community partners went well beyond preserving architectural history and integrity; therefore, landmark designation and regulatory review by the Landmarks Preservation Commission were not sufficient tools. We found that, to address issues of social inclusion, historic preservation practitioners need to acknowledge and embrace community goals beyond aesthetics, to think outside the traditional preservation toolbox, and to listen to community voices.

Pratt Center's work in downtown Brooklyn sought to secure the future of Fulton Street Mall—located on Fulton between Flatbush Avenue and Adams Street—as a vital public place. Attracting as many as one hundred thousand shoppers daily, the street has been an important commercial

33
The Gibb Mansion is a supportive housing facility in a historic Clinton Hill mansion developed by IMPACCT Brooklyn; Urban Horizons is a housing and social services facility in the former Morrisania Hospital complex developed by the Women's Housing and Economic Development Corporation.

34
This theory of a values-based approach to historic preservation was developed and has been put into practice by a number of preservation and planning scholars and practitioners during the past decade. The author's education in values-based preservation came from reading the work of—and working in partnership with—Randall F. Mason and Erica Avrami, to whom she is greatly indebted.

35
Many incredibly committed and talented community experts and Pratt planners, instructors, and students have participated in applying a values-based approach in places like Downtown Brooklyn; Cypress Hills and Crown Heights; the public housing site Markham Gardens, on Staten Island; Manhattan's East Village; and Mott Haven, in the Bronx.

The central portion of
downtown Brooklyn's
Fulton Street shopping
corridor runs the
length of Adams Street
to Flatbush Avenue
Extension, a stretch of
some eight blocks. It
was dubbed the Fulton
Street Mall when it was
closed off to vehicular
traffic in the 1970s. The
corridor also included
the indoor Albee
Square Mall, built in the
former Albee Theater
in 1977, which was
demolished in 2004 to
make way for the City
Point shopping center,
which now occupies
the site. In this essay,
the entirety of the
Fulton Street shopping
corridor is referred to
as the Fulton Street
Mall or the Fulton
Street corridor.

corridor since its development in the late 1800s as a destination shopping area. Transformed into something of a pedestrian mall in the 1970s, the Fulton Street Mall has been most popular with a constituency of Black Brooklynites who live in the northeastern neighborhoods of the borough. 36

Our project had its roots in the public review process for the 2004 Downtown Brooklyn Redevelopment Plan, which sought to create office and residential space in areas surrounding the shopping corridor. While the plan didn't propose significant changes to Fulton Street itself, it was clear that the city's desire to transform the area would have a major impact. Several preservation organizations took an interest in the corridor's historic architecture and began a campaign for its protection. Though the use of landmark designation offered potential protection for several architecturally distinct buildings, it was clear that it would not preserve the *place*. The character of Fulton Street Mall was not derived from its architecture alone: it emanated from the businesses that occupied the buildings and, most importantly, from its use as a shopping and gathering place.

While the economy on this stretch of Fulton Street was thriving, there was a prevailing sense among city planners and business leaders that it needed dramatic improvement. Some essentially called for the reinvention of Fulton Street—to entirely replace its cacophonous mix of businesses, shoppers, and signage with a more "comfortable" and sanitized (i.e., white) feel. The impulse of preservation organizations to vouchsafe the area's architectural history had already touched a nerve with policy-makers who felt the "improvement" of the downtown business environment might be thwarted by landmark designation. On one side, a handful of groups were speaking out against the potential demolition of architectural structures; on another, decision-makers were arguing that the structures might be standing in the way of economic progress.

Both parties may have had valid opinions, but where, in this dialogue, was the voice of the large number of people who comprised the street culture and commerce of Fulton Street Mall? What, in their view, would be worth preserving? What kinds of "improvement" were they hoping for? The opinions of shopper-stakeholders seemed to us to be critical to defining the place's character, strengths, and weaknesses. And yet those opinions were being ignored. We designed our study to bring these voices into the dialogue, in order to understand the *whole* significance of the place. We felt that looking beyond the narrow interests of one constituent group or another, one aspect of significance or another, was necessary to ensuring that this key Fulton Street constituency did not get frozen out of the debate.

Over a year's research and consultation, we found that the Fulton Street corridor had long supported social bonds woven out of economic activity and cultural expression. Like the Greek agora, Arab souk, or Middle Eastern bazaar, Fulton Street is an economic marketplace that fosters many types of interaction, functionally serving as a public square. While by no means considered perfect, it was popular, profitable, and historically relevant to a diverse range of shoppers and visitors. At the same time, it was maligned by many who lived or worked nearby as a place in need of radical transformation. We unearthed many negative perceptions of the corridor among nonusers as well; white newcomers to the area

37
To read the Fulton
Street Mall report,
visit https://
prattcenter.net/
projects/building-
resilient-communities/
fulton-street-mall.

FIG. 6: The Fulton Street Mall study at Pratt Center posits that historic
preservation is just one of many approaches needed to preserve all of the ways
in which this dynamic retail corridor in Downtown Brooklyn is valued by a
broad spectrum of constituents—including its shoppers. Image is property of
Pratt Center for Community Development.

shared perceptions grounded in racial stereotypes and fears about living
near a Black shopping district. These stood out as a significant challenge
to preserving the culture of the corridor and nurturing its future. In
reporting on a sizable community outreach effort, we pointed to the racial
disparity in opinions about what was "needed" at Fulton Street Mall.

We analyzed our findings and proposed strategies aimed at
improving Fulton Street for its current users and increasing its appeal
to those in the areas immediately adjacent to it. 37 FIG. 6 We strove to
develop recommendations that would achieve some balance between
old and new within the corridor. While some of our recommendations
were realized, the most gratifying outcome was that we were able to
intervene in a one-sided dialogue about the future of what had long been
a contested place. In total, a number of historic department store buildings were designated as New York City landmarks and redeveloped for
mixed use; an urban design plan significantly improved the public realm
for the hundreds of thousands of shoppers who visit the corridor daily;
and new development is bringing more and better retail options to the
area. It's impossible to know if these changes would have come without
our report (arguably, they would have), but ours was the only effort to
engage shoppers in the discussion. Since that time, the development
of market-rate residential towers and more upscale businesses around
Fulton Street has drastically changed the area. But when one visits the
corridor today, the essential character of the place—as evinced by its
racially diverse shopping constituency, vibrant street culture, sometimes
garish signage, and distinctly urban retail offerings—is much the same
as it was then. By seeking to meet the needs and interests of a broad
spectrum of stakeholders, much of what users valued about Fulton Street
has been preserved despite the changes.

38
The Mott Haven studio project was conducted under the auspices of the Graduate Center for Planning and the Environment in the School of Architecture at Pratt Institute. The community-based organization South Bronx Unite served as the studio's community "client." South Bronx Unite's strong leadership, expertise, local knowledge, and considerable prior work provided vast resources for the project, and the author is grateful to have had the opportunity to work with them.

In a Neighborhood Preservation Studio course focused on the Mott Haven section of the Bronx, Pratt Institute graduate students in historic preservation, city and regional planning, urban place-making, and sustainable environmental systems were invited to work with a community-based organization that was looking for support in its efforts to address the significant lack of open space, high rates of asthma, and decreasing affordability of housing in the community. 38 While the HP students began with a fairly traditional documentation study—looking at historic maps and census and other public records and identifying how the current built environment of Mott Haven came to be—they found the story of the South Bronx neighborhood's decline during the 1970s and citizen-led resurgence in the 1980s to be the central historical marker and the most important jumping-off point for the project. The community's grassroots organizations—which preserved much of the physical fabric and sustained the community of Black and Latino residents in the face of disinvestment and urban renewal—were identified by the students to be among its greatest historic assets. A community survey effort forced all of the students out into the neighborhood, where they observed and interacted with residents and business owners. Working with teachers from a local public school, a number of students were able to share information and engage with middle and high school students whose views and creative ideas informed and inspired them.

The students struggled with the multitude of voices they heard throughout the semester and with the seriousness of the issues facing the community—from the over-policing experienced by youth and adults alike, to the unacceptably poor condition of the local health facilities, to the overcrowding of playgrounds and city-owned open spaces, to the fear of gang violence in many pockets of the neighborhood. However, community members also shared stories that prompted the students to develop potential strategies to address these challenges: stories of the Young Lords public health advocacy and their temporary takeover of a public hospital in 1970, of the resident-led occupation of rubble-strewn lots for urban farming, and of the grassroots effort to reclaim the neighborhood's waterfront. The heritage of the community as a place of progressive civic engagement and its history as a pillar in the community development movement were important sources of ongoing community power. This heritage inspired the students to suggest that the tools of planning and preservation could—and should—be used to assist the community to remember, identify with, and perpetuate its legacy of self-determination.

Pooling their research and ideas, many of which came directly from their interactions with community members, the students developed a number of proposals for short-, medium-, and long-term community preservation and planning activities. Some of these were place-based, such as a proposal to adapt a soon-to-be-vacated police precinct into a community justice center. Others were programmatic, such as collecting oral histories from generations of community gardeners and sharing these histories with local schoolchildren to inspire the next generation of gardeners. In presenting these ideas to our community partners, the students argued that Mott Haven's past as a hotbed of locally-led improvement and sustainability provided a powerful foundation for the development of strategies to protect and improve it into the future.

With all that is at stake in our communities—in New York City and all over the United States—it is hard to imagine that historic preservation practice can remain singularly focused on one aspect of the urban environment and stay relevant. The challenges that community developers and community preservers faced in mid-twentieth-century New York seem remote in today's economic boom, but that boom brings its own difficulties. By broadening our purview to consider other-than-architectural treasures in our communities and by centering some of the city's most vulnerable residents—many of whom are, themselves, community treasures—preservation practitioners can find incredibly purposeful applications for their knowledge, interests, and skills. This is the approach we are taking at Pratt, both within professionally led community projects and in the field with our students. We believe it is helping us to find—and invent—new policy directions to meet our most ambitious goals. The resulting energy, ideas, and outcomes remind us that a path to community preservation that is fully community engaged and that embraces social inclusion is one well worth taking.

The research briefly shared in this volume began in 2004 with the Fulton Street Mall study, funded by the J. M. Kaplan Fund. A midcareer grant from the James Marston Fitch Charitable Foundation enabled further research on the evolution of community development and historic preservation as urban social movements in New York City. I am grateful to my colleagues and students at Pratt for their important contributions to the exploration of these issues.

Pullman Revitalization, Historic Preservation, and Community Engagement

An interview with Ciere Boatright

Connecting to Community Development

ERICA AVRAMI
Your work with Chicago Neighborhood Initiatives (CNI) is situated within a mission of economic and community development, but the organization emphasizes place-based approaches that capitalize on neighborhood assets. Can you speak to the ways in which your projects engage heritage assets in these broader efforts, especially in the historic Pullman neighborhood?

CIERE BOATRIGHT

At CNI, we think about all our assets—land, architecture, proximity to rail, water, and the expressway—and leverage them to transform disinvested and under-resourced communities into places where more people will want to live, work, and do business. A neighborhood like Pullman, for example, has everything it needs to become vibrant once again. It was one of the nation's first planned industrial communities, built in the 1880s by Pullman's Palace Car Company. Its historic row homes and buildings are huge assets that we can leverage. It's not just about spurring new development—it's also about investing in existing historic structures for future generations. Without the investment, the time, and the energy to restore these buildings, that rich history will get lost. FIG. 1

When I think about economic development and investment in Pullman, I always look at it through three lenses: historic preservation; the strategic, economic investment and infusion of dollars; and community engagement. For historic preservation, that means thinking about our heritage and understanding how our buildings are assets to the community and to the city. We couldn't do the work that we do without thinking about it that way.

Does CNI's perspective reflect that of the community? Do the people who live in Pullman see those buildings as assets as well?

Absolutely. Overall, I think most of the people who live here chose to do so because of Pullman's rich history. Many of them are fourth- and fifth-generation residents of Pullman. They value the authenticity and the history of the built environment. People in the historic district take tremendous pride in their homes and want to maintain their historic and architectural character. That pride is on display every year during the Historic Pullman Foundation's house tours. And many of the people who visit Pullman want to learn more about that history. Once the National Monument site is complete, we expect it will draw more than 300,000 visitors a year. They will learn more about this factory town where the labor movement gained traction and where the nation's first Black union was formed. And they'll see first-hand how the community has been revitalized over the last ten years.

We value transparency and community involvement—we want to know what residents think, even if that involves pushback. For example, we're working on the Pullman Artspace Lofts, a new artist live/work housing development. It includes the renovation and adaptive reuse of two historic buildings from the late 1800s, plus new infill development on a lot vacant for more than 70 years. The community came to us and asked that the new construction complement the existing historic buildings.

And they were exactly right. Residents are thinking about history and architectural fit at every turn, even when it comes to new construction. How will a structure fit in without simply replicating the past? Will it complement what's there? Will it look so new and iconic that it's a distraction? Our community is very vocal about these things, and we worked closely with them and the architect to refine the design accordingly.

FIG. 1: *The Pullman Clock Tower and Administration Building will serve as the visitor center for the Pullman National Monument, recognizing the first planned industrial community in the United States. Along with the Pullman factory, which produced railroad cars, the model town housed a diverse community—more than half of residents were foreign-born—with a population of over 8,000 at its peak in the mid-1880s. The 1894 Pullman Strike was a historic turning point in US labor law. When Pullman workers went on strike after a reduction in wages, other members of the American Railroad Union supported their cause by refusing to add or remove Pullman cars from trains, thereby disrupting rail service across the country and prompting the first-ever federal injunction to block a strike. Image courtesy of Marc PoKempner.*

The work of the heritage field represents the best of intentions when it comes to ensuring that cultural significance is communicated through the physical preservation of buildings, but it takes a lot of investment. The cost-benefit balance can sometimes be a real challenge. Can you talk about the challenges and the opportunities you've encountered as you negotiate between economic development and some of these preservation interests?

I think acknowledging existing community assets and knowing that we can't just focus on vacant land is crucial in terms of new construction. We're converting 180 acres of abandoned and vacant land in Pullman into new commercial and industrial spaces, as well as a new year-round, 135,000 square foot indoor sports and education complex. Creating a holistic and comprehensive neighborhood requires generating investments for a wide variety of different developments. In turn, we've had to get creative and use every tool in our belt to incentivize developers and cultivate investment. That includes new market tax credits and tax increment financing. We're also using low-income housing tax credits, historic tax credits, and partnering with public and private entities.

Historic preservation guidelines add an extra layer that takes a little bit more energy and coordination, but it's absolutely essential when you realize the benefits of preserving the rich history of Pullman. We can't neglect these historic row homes. We can't neglect these unique structures. We can't neglect the stories they contain. Is it hard? Sure. But it's completely worth it when you can take buildings that have been vacant for decades and restore them to productive use. Or when you can save precious natural resources by renovating instead of demolishing buildings. Or when you can turn renters into new homeowners and help them build wealth and a brighter future. And it's really worth it when you can energize entire vacant blocks by renovating one or two structures at a time. FIG. 2 Comprehensive development means focusing on these historic spaces *and* essential services like health care, recreation, education, and the cultural activities that are typical of a strong, healthy community.

FIG. 2: *Rehabilitation of a historic row house in north Pullman. Image courtesy of Marc PoKempner.*

You are a strong proponent of "authentic engagement" to understand the needs of communities and to promote inclusive development. Tell us what that looks like and how engagement processes change when heritage is part of the scope.

When I say "authentic engagement" I mean conducting more than one community meeting or prepping for a meeting with the city council. It's really digging deep and listening, more than anything else. I'll give an example of how that looks on the ground: when CNI was established, before we created any plans or built anything, we listened to residents for an entire year. We went to community meetings. We went to block club meetings. We went to churches. We went to different community organizations. And we asked: "What do you want? How should it look?"

We didn't focus only on historic assets. We had to understand the community's overall needs and interests. For example, Pullman was known as one of the city's largest food deserts. There wasn't a single grocery store there. Residents had to leave the community and head to the south suburbs, nearly 30 minutes away, for affordable, fresh food. Or they went to the gas station for an expensive gallon of milk or a cup of coffee. Things that many people take for granted just didn't exist here.

There was also a need for more jobs. With every project we do, we think in terms of how many jobs it will create and the hiring requirements—for example, new hires must come from the surrounding zip codes. How do you develop a strong, sustainable community if you don't ensure that residents have access to the benefits from new jobs? Our community benefits agreements (CBAs) are tied to hiring and are critical as new businesses come into the community. Also, the hiring requirements that are placed on these companies help hold them accountable for the financial incentives they receive in the form of tax increment financing. So it works full circle. You're building, you're attracting additional economic development, and the folks who live here are also benefiting firsthand from the new development.

The community also wanted more housing—specifically, affordable housing. And they asked for recreation options. Would we have known these things if we hadn't really engaged the community? No way. Many developers come in with a preconceived idea of what they want to build. But we took the time to listen to the community. And that listening allowed us to plan with the community.

With these kinds of developments, there can often be a range of stakeholders and interests. How do you manage diverse interests, build trust, and sustain engagement over time?

We love new residents, but we're really developing the neighborhood for the residents who already live here. They're the ones who should get the jobs. For instance, when it comes to construction contracts, we ask, "How we can focus on local contracting? How do we ensure that the people who live here and have businesses are able to directly benefit from our projects?"

FIG. 3: *Method soap factory in Pullman. Gotham Greens operates a 75,000 sq.ft. hydroponic greenhouse on the roof. Image courtesy of Marc PoKempner.*

Authentic, honest engagement allowed us to do that. It held us accountable. And the community knows that we're really invested in hearing their ideas and suggestions. I also think that, for us as a developer, it's important to say, "Hey, here's what we've done. Here's where we are. It's time to check in. Are we getting it right? Does this feel right?"

As a developer, we rely on existing relationships in these communities. When we do development, we look to partner with other developers and stakeholders who have good relationships with local organizations and residents. We never go into a community and plan *for* the community. Instead, we plan *with* the community. In Pullman, there are many different organizations we work with. One thing that's really helped the engagement and community planning process is having an "umbrella" organization that pulls all of them together. For example, the Pullman Civic Organization will say: "We're starting our next phase of neighborhood development. We've got a 10,000-square-foot building with five spaces. Who should we reach out to? What type of retail do we want to see? What do you want to see? And if you have relationships with small businesses, please introduce us. We're happy to reach out to them as well." There's a careful balance between having national tenants and supporting the small businesses that believe in the community, that know they can be successful in the community, and that want to be a part of it.

One of Pullman's greatest assets is its very engaged community. It's a breath of fresh air. They are our sounding board for the work that we do. Virtually nothing gets done in Pullman by CNI without the project being fully vetted by the community. The Pullman Artspace Lofts is a good example of how engagement really works—of how, when you get pushback, you respond. When we first planned it, we thought it was going to consist of 45 units of housing. But after we hosted a design competition with community residents on the jury, they selected an architect and helped refine the preliminary designs. We told them, "Mark up what you like. Mark up what you don't like. Show us what's working and show us what isn't." Their feedback was that the building felt too tall and had too many units. So we went back and reduced the number of units to thirty-eight and decreased the height of the building. That's what I mean when I say, "authentic engagement." It's not just kind of listening and saying, "Yeah, yeah, yeah." It's being responsive and respectful to the community and their concerns.

Before we get too far in the design of a space, we make sure that the community is on board. Once we get the buy-in, then we do the design, we engage all the consultants, and we go through the process for all the necessary approvals. But we start with the community. There are times when we engage other consultants, small businesses (including minority- and women-owned businesses), and local partners to work with us during the community outreach part. But to be completely honest with you, a lot of the work that we're doing on the community engagement side is really just us reaching out—not people coming in and doing professional focus groups. It's us saying: "Hey, community, we're back at you again."

How do you cultivate a development team that has the skills to engage with communities?

Before we were CNI, we were a subsidiary of a large bank. A lot of the team members came from that bank and brought experience with them from the community and economic development worlds. I came from a financial institution with a city planning background. I have colleagues in the CNI Micro Finance Group who are making capital available to growing small businesses. We also have college students who are interested in urban planning. It's a marriage between those that are focused on finance, those focused on urban planning, and those working in community development. This range of skills allows us to keep our ears to the ground and look at development through many lenses.

When we need to do additional hiring, we want a team that is committed and passionate about historic preservation and community engagement, but that understands the importance of economic development and strategic investment in the area.

Addressing inequity is a guiding principle of CNI, whether that's through ensuring fair hiring practices or prioritizing the existing community in your development efforts. In what ways did some of the historic inequities represented in Pullman—especially regarding its labor history—play a role in the redevelopment process?

I keep going back to job creation because it's so important when you think about economic development and leveling the playing field. Pullman's known for labor issues, historically. When we think about development, we think about attracting new businesses and entrepreneurs to the area— whether it's manufacturers and distributors like Method Home Products, Gotham Greens, and the Whole Foods Midwest Distribution Center, or new retail like the Walmart at Pullman Park, or the three restauranteurs at the new One Eleven Food Hall. FIG. 3 These businesses and others have created more than 1,500 jobs in Pullman. Working with Alderman Anthony Beale, we not only secured jobs for local residents but also at higher wages when compared with other Walmart workers nationwide.

But it's not only about jobs. When we think about housing, for example, we have rental options. But we also think about how to create affordable home ownership opportunities. That way, we can start building appreciable wealth in the community. And that also happens through developing new small businesses. How do we support retail in the community? How can we get entrepreneurs to partner with our microfinance group to obtain the capital they need to grow their business?

We recently developed a 10,000-square-foot building in Pullman. When we went to the community to discuss the project, we heard over and over that people wanted restaurants and additional food options. Of the five spaces in the building, one is about 2,300 square feet, and we talked to a few different restaurant owners about it, all African American, all small businesses that are successful in their own right. What we heard from them was: "The space feels a little big. I don't know that I'm *there* yet." So, we thought creatively: Why don't we, CNI, divide the 2,300-square-foot space into three separate spaces and allow them to operate their own businesses individually? They can drive traffic to one another. And we can have some shared common space for folks to sit down and dine. In essence, it becomes a restaurant incubator. Our vision is that these restaurants will be so successful, they'll grow out of these shared spaces and eventually want to go into our next phase of development. We can't adopt a one-size-fits-all model for development. We have to understand the neighborhood's unique challenges, but also recognize the assets—our businesses, our people, our land, our proximity to downtown and other communities—and the value that uniquely is here. FIG. 4

So we look at jobs, but we also think about attracting new businesses. And we think about home ownership. And we think about the

FIG. 4: New retail at the 180-acre Pullman Park site has combated the food desert in Pullman. Image courtesy of Marc PoKempner.

preservation of affordable housing. And we think about the preservation and restoration of historic buildings. All those things are necessary to a healthy community. It can't just be one thing.

With Pullman's proximity to downtown, its tremendous assets, and good investment and job opportunities on the horizon, how does CNI work to ensure that no one gets left behind and that the risk of displacement is minimized? Especially with the planned opening of the Pullman National Monument Visitor Center, how are you anticipating change so as to preserve a sense of place and community?

We're looking at decades of investment in Pullman, so we're still pretty far away from displacement or gentrification. The average price of a home in the neighborhood is half that of the rest of the city. That said, we are thinking proactively and trying to create density. Our Pullman Artspace Lofts project will bring more people to the community. We're working with groups like Neighborhood Housing Services of Chicago and others to provide the information and resources renters need to become homeowners. When we think about historic properties, how do we put them back in productive use with folks from the community and so they want to live here? It's about being intentional and knowing that it can happen. But we're being thoughtful about it, and I think housing is one way we're being very thoughtful.

As a result of where the community is situated in proximity to 111th Street, it's the gateway into the Pullman National Monument site. So when we think about development, we're thinking about it in terms of the people that are here as well as the visitors. We're responsive to the needs of the people that are already here and trying to build new developments that lead to a better Chicago. Throughout the year, visitors come here just to learn about George Pullman, the labor movement, and the Pullman Porters. As I mentioned earlier, an economic feasibility study projects three hundred thousand annual visitors to the monument by its tenth year in operation. That's a lot of economic power. How do we keep some of those dollars here? When we think about development, we want to make sure there are restaurants, stores, hotels, and everything else that creates an awesome experience.

So again, we're thinking proactively. How do we create a space so that people don't have to go downtown after they visit the national monument? How can we create retail and restaurant options, coffee shops and ice cream shops, so that people can stay here and spend locally? And how do we partner with local entrepreneurs so their small businesses can thrive in these spaces? We're not necessarily saying no to national tenants, but we really want those small local businesses to be the face of retail here.

What are the most important lessons we can learn from Pullman about the integration of inclusive development and historic preservation?

Over the last eight to ten years, we've coordinated more than $350 million of investment. That's created about 1,500 jobs. When you have a long-term commitment to a neighborhood and a focus on authentic engagement, it really can pave the way for other strategic investments. And I think Pullman is a terrific example. Of course, there's more work ahead of us, including another 60 acres to develop. But I think there's something to be said for what we've accomplished through these dynamic partnerships.

I'm often asked to talk about Pullman and how it works. And I always stress that this model for community renewal is not unique and can be replicated. When developers have a commitment to listen to the community and work closely with the community, they understand the value of public-private partnerships. Pullman doesn't have to be an anomaly. It can happen throughout Chicago and across the country. Each neighborhood has it owns assets that can be leveraged to create and attract new opportunities. And the benefits can be significant. Here in Pullman, we're one of the only neighborhoods on Chicago's south and west sides experiencing declines in poverty, unemployment, and violent crime—and increases in population and property values.

Connecting Historic Preservation and Affordable Housing

Caroline S. Cheong

Connecting to Community Development

The United States is facing an escalating affordable housing crisis. [1] According to the National Low Income Housing Coalition, in 2018 no state had enough rental housing for those with household incomes at or below the poverty line or 30 percent of median area income. [2] In 2017 almost half of all renter households were cost burdened, spending more than 30 percent of their annual household income on housing, with 11 percent spending more than 50 percent. [3] These figures parallel a growing crisis in income inequality: in 2017 the top 20 percent of households held 52 percent of the country's income, while the top 5 percent captured 22 percent of the country's income. In other words, the top 10 percent have, on average, more than nine times the income of the bottom 90 percent. [4]

Such income disparities and the consequent gap in access to affordable housing have dire consequences for socioeconomic integration, creating cityscapes that are defined by pockets of wealth and poverty and segregating populations by race and class. The far-reaching impacts of such socioeconomic and spatial isolation are well documented. [5] This exclusion is tied to a diversity of interconnected and mutually reinforcing challenges, including unemployment, poverty, lack of access to physical and socioeconomic services, and housing. [6] As housing is both a human right and a tool for wealth-building, increasing the supply of affordable homes is essential to decreasing socioeconomic exclusion for many marginalized populations.

At the same time, nationwide, 3.5 million housing units built before 1950 are vacant. [7] As N. Edward Coulson and Michael Lahr observe, "nearly all of the US's historic building stock is located in cities and, moreover, older neighborhoods often are the parts of cities in greatest need of external stimuli." [8] Converting these underutilized structures into affordable housing units is an obvious response to the 7.2 million-unit deficit for renters alone, yet preservation and affordable housing have, more often than not, been pitted against each other: many people believe that preservation decreases the availability of affordable housing, thereby increasing socioeconomic exclusion. [9] Though the convergence of historic preservation and affordable housing projects is infrequent and atypical, aging city centers have the supply to address the demand for affordable housing. Capitalizing on the opportunity to integrate historic preservation with the affordable housing field would counter the discipline's reputation for socioeconomic exclusion in both process and outcome.

Given the co-location of designated historic assets within deteriorated city centers and the growing need for affordable units, at first glance it seems obvious that historic preservation should have a symbiotic relationship with affordable housing. In practice, however, combining these two goals is a much more complex endeavor. Long-standing and outdated misperceptions of the preservation field on the part of the affordable housing sector and a lack of knowledge about affordable housing tools on the part of preservationists hinder efficient partnerships. An ample body of literature condemns historic preservation for limiting affordable housing stock and initializing gentrification and displacement. These approaches take an overly simplistic approach, however, and an equally robust body of research finds a host of other factors contributing to inadequate affordable housing and gentrification—preservation cannot be

1
This article uses the US Department of Housing and Urban Development's definition of affordable housing: families spending more than 30 percent of their annual income on housing are "cost burdened, and may have difficulty affording necessities such as food, clothing, transportation and medical care." This figure is a general guide, as some localities, particularly high-density metropolitan areas, may define affordable housing according to locally determined criteria.

2
Andrew Aurand et al., The Gap: A Shortage of Affordable Homes (National Low Income Housing Coalition, 2018).

3
Joint Center for Housing Studies, The State of the Nation's Housing 2017 (Cambridge, MA: President and Fellows of Harvard College, 2017).

4
Kayla Fontenot, Jessica Semega, and Melissa Kollar, "Income and Poverty in the United States: 2017," US Census Bureau (2017).

5
See, most famously, William Julius Wilson, The Truly Disadvantaged (Chicago: University of Chicago Press, 1990).

6
Nicola Calavita and Alan Mallach, Inclusionary Housing in International Perspective: Affordable Housing, Social Inclusion, and Land Value Recapture (Cambridge, MA: Lincoln Land Institute, 2010).

7
Donovan Rypkema, "Historic Preservation—Part of the Solution to the Affordable Housing Crisis," Alliance Review (Fall 2018): 27–33.

8
N. Edward Coulson
and Michael L. Lahr,
"Gracing the Land of
Elvis and Beale Street:
Historic Designation
and Property Values in
Memphis," *Real Estate
Economics* 33, no. 3
(September 2005): 487.

9
Aurand et al., *The Gap.*

10
Patrice Frey,
"Why Historic
Preservation Needs
a New Approach,"
CityLab, February
8, 2019, https://
www.citylab.com/
perspective/2019/02/
tax-credit-historic-
preservation-old-town-
main-street/581989.

11
Stephanie Ryberg-
Webster, "Beyond
Rust and Rockefeller:
Preserving Cleveland's
African American
Heritage," *Preservation
Education and
Research* 9 (2017):
7–23.

blamed as the singular cause of either. The literature makes plain the risks of combining affordable housing and preservation, whereas it obscures the benefits of collaboration.

Research regarding the synergy between historic preservation and affordable housing is in its beginning stages, with the majority of publications coming from government, practitioners, professional organizations, or think tanks. The scant research-based literature that does exist is largely composed of evaluations of the efficacy of Federal Historic Tax Credits (HTC), graduate thesis research, commissioned research reports, and minor mentions within the context of parallel phenomena such as urban revitalization. Journalistic opinion pieces touting or condemning preservation's contributions to affordable housing and gentrification also contribute to this dialogue. While popular conception holds that the decline of affordable housing and resultant displacement are de facto outcomes of preservation, in fact, historic preservation has the capacity to generate, rather than limit, inclusionary housing—and contribute to the creation of inclusive, sustainable urban spaces.

— PRESERVATION AND AFFORDABLE HOUSING:
   PAST AND PRESENT

Historic preservation is at a crossroads. Encumbered by legacies of exclusionary and elite-driven processes, over the last three decades many of the field's advocates, researchers, and practitioners have advanced a form of inclusionary preservation that represents the diversity of local communities. Recent research from leading preservation organizations advocates an inclusive, socially based approach to the historic built environment. For example, the National Trust for Historic Preservation—the country's most prominent national preservation organization—has an entire research arm dedicated to uncovering the historic built environment's contributions to economic and community development. Much of the National Trust's work (and the work of others) demonstrates that preserving a neighborhood's older buildings can be an effective vehicle for development that includes, rather than excludes, low-income and marginalized populations.

Despite these advancements, there is a disparity between preservation ideology and practice, chiefly because of the discipline's reliance on materially based preservation policies. This adherence, particularly at the local level, perpetuates outdated perceptions of historic preservation as exclusive and architecturally driven—that is, prioritizing material values over all others. This emphasis on materiality is present in both designation criteria and treatment standards. The historic register system at all levels functions in a binary: historic or not. [10] As Stephanie Ryberg-Webster observes, there is "a pressing need to question the applicability and usefulness of long-standing preservation tools when working in communities that lack high architectural value and material integrity but have a rich cultural heritage and historic significance." [11] Further, as Patrice Frey points out, the Secretary of the Interior's Standards for the Treatment of Historic Properties, which has not been significantly revised since 1977, remains the guiding document for the vast majority of decision-makers despite significant changes in governance, financing, and cultural values. Preservation is thus trapped within a self-fulfilling prophecy. Decision-makers continue implementing outdated and ill-fitting policies that prioritize material significance over all else. The result is that communities around the country describe how preservation commissions have demanded adherence to architectural authenticity at the expense of very real socioeconomic or environmental challenges, or have allowed the demolition of structures that were deemed historically insignificant but that held acute value for the local community. In doing so, the field provides preservation's critics with ample material to denounce it as an elite-driven, restrictive force of urban exclusion.

Historic preservation is therefore not commonly perceived to be a vehicle for creating affordable housing. Critics claim that preservation regulations limit affordable housing by reducing supply, as developers are unable to build or are discouraged from building in heavily regulated areas. Many consider preservation to be a catalyst and a driver of gentrification and displacement, envisioning a preservation that prioritizes elitist history—that is, the stories of white, wealthy, and usually male leaders—over all else. 12 Carol Rose notes, "[t]he displacement of low-income residents... may be the albatross of the modern historic preservation movement, evoking... overtones of snobbery and special interest that have long dogged preservationists." 13 In her analysis of Washington, DC, communities that opposed historic designation, Sarah Conde observes how perceived connections between designation, gentrification, and declines in affordability influenced the communities' decision-making process. 14 James Cohen begins his analysis of preservation and class integration in Baltimore's Butcher's Hill neighborhood by asserting that preservation usually leads to permanent displacement of adjacent low-income residents. 15 Twenty years later, in 2018, *CityLab* writer Kriston Capps reiterated this perception, contending that historic districts are among the primary culprits in the country's lack of affordable housing. Capps opines that preservation should not regulate private homes that were previously accessible only to the beneficiaries of race-based housing policies. He notes that when governments create historic districts, "they do not always simply protect culture, architecture, and history. Sometimes they also shore up wealth, status, and power." 16

Gentrification and Affordable Housing: A Closer Look

Preservation is thus understood to be an exclusive force of urban change that leads to gentrification, a decline in affordable housing, and the displacement of low-income, marginalized populations. Economists perpetuate these popular perceptions, applying oversimplified theories to depict historic preservation within the urban landscape. However, a growing body of research contradicts this framework. While some researchers acknowledge the multitude of factors leading to gentrification beyond preservation, others have simply been unable to find a direct, causal link between preservation and affordable housing or between gentrification and displacement. The connections between these urban processes are muddled and ill-defined; preservation should therefore not be assumed a direct barrier to affordable housing.

12
See for example, Neil Smith, "Comment on David Listokin, Barbara Listokin, and Michael Lahr's 'The Contributions of Historic Preservation to Housing and Economic Development': Historic Preservation in a Neoliberal Age," *Housing Policy Debate* 9, no. 3 (1998): 479–485; James R. Cohen, "Combining Historic Preservation and Income Class Integration: A Case Study of the Butchers Hill Neighborhood of Baltimore," *Housing Policy Debate* 9, no. 3 (1998); and Edward L. Glaeser, *Triumph of the City: How Our Greatest Invention Makes Us Richer, Smarter, Greener, Healthier, and Happier* (New York: Penguin, 2011).

13
Carol M. Rose, "Preservation and Community: New Directions in the Law of Historic Preservation," *Stanford Law Review* 33, no. 3 (1981): 478.

14
Sarah N. Conde, "Striking a Match in the Historic District: Opposition to Historic Preservation and Responsive Community Building," *Georgetown Law Historic Preservation Papers Series* (2007): 24–38.

15
Cohen, "Combining Historic Preservation and Income Class Integration," 663.

16
Kriston Capps, "Why Historic Preservation Districts Should Be a Thing of the Past," *CityLab*, January 29, 2016, https://www.citylab.com/equity/2016/01/why-historic-preservation-districts-should-be-a-thing-of-the-past/431598.

17
Andrew Hurley, *Beyond Preservation: Using Public History to Revitalize Inner Cities* (Philadelphia: Temple University Press, 2010).

18
Conrad Weiner, *Philadelphia: Neighborhood, Authority, and the Urban Crisis* (New York: Praeger, 1967).

19
Christopher Klemek, *The Transatlantic Collapse of Urban Renewal: Postwar Urbanism from New York to Berlin* (Chicago: University of Chicago Press, 2011), 93.

20
Klemek, *Transatlantic Collapse of Urban Renewal*, 94.

21
Robert A. Beauregard, "Trajectories of Neighborhood Change: The Case of Gentrification," *Environment and Planning A* 22, no. 7 (1990): 855–874.

22
John R. Logan and Harvey Luskin Molotch, *Urban Fortunes: The Political Economy of Place* (Berkeley: University of California Press, 1987), 177.

23
David Listokin, Barbara Listokin, and Michael Lahr, "The Contributions of Historic Preservation to Housing and Economic Development," *Housing Policy Debate* 9 (1998): 431–478; and Smith, "Comment on David Listokin, Barbara Listokin, and Michael Lahr's 'The Contributions of Historic Preservation to Housing and Economic Development.'"

In many ways, historic preservation's naysayers have reason to be wary. Governments and urban elites have repeatedly used preservation as a vehicle for community fragmentation rather than preservation. In the mid-twentieth century, many city leaders used historic buildings as a centrifugal force for urban revitalization, resulting in the relocation of hundreds of families. [17] Capitalizing upon the aesthetic charm and human scale of many historic neighborhoods, city leaders revitalized low-income urban areas by restoring buildings to their historic state and actively encouraging middle- and upper-income residents to relocate into the neighborhood. In Philadelphia, for example, Edward Bacon and William Rafsky's plans to preserve the central business district, upgrade the slums, create new housing, prevent deterioration in other neighborhoods, improve transportation, and foster industry were emblematic of such efforts. [18] From 1949 to 1970, Bacon famously embarked on an ambitious urban renewal program to "reinvent Society Hill through managed preservation", or gentrify the neighborhood through historic preservation. [19] He delivered one of the earliest American examples of preservation as an exclusionary tool in both practice and outcome: local residents were not part of the preservation process and were effectively excluded and removed from enjoying the fruits of the changed neighborhood. The project restored hundreds of homes to their former Georgian glory, built three new residential towers as well as a handful of commercial structures, and successfully lured wealthy, suburban families back to the city. These "benefits" came with significant costs. By the end of the initiative, out of the 2,197 extant structures in the area, only one-third were retained, a tribute to the image of the neighborhood's historic fabric rather than its reality. To make room for the incoming affluent residents, hundreds of working-class families were evicted; as many households were displaced as if the neighborhood had been completely demolished. [20] Similar programs took place in historic neighborhoods around the country.

Writing in 1990, Robert Beauregard cites the extensive use of the Federal Historic Tax Credit (HTC) as a catalyst for the gentrification of Philadelphia's Spring Garden neighborhood. [21] Spring Garden was placed on the National Register of Historic Places in 1979; during the subsequent decade, three developers rehabilitated 74 percent of the 582 historic units approved for the historic tax credit. All of the renovated units were marketed to investors who rented them as upscale, luxury condominiums, eliminating a significant number of affordable housing units. In this case, developers—enabled and unchecked by government—used a historic preservation tool to facilitate the displacement of a prominent Hispanic community. Beauregard's research exemplifies common perceptions and realities of the preservation field at the time, representing a disciplinary identity that many contemporary preservationists have spent the last few decades contesting.

According to John Logan and Harvey Molotch, the purported tax benefits of historic preservation due to increased property values may be overinflated, with historic preservation ultimately costing more than is believed. They argue that the financial benefits of preservation rarely materialize because governments and the urban elite—those in power—do not reassess the properties or provide further subsidies out of fear of discouraging future investors from coming into the neighborhood. They continue: "given the high demand such places make for services… the preciously gentrified districts may be net fiscal losers, regardless of the social costs paid by those displaced. Although they might be artistically successful, many of these districts are, in social and fiscal terms, the work of philistines." 22 From this perspective, preservation is an expensive way to benefit the elite—favoring opportunistic developers and inducing displacement and gentrification but providing minimal financial benefit to the government and the general public.

This line of simplistic criticism—firmly confined to economic models—describes a form of preservation that operates unchecked within a market-based society. Lacking a wider, system-based lens, it does not consider other policy or financial interventions—such as tax abatements, community benefits agreements, tax increment financing districts, work-force development programs, and a myriad of other common planning tools—that can be integrated into the preservation process so as to serve multiple goals and outcomes. Responding to the work of David Listokin, Barbara Listokin, and Michael Lahr promoting preservation's contributions to economic development, Neil Smith maintains that the HTC is an inefficient means of providing affordable housing, which would be more productively delivered through direct subsidy. 23

According to Edward Glaeser, one of preservation's most vocal critics, "as if it weren't enough that large historic districts are associated with a reduction in housing supply, higher prices, and increasingly elite residents, there's also an aesthetic reason to be skeptical about them: they protect an abundance of uninteresting buildings that are less attractive and exciting than new structures that could replace them." 24 Glaeser also questions whether historic districts should even exist, as "no living city's future should become prisoner to its past." 25 Dan Bertolet points to laws of supply and demand to explain the increase in property values, noting that preservation regulations—which he likens to exclusionary zoning—stymie the market by decreasing supply and driving up demand, resulting in inflated home prices that are out of reach for the most vulnerable segments of the population. 26 A number of studies have corroborated Glaeser's conclusion. In these studies, researchers found that a location within a historic district is correlated with a greater increase in property value than similar properties outside districts. 27 Others view historic districts as "a municipal weapon to gentrify vibrant, hardworking communities or to turn neighborhoods into museums to attract tourist dollars." 28

Countering these narratives, some researchers observe that preservation regulations, like districting, actually improve and retain affordable housing stock. In this body of research, preservation is dynamic and inclusive, contributing to affordable housing stock and diverse neighborhoods. As increased restrictions on properties limit what owners can do, sellers are forced to lower their asking price. Some real estate agents noted that older properties with heavier restrictions often sold for less than properties without restrictions. 29 Further, taking a more urbanistic approach, Donovan Rypkema cautions that in most historic, gentrifying neighborhoods, an increase in property values is caused not by designation

24
Edward Glaeser, "Preservation Follies," City Journal 20, no. 2 (2010), https://www.city-journal.org/html/preservation-follies-13279.html.

25
Glaeser, Triumph of the City, 119.

26
Dan Bertolet, "When Historic Preservation Clashes with Housing Affordability," Sightline Institute, December 19, 2017, https://www.sightline.org/2017/12/19/when-historic-preservation-clashes-with-housing-affordability.

27
See Andrew Narwold, Jonathan Sandy, and Charles Tu, "Historic Designation and Residential Property Values," International Real Estate Review 11 (2008): 83–95; Donovan Rypkema, "Heritage Conservation and Property Values," in The Economics of Uniqueness: Investing in Historic City Cores and Cultural Heritage Assets for Sustainable Development, ed. Guido Licciardi and Rana Amirtahmasebi (Washington, DC: World Bank, 2012): 107–141; and Robert Shipley, "Heritage Designation and Property Values: Is There an Effect?," International Journal of Heritage Studies 6 (2000): 83–100.

28
Gregory Heller, "We're History: Why Historic Preservation Efforts Are Vital in Low-Income Neighborhoods," Philadelphia City Paper (2005), http://www.hellergreg.com/writings/were-history-why-historic-preservation-efforts-are-vital-in-low-income-neighborhoods-source-philadelphia-city-paper-date-may-19-25-2005-byline-gregory-heller.

29
Michelle Higgins,
"The Teardown
Wars," *New York
Times*, June 16, 2006,
http://www.nytimes.
com/2006/06/16/
realestate/16tear.
html?pagewanted=all.

30
Donovan D.
Rypkema, "The
Oversimplification of
Gentrification," *Forum
Journal* 18 (2004):
26–34; Rypkema,
"Heritage Conservation
and Property Values."

31
Rypkema, "The
Oversimplification of
Gentrification," 31.

32
Stephanie Meeks
and Kevin C. Murphy,
*The Past and Future
City: How Historic
Preservation Is
Reviving America's
Communities*
(Washington, DC:
Island Press, 2016),
219–220.

33
Jeremiah Jensen,
"Rentcafé: 87% of Units
Delivered in 2018 Are
Luxury," *HousingWire*,
September 28,
2018, https://www.
housingwire.com/
articles/46957-rent-
caf%C3%A9-87-of-
units-delivered-in-
2018-are-luxury.

34
Sharon Zukin,
"Gentrification: Culture
and Capital in the
Urban Core," *Annual
Review of Sociology* 13
(1987): 129–147.

35
Jacob L. Vigdor, "Does
Gentrification Harm the
Poor?," Brookings-
Wharton Papers on
Urban Affairs (2002);
Lance Freeman, *There
Goes the 'Hood: Views
of Gentrification
from the Ground Up*
(Philadelphia: Temple
University Press, 2006).

36
Allyson Atwood, "A
New Understanding
of Gentrification and
the Role of Historic
Preservation," *The
Historic Dimension
Series* (2006), 4.

itself but likely by a multitude of exogenous factors, including improved public services and facilities, infill construction, and enhanced commercial activity. 30 He also notes that incoming residents are rarely attracted to a neighborhood because of its historic designation; rather, they choose the neighborhood because it is already an attractive option—"it is not the historic designation that makes a great neighborhood—it's already a great (or potentially great) neighborhood." 31

Stephanie Meeks responds to claims that historic preservation regulations are to blame for the market's unwillingness to create affordable housing by noting that the majority of new construction is geared toward luxury housing, whether in historic districts or not. 32 In her analysis, the problem is not that builders are unable to build affordable housing in historic neighborhoods—it is that they do not want to. Luxury rentals, Class B and above, continue to dominate residential construction: of the eighty thousand large-scale development projects underway across 130 metropolitan areas in 2018, more than 80 percent were estimated to be luxury units. The previous year, 79 percent of new rental construction fell into the luxury category. 33 Meeks's assessment points to the absence of policy or financial incentives used in conjunction with preservation practice; developers need to be compelled to build affordable housing in historic neighborhoods. Without such interventions, developers will continue building luxury units in both historic and nonhistoric areas.

Corroborating these fears, Sharon Zukin notes that historic preservation may encourage displacement, but ultimately, a household's departure is a function of rising rents and higher sale prices. 34 Similarly, in studies in New York and in Boston, Lance Freeman and Jacob Vigdor's analyses, respectively, found that low-income residents may actually stay in gentrifying areas in order to take advantage of the improved amenities. 35 Further, "historic districts are likely to experience a certain degree of stabilization and protection from extremely modulating property values," which may provide low-income residents with a degree of protection in a volatile market. 36 A 2016 study for New York City's Historic Districts Council, produced by ThinkBrooklyn, confirmed these findings. Using regression analysis, the study found that between 1970 and 2010, historic district designation had no statistically significant impact on the rental rates or the number of rent-burdened households, though there was a correlation between designation and an increase in household income in some areas. 37 In their analysis of Fort Worth, Texas, Edward Coulson and Robin Leichenko found that historic designation does not lead to displacement and that "while there is some evidence that areas are chosen for preservation efforts with neighborhood revitalization in mind, the decade or so following designation produced no significant change in neighborhood demographic composition."38 Similar to residents in New York and Boston, the original low-income residents seemingly desired to stay in their revitalized neighborhood to take advantage of the improved quality of life. Rypkema also analyzes a study conducted by the US Department of Housing and Urban Development that examined neighborhoods that had maintained economic and racial diversity over an extended period of time; Rypkema concludes that nearly all of them were historic districts. 39

These findings refute claims that historic preservation always leads to homogenous, elite enclaves and indiscriminately produces a decline in affordable housing. In instances where gentrification does follow historic preservation, "only where the safeguards against displacement, possible through government action, are not used is this accelerating movement a problem."[40] Roberta Gratz and other preservation advocates position historic preservation as a tool with the potential to preserve a neighborhood's physical assets in addition to its economic and social resources. In fact, Listokin notes, "over the past two decades, preservationists have done yeoman's work in trying to reduce displacement pressures."[41] Rypkema postulates that the adaptive reuse of historic buildings for low-income households adds to a community's affordable housing stock by producing quality units in a diversity of styles and sizes to accommodate a mixture of incomes, household structures, and populations. [42] Arguments such as these highlight historic preservation's potential as a tool for equitable development and the creation of affordable housing when a community's social values and economic needs are placed on par with the preservation of a neighborhood's heritage values.

Preservation and Affordable Housing: Synergies

Given the presence of historic buildings in low-income city centers, there are ample opportunities to merge historic preservation values with those of community development and affordable housing. The federal government acknowledged this synergy as early as 1995, when the Advisory Council for Historic Preservation adopted its first "Policy Statement on Affordable Housing and Historic Preservation." Updated in 2006, the policy is intended to guide federal agencies and State Historic Preservation Offices (SHPOs) in their review of affordable housing projects subject to preservation regulations and Section 106 review. The statement encourages programmatic and ideological flexibility, recommending that federal and state agencies, housing developers, and preservationists in general "actively [seek] ways to reconcile historic preservation goals with the special economic and social needs associated with affordable housing [in order to address] one of the nation's most pressing challenges."[43]

A number of studies observe that historic structures—designated and undesignated—are already meeting some of the affordable housing demand, offering more housing options than newer areas. In 2017 the National Trust for Historic Preservation's Research and Policy Lab found that when compared to areas with larger and newer structures, character-rich blocks of older, smaller, mixed-age buildings in Los Angeles, Chicago, and Detroit have more than twice, one-quarter, and nearly one-third more units of affordable housing, respectively. [44] Rypkema finds that, nationwide, 57 percent of pre-1950 housing units cost less than $1,000 a month. He observes that for every household income bracket below $50,000, a greater proportion of households lives in housing built before 1950 as opposed to after 1999. Millennials have further increased demand for historic housing. With seventy-three million millennials scheduled to outnumber the seventy-two million baby boomers in 2019, in 2017 this younger generation accounted for more than one-third of all home buyers nationwide. That same year, 44 percent of buyers purchased homes built

37
ThinkBrooklyn, *The Intersection of Affordable Housing and Historic Districts* (New York: Historic Districts Council, 2016).

38
Edward Coulson and Robin Leichenko, "Historic Preservation and Neighbourhood Change," *Urban Studies* 41, no. 8 (2004): 1598.

39
Rypkema, "Oversimplification of Gentrification."

40
Roberta Brandes Gratz, *The Living City: How America's Cities Are Being Revitalized by Thinking Small in a Big Way* (New York: Wiley, 1994), 67.

41
Listokin, Listokin, and Lahr, "Contributions of Historic Preservation," 465.

42
Donovan D. Rypkema, *Historic Preservation and Affordable Housing: The Missed Connection* (Washington, DC: National Trust for Historic Preservation, 2002).

43
Advisory Council on Historic Preservation, "Final Advisory Council on Historic Preservation Policy Statement on Affordable Housing and Historic Preservation," *Federal Register* 72, no. 31 (2007): 7387.

44
Preservation Green Lab, National Trust for Historic Preservation, *Untapped Potential: Strategies for Revitalization and Reuse* (Washington, DC: National Trust for Historic Preservation, 2017), 34–42.

45
Donovan Rypkema, "Historic Preservation—Part of the Solution."

46
US Department of Housing and Urban Development, "Using the Historic Tax Credit for Affordable Housing," https://www.hudexchange.info/programs/environmental-review/historic-preservation/tax-credit.

47
See Listokin, Listokin, and Lahr, "Contributions of Historic Preservation"; Thomas R. Curran Jr., "Historic Preservation, Affordable Housing, and Community Development: Structuring Rehabilitation Tax Credit Projects," *Journal of Affordable Housing & Community Development Law* 7 (1997): 145–156; David Listokin and Michael L. Lahr, "First Annual Report on the Economic Impact of the Federal Historic Tax Credit" (2010); Harry K. Schwartz, "State Tax Credits for Historic Preservation: A Public Policy Report Produced by the National Trust for Historic Preservation's Center for State and Local Policy" (2010); Donovan Rypkema and Caroline Cheong, "Measuring Economic Impacts of Historic Preservation: A Report to the Advisory Council on Historic Preservation" (2011); Stephanie Ryberg-Webster and Kelly L. Kinahan, "Historic Preservation in Declining City Neighbourhoods: Analysing Rehabilitation Tax Credit Investments in Six US Cities," *Urban Studies* 54, no. 7 (2017): 1673–1691; and US Department of Housing and Urban Development, "Using the Historic Tax Credit."

between 1913 and 1960, and 58 percent of houses sold were built before 1912. Millennials' purchasing preferences and their purchasing power indicate a strong demand for affordable historic housing. [45] In other words, extant older housing stock is already meeting the needs of moderate- and low-income populations, though not to its fullest extent. While it is impossible to disaggregate designated from undesignated historic structures—those subject to preservation policy and those not—these figures, combined with the expansion in preservation policy to include vernacular structures, indicate a market preference for older homes.

In a shift from Beauregard's previously discussed 1990 critique that the HTC generates primarily luxury units, tax credits have, in recent years, received attention for enabling the rehabilitation of many older buildings into affordable housing, particularly when combined with Low Income Housing Tax Credits. According to the US Department of Housing and Urban Development, the HTC has created 153,225 low- and moderate-income housing units since its inception in 1976. [46] The HTC remains one of preservation's most powerful tools in creating affordable housing, and numerous studies detail its effectiveness. [47]

— THE WAY FORWARD

For the preservation field to become more inclusive both in process and outcome—to include traditionally marginalized people in the process of deciding what is preserved, thereby creating more socioeconomically and spatially inclusive communities—the field needs to align itself more strategically with the goals and methods of the affordable housing sector, among other community and economic development disciplines. Doing so requires preservationists to move away from strict adherence to architecturally driven preservation guidelines. In this paradigm, preservation practice would decenter architecture to be inclusive of social, cultural, economic, and architectural values and rely on socially driven, bottom-up tactics. Many researchers and practitioners already assess preservation's role in minority communities. [48] However, such an inclusive approach is not yet pervasive throughout the discipline, as indicated by the 2017 elimination of the 10 percent tax credit in favor of retaining the 20 percent HTC credit. Given that the HTC requires both eligibility for the National Register and adherence to the Secretary of the Interior's standards—both of which prioritize physical and structural values over all others—the decision to only retain this financial incentive narrowly focuses preservation policy on architecturally-driven outcomes. While the smaller credit applied to nondesignated buildings built before 1936 and required looser adherence to architectural standards than the larger credit, the decision to sacrifice the incentive implicitly reinforces the primacy of National Register and materially driven criteria over local, perhaps less exceptional, values.

Implementing an inclusive preservation approach thus necessitates expanding the preservation toolkit to incorporate spatial, social, and economic context. To develop these tools, Frey calls for a multidisciplinary exchange of ideas including from those working in finance, affordable housing, community development, sustainability, and other allied fields. [49]

In other words, in order to shift historic preservation from exclusionary to inclusionary—and give the field's naysayers less cause for criticism—researchers and practitioners need to embrace research methods and tools from other fields. By placing less primacy on materials and more emphasis on the values of underserved communities, "preservation becomes more viable in low-income community development... When concerns regarding materiality drive the process... affordability loses out. When redeveloping low-income historic neighborhoods, affordability must be given priority."[50]

Incentives and Regulation

Preservationists can encourage the reuse of historic buildings for residential occupation by low-income households in multiple ways. At a local level, preservationists can encourage governments to fast-track the acquisition and redevelopment of vacant, abandoned, or foreclosed properties and to prioritize older or historic neighborhoods for infrastructure enhancements and improved social services.[51] Preservationists can advocate that governments nudge local businesses to relocate to historic buildings by providing short-term financial incentives such as subsidies or grants, perhaps by creating a revolving fund. From a regulatory perspective, preservationists can encourage governments to alter zoning codes or provide variances for projects that create affordable housing.[52] Within the redevelopment of historic structures, governments can use the "stick" of regulation with the "carrot" of incentives to encourage developers to dedicate a percentage of units to house low-income households in the neighborhood.[53]

At a state level, public bodies could create or continue funding tax credits for residential rehabilitation, favoring projects that produce affordable housing. Projects that combine the Federal Historic Rehabilitation Tax Credit with the Low Income Housing Tax Credit or the New Markets Tax Credit could be prioritized and offered an additional credit or deduction. Nationally, the federal government can similarly favor projects that achieve historic preservation with affordable housing. In the United States, communities would also benefit from the creation of a federal tax credit that focuses on the rehabilitation of residential structures.

Shared Equity Models

At a local level, historic preservationists can encourage community-based housing, in which local communities own, operate, and manage housing stock. In this scenario, authority and control is shifted away from government or developers toward community members, allowing them to dictate the future of the resources and reap the benefits of rehabilitation themselves. Such programs have gained popularity under the term "shared equity housing," which John Davis calls:

a generic term for various forms of resale-restricted, owner-occupied housing in which the rights, responsibilities, risks, and rewards of ownership are shared between an income-eligible household who buys the home for a below-market price and an organizational steward who protects the affordability, quality, and security of that home long after it is purchased.[54]

48
See Ryberg-Webster, "Beyond Rust and Rockefeller"; Gail Lee Dubrow, "Feminist and Multicultural Perspectives on Preservation Planning," in *Making the Invisible Visible: A Multicultural Planning History*, ed. Leonie Sandercock (Berkeley: University of California Press, 1998); Owen J. Dwyer, "Interpreting the Civil Rights Movement: Place, Memory, and Conflict," *Professional Geographer* 52, no. 4 (2000): 660–671; Antoinette J. Lee, "The Social and Ethnic Dimensions of Historic Preservation," in *A Richer Heritage: Historic Preservation in the Twenty-First Century*, ed. Robert Stipe (Chapel Hill: University of North Carolina Press, 2003); Ned Kaufman, *Place, Race, and Story: Essays on the Past and Future of Historic Preservation* (New York: Routledge, 2009); and Toni Lee, "Cultural Diversity in Historic Preservation: Where We Have Been, Where We Are Going," *Forum Journal* 27, no. 1 (2012): 20–34.

49
Frey, "Why Historic Preservation Needs a New Approach."

50
Rebecca Sohmer and Robert E. Lang, "Beyond *This Old House*: Historic Preservation in Community Development," *Housing Policy Debate* 9, no. 3 (1998): 428.

51
Rypkema, *Historic Preservation and Affordable Housing*.

52
Norma E. Rodrigo-Cervantes, "Urban Conservation in Mexican Colonial Cities: The Historic Center of Morelia," in *Designing Sustainable Cities in the Developing World*, ed. Roger Zetter and Georgia Butina Watson (Burlington, VT: Ashgate, 2006): 69–84.

53
Rypkema, *Historic Preservation and Affordable Housing*.

54
John Emmeus Davis,
"More Than Money:
What Is Shared in
Shared Equity Home-
ownership?," *Journal
of Affordable Housing
and Community Devel-
opment* 19 (2010): 272.

55
Meagan M. Ehlenz
and Constance
Taylor, "Shared Equity
Homeownership in the
United States: A Litera-
ture Review," *Journal of
Planning Literature* 34
(2019): 3–18.

56
Davis, "More Than
Money."

57
J. Peter Byrne, "Two
Cheers for Gentrifi-
cation," *Howard Law
Journal* 46 (2002):
405–432.

58
Emily Milder, "Histori-
cally Affordable: How
Historic Preservation-
ists and Affordable
Housing Advocates
Can Work Together to
Prevent the Demolition
of Rent-Stabilized
Housing in Los
Angeles," *Journal of
Affordable Housing* 25,
no. 1 (2016): 104–130.

59
Rypkema, "Heritage
Conservation and
Property Values."

Primary forms of shared equity housing include community land trusts, limited equity cooperatives, and resale-restricted homes with affordability covenants lasting longer than thirty years. The key characteristics of such housing models are their shared goals of maintaining housing affordability and facilitating homeownership—considered to be a primary avenue of building wealth—through innovative ownership models. 55 In conventional markets, gains from community improvements unrelated to the property owner's actions are embedded in a home's resale value. In shared equity models, however, this value is locked into place when the community land trust, limited equity cooperative, or other model is created so that residential properties become depositories for subsidies and other accrued gains.

In these models, the shared equity organization owns the land or building. When homeowners buy their homes, they do so at rates lower than market value as they are not purchasing the land or the building itself. Further, the home's appreciation rate is locked in such that when they sell their homes, they recoup only the equity gained from their own labor or investments and whatever the predetermined appreciation rate was. Doing so limits the amount of speculative value an individual can claim, lowers initial home-purchasing costs, and maintains housing affordability for future generations. 56

Shared equity models could be applied to historic low-income neighborhoods. Preservation of the historic structures could be built into the purchase agreements in order to retain their cultural values. By providing avenues for homeownership and wealth building, these models preserve not only a neighborhood's physical assets but also the social and cultural resources embedded in the community and continuity in an otherwise volatile environment. Such tools can be implemented in neighborhoods experiencing decline or gentrification, with the housing trust providing an anchor to slow increasing property values and retain affordability. In both scenarios, the shared equity institution must be dedicated to including populations at risk of economic or social exclusion.

Economic Integration

Regarding the retention of existing structures, rent controls—for all their controversy—have proven to be an effective means of facilitating economic integration in gentrifying areas. 57 In Los Angeles, Emily Milder examined rent stabilization as a tool through which historic preservation and affordable housing goals combine. Though she found preservation and affordable housing to work in tandem, she cautioned that this reciprocal benefit was highly contextual and that trade-offs are common and necessary. 58 Similar to shared equity models' emphasis on regulating appreciation, preservationists can encourage policies that stipulate incremental increases in rent or tax deferment policies. In a similar vein, preservationists can aid in the creation or management of organizations that help renters become owners of historic structures. 59 Such programs could include rent-to-own housing funds or increased access to financing.

Preservationists could also lobby for increased use of tax increment financing to subsidize the rehabilitation of existing historic structures or subsidize tax payments or rents for low-income households in historic neighborhoods. These methods would increase both the quantity and the quality of affordable housing in the neighborhood and facilitate the retention of existing residents. Additionally, public and private sector groups could explore housing microfinance, which has gained traction in the Global South for supporting low-income households that may otherwise be excluded from traditional housing finance markets. 60

As housing and employment are inextricably connected, labor policy has also gained traction as a way to retain existing residents. Examples include mandating the hiring of local workers in adaptive reuse construction projects, instituting a wage floor, and creating training linkage fees in which developers who receive concessionary land, historic structures, or subsidies contribute on a per-square-foot basis to a fund that will help local low-income community members find and keep work. 61 Job training programs would focus on the development of conservation techniques in order to build locally applied and valued skills, in addition to fostering a greater appreciation for historic assets.

The retention of local residents via the creation of affordable housing is at the heart of all these initiatives. Savannah, Georgia, stands out as a city that has been able to capitalize on its historic assets to improve quality of life without sacrificing housing affordability for low-income residents. The community organization Savannah Landmark Rehabilitation Project, founded in 1975, did so by creating a historic district and a revolving fund for rehabilitation, in addition to taking advantage of low-interest rehabilitation mortgage funds, low-income rent subsidy, and federal Comprehensive Employment and Training Act funds. 62 Savannah's multifaceted approach demonstrates how the combination of adaptive reuse and rehabilitation, job training, innovative financing, and community education can revitalize communities and protect affordable housing. Today, the historic district and surrounding neighborhoods face gentrification pressures, but the success of their initial efforts demonstrates that equitable development and conservation can mitigate the impacts of preservation-based revitalization.

Countless historic downtowns face higher-than-average residential and commercial vacancy rates and are in need of neighborhood-scale regeneration. Many so-called postindustrial Legacy Cities still face sustained job and population loss. Despite the ample supply of historic buildings that can meet the country's critical demand for affordable housing, preservation and affordable housing are seen more often as enemies than as allies, and preservationists' continued adherence to architecturally driven standards is partially to blame. While those in the affordable housing sector could certainly be more appreciative of the historic environment's contributions to creating healthy, vibrant urban centers, preservationists must be similarly flexible and receptive to the needs of the affordable housing community. Historic preservation practitioners and researchers need to implement a comprehensive, dearchitecturalized strategy that places social responsibility at its core and anticipates the need to mitigate the potentially harmful impacts of preservation regulations, such as displacement. Preservationists can encourage greater symbiosis between the preservation and affordable housing fields. Still, further research on tools that can meet the needs of the historic environment and low-income, underserved communities is a vital step toward an inclusive preservation practice and the creation of sustainable, inclusive cities.

60
Brian Hoyle, "Urban Waterfront Revitalization in Developing Countries: The Example of Zanzibar's Stone Town," Geographical Journal 168 (2002): 141–162.

61
Laura Wolf-Powers, Jeremy Reiss, and Margaret Stix, "Building in Good Jobs: Linking Workforce Development With Real Estate-Led Economic Development," Departmental Papers (City and Regional Planning) 42 (2006).

62
Gratz, Living City.

Toward Equitable Communities:
Historic Preservation in Community Development

An interview with Maria Rosario Jackson

Connecting to Community Development

ERICA AVRAMI

Much of your work centers on the integration of arts and culture into
strategies that seek to address urban inequality. For more than 25 years
you have focused on a wide range of community planning and development
strategies across the United States, particularly with low-income com-
munities and most often with communities of color. This was long before
the popularization of creative place-making in community development.
Could you explain how you came to focus on the arts and culture as a tool
for community development?

MARIA ROSARIO JACKSON

I grew up with a very strong consciousness around racial/ethnic identity.
My parents raised us around arts and culture, not because they were
wealthy patrons or "art people" but because—as an African American
father and a Mexican immigrant mother—they were deeply concerned
that my brother and I had a good understanding of where they came
from and what their cultural heritage was. They taught us about art that
reflected their cultures—the history and magnificence of people who
were mostly absent, maligned, or stereotyped in mainstream representations. They didn't think we were going to get that in school. It was
very important to them.

In a world where race matters, being equipped in that way was an
important part of my formative years. As an urban planner, I started to
wrestle with questions about what makes for equitable places and spaces
where people can thrive. Art and culture provide critical perspectives
on the root causes and consequences of inequity and the ways in which
people have survived—and sometimes even thrived—in spite of systemic
oppression and dire circumstances. Art and culture also offer ways of
imagining new possibilities. They are critical to a grounded and hope-
ful life and to the development of strategies that can address historical
and current injustice. They seemed like really important components
that I kept seeing missing as I embarked on that career; urban planning
didn't value the arts in thinking about comprehensive approaches to
communities.

Your career has led you to work in several spheres: you are an academic,
you've worked with foundations, you've served on government boards,
and more. In working toward the integration of arts and culture into
community development from these various perspectives, what have been
some of the challenges?

There are several. One of the principal challenges is that, as a society,
we've been conditioned to think of art and culture in really narrow ways.
Those ways include thinking almost exclusively about art as a product
or culture as a product, rather than as a process or an approach to other
dimensions of life. That default gets in the way. Another thing that gets
in the way is the sense that arts and culture happen only in cultural
organizations or presenting organizations, like museums and theaters.
I think presenting organizations can be a really important part of our
public and civic life. But presentation and consumption are not the only

ways art exists. If we keep thinking that, we do ourselves a disservice. That's a big challenge, getting people beyond default notions of art and culture. The work that I've been advancing over the past decades suggests that some change is happening, but that it requires you to set aside those default notions.

Another notion that gets in the way is that from a planning or community development perspective, economic development is the most important or the singular value of arts and culture. I think, certainly, that the arts and cultural activity can contribute to economic development at times, but their contributions are far more complex. Again, we do ourselves a disservice by defaulting to blunt interpretations of why art matters. By looking exclusively at economic impacts, we fail to consider other things that also matter, such as things that have to do with control over narrative, cultural self-determination, and individual as well as collective agency. These are contributions that historically have not been on the community developer's or planner's lists of how to gauge impact or progress. Frankly, it hasn't even been a priority of the arts sector in asserting the value of the arts. I understand why that is the case. Economic development and related concepts are the currency of the policy debate. But we have to move beyond that.

Akin to the notion of arts and culture as products rather than processes, historic buildings and heritage places are often viewed solely as physical assets, and the work of preservation focuses heavily on materially preserving the place as product. How might we begin to better value process as a social dimension of heritage? And how might the processes of preservation play a more instrumental role in questions of equity and inclusion?

Heritage isn't something that we've focused on as a dimension of equity or even as a dimension of communities. For example, when we think about the characteristics of a more just society or a more equitable community or places where everybody can thrive, we're not paying attention to the ability to transmit heritage from one generation to the next.

One of the markers of an unjust society is that the ability to transmit heritage has been hampered, as is the case with a lot of marginalized communities. It's not just in the United States. It's all around the world and throughout the ages. In strategies to disempower or oppress groups, the oppressor hinders the ability to make meaning—to assert and control one's own narrative—and by extension to freely pass on heritage to the next generation. I think there is evidence of this among groups that I have affinity with, like African Americans. We have been able to pass on heritage, but it has often been an act of defiance, an act of resilience, and in spite of circumstances, not because of them. A significant shift would be expanding criteria for what constitutes a historic place or space, being inclusive of these considerations around heritage to enable cultural self-determination.

There is a growing intersection between heritage and broader urban planning and community development through creative place-making, which has positive and negative aspects. Do you see any lessons from the application of creative place-making for community development that could inform policy thinking in preservation?

Over the last few years, in particular, creative place-making has begun to get in the water in community development and planning. Place-making comes out of urban design and planning. That concept is not new. The creative part, which is the explicit focus on arts and culture as dimensions of planning and community development practice, is newer.

The lessons of the creative place-making experience, to date, have to do with ethical practices: the importance of having a historical analysis of socioeconomic conditions and root causes and a power analysis of the places where creative place-making initiatives happen. The other piece that is more accepted now is the fact that people who live in the communities where the work is happening have the greatest stakes in what happens there and they have to be central to art- or heritage-based community development.

Another lesson has to do with the mitigation of displacement and loss of affordability—what people think of as gentrification concerns. Those concerns are real. They're more significant and valid in some real estate markets than others. But they're real. Creative place-making shouldn't happen without consideration of outcomes that could lead to a loss of affordability, or of further marginalizing communities that have already been historically marginalized, or of how the benefits of those initiatives are made available to residents who may have limited opportunities for lots of reasons, structural reasons. Without taking those considerations seriously, it's not ethical practice.

> *You've highlighted the importance of ensuring that those who live in a place have a stake in planning and preservation processes, and also that they benefit equitably from the outcomes. An ethical process does not necessarily ensure just outcomes. How might the work of planners and preservationists internalize considerations of both process and outcomes to promote inclusion?*

There has to be a concern for both process and outcome. I don't want to get sucked into something that can be touted as equitable process or engagement and that reads like "best practice," but in the end, material conditions haven't changed. I am an advocate of good, thoughtful, and meaningful process. But, at some point, the question has to be asked: what's different as a result?

It's also imperative to open our aperture and understand that progress is more nuanced than simple economic development or advancement. Not that we should not aspire to see economic progress in those communities that have seen disinvestment or that have been marginalized in many other ways. I'm not advocating that at all. I think we should press for that. But I also think that we have to be concerned with other kinds of damage that have been and continue to be done. We don't reckon enough with the range of harm that has been endured. One of the harms that we don't reckon with is the violence that has been done to marginalized people's root culture and to heritage. It's critical that we think more expansively about change, about how things have happened and what markers of progress could and should look like.

When we're doing an examination of a neighborhood—"we" being the planners, community developers, scholars, or researchers that contribute to this body of work—a lot of times we focus exclusively on the descriptive characteristics of a community, what I think of as the *what*. What's the socioeconomic status? What are the demographic characteristics? These are very common ways of describing a community. We don't often reckon with *why and how*. Not to say that socioeconomic, demographic, and other descriptors are not important. They are. But reckoning with why things are the way they are is part of the analysis that sometimes gets short shrift, if it gets any attention at all. When you reckon with the why, then you're starting to look at some of the structural causes and consequences.

> *When we talk about some of those structural causes and consequences at the level of policy, are there any approaches or practices that are addressing this question of inclusion—particularly in communities grappling with legacies of spatial injustice—in innovative ways?*

That's a good question. It is a challenging question to think about in a general way because I think that, depending on what the intervention is, there's a different suite of policies that might be available to advance the intention. If you wanted to reckon with some of the structural causes and consequences of housing inequality, let's say, and you wanted to frame the issue differently, it could be interesting to enlist the assistance of an artist to help do that—to help think through how this issue might be presented in a different way that might bring about a different kind of response. Questioning how we frame issues is crucial.

I was talking with a community organizer, Joseph Larios from Phoenix, Arizona, some months ago about this issue of framing. The example he brought up was that when you use the term "food desert," which in planning and community development refers to places with inadequate access to healthy food, it may trigger one response that has to do with meeting immediate needs. But if you think of the "food desert" as a "nutrition deprivation zone" instead, that framing could trigger a different response, one that has more to do with the structural sources of the problem. I think that artists can be particularly effective as truth seekers and truth tellers, informing how we frame policy issues and program design.

> *Around this idea of reframing, you're not someone who sits squarely within the realm of historic preservation or heritage; you've worked in areas that connect with it. How do you see preservationists potentially tackling this kind of reframing? How do you see the heritage field shifting the way it talks about itself and with others, to engage more robustly in some of these equity-related questions?*

A question that echoed during the symposium was, can preservation be an instrument for addressing or for advancing equity? In order for that to be the case, the preservation field can't operate in a bubble. For preservation to be an instrument for advancing equity, it has to be connected to other concerns, policy issues, and fields of practice.

I might ask the following questions: How are preservationists being trained? Are they acquiring the skills, the intellectual curiosity, and even the human inclination to want to do that work? Are they able to collaborate with community developers and planners, organizers, and people in social welfare and in all of the professions that are implicated in building healthier communities? Are they equipped to work at the grassroots level with people who have an interest in reclaiming their narrative? Do they have the skills to help with the healing that has to happen because violence was done to a cultural root? Those kinds of questions trigger perhaps a different way of thinking about how training happens and how one may think about standards of excellence in the field.

— Appendices

During the symposium in February 2019, intensive discussions helped to cultivate the ideas explored in the preceding chapters of this volume. To help move those ideas from the realm of discourse toward collective agency and practical implementation, participants were asked to consider how inclusion might be enacted through the institutions and policy infrastructures of preservation. While an increasing number of projects and programs around the country are experimenting with and implementing new approaches to inclusive preservation, there is still much work to be done to foster systemic change.

In considering how to confront institutionalized bias and legacies of exclusion, several modes of action were discussed during the two-day dialogue. In breakout groups, we challenged participants to identify specific actions and actors that could promote change:

- *Points of leverage*: positions in institutions and/or junctures within governance processes where change might be effectively influenced
- *Bridges*: connections within and/or beyond institutions and across fields to integrate and internalize change
- *Ethical engagement*: participatory processes to reorient institutions toward shared and equitable decision-making with communities
- *Subversive acts*: challenges to the status quo to prompt institutional and/or policy change

While neither a formal set of recommendations nor a consensus in the field, the following ideas serve as a provisional agenda to encourage innovative thinking about the pathways toward systemic shifts in preservation policy and institutional frameworks.

Reposition Preservation
The past half century has seen the establishment of preservation in the United States as a discrete professional field, academic discipline, and aspect of public policy. While this distinction has helped to legitimize preservation, it likewise contributes to its exclusivity. Preservation has historically allied itself with architecture, the arts, the humanities, and to some extent the material sciences, but the challenges of inclusion compel more robust connections to the social sciences—in both university and professional environments—so as to better understand intersectionality in heritage work. To forge stronger links to urban planning, community development, sustainability, environmental justice, and other policy arenas with shared goals, preservation needs to reposition itself as an embedded field: embedded in spaces, activities, disciplines, and institutions outside the traditional sphere of heritage work.

Restructure Professional Education

To complement existing education in the multifaceted dimensions of significant places, preservation curricula in universities should be restructured to better prepare students to work with *people* in a range of socioeconomic and cultural contexts. Beyond the generic call for community participation and a recognition of diverse stakeholders, professional heritage education should incorporate more robust training in the ethics of working with diverse publics, including how to develop cultural competence, establish trust, share decision-making, minimize risk (especially to vulnerable or marginalized populations), create safe spaces, break down language barriers, and more. This curricular orientation toward the methods and principles of inclusion means building the capacities of educators in these areas as well. Forming stronger bridges through networks of educators—for example, by working through the National Council for Preservation Education—would facilitate the sharing of knowledge and best practices, as would mentorship programs and more open-source scholarship.

Educate Beyond the University

While curricular changes at the university level would help to prepare future generations of preservationists to better address the intersection of heritage and inclusion, existing professional and advocate communities still need to build capacity. Training in inclusion ethics and methods could be offered as part of continuing education credits from professional organizations such as the Association for Preservation Technology, the American Institute of Architects, and others. The staff and boards of local historical societies, preservation commissions, and similar organizations, whether government- or civil society-based, could likewise benefit from training opportunities that address inclusion issues in the context of preservation. State Historic Preservation Offices could require such training as part of the Certified Local Government Program as a point of leverage in systemic policy change.

Build Diversity from Within

A fundamental issue in promoting more inclusive preservation in the United States is the demographics of heritage-related organizations and institutions. Perceptions of and research about preservation suggest that its promoters tend to be disproportionately older and more likely to be white, wealthy, and highly educated. Beyond diversifying whose stories are told or which communities are engaged in preservation processes, the institutions that form the infrastructure of heritage policy must work to reflect more racial, ethnic, cultural, and socioeconomic diversity in their staffs, boards, consultants, and project teams. Preservationists should be proponents for the establishment of diversity and equity officers and/or agendas within public and private heritage organizations. University preservation programs should work to establish scholarships and fellowships for people of color and others underrepresented within the field.

Challenge Metrics of Success

While the preservation enterprise involves a broad range of policy tools, municipal agencies tend to focus on designation and design review. The physical protection of a place is a significant driver of decision-making and resource investment, but all too often it serves as the primary metric of success. Questions of how people encounter, engage, interpret, and use such places—that is, how heritage reflects and thus creates a sense of self and community—are an underappreciated aspect of policy implementation and assessment. There is a need to create new expectations and metrics for designated sites given the public investment such listing incurs. Promoting more inclusive preservation policies means understanding—through more intentional research and evaluation—who is benefiting, who is not, and how. It likewise means analyzing how normative tools such as the Secretary of the Interior's Standards and Guidelines and the National Register criteria, which have an outsize influence on municipal policy, may require revision in order to be more inclusive.

Educate Donors and Reorient Funding Criteria

Preservation in the United States is both a public and a private enterprise. Grants, matching funds, revolving loans, tax credits, and similar financial incentives play a significant role in the physical stewardship of heritage in urban contexts. Promoting more inclusive preservation policy means incorporating a focus on people, not just places, in such funding structures. There is a need to educate donors and other funding agents and to think creatively about how inclusion-oriented criteria might be incorporated into project selection and funding requirements, such as diversity in hiring and contracting, community engagement provisions, inclusion training, and support for outcomes studies. It is likewise necessary to recognize how preservation does happen in less advantaged communities—for example, by assigning value to volunteer labor and leadership. Finally, motivating systemic change entails robust collaboration and communication among diverse actors, and such coming together depends on support from progressive funding agents who see potential in more inclusive preservation policy.

Spark Conversations in Place

While this initiative focuses on systemic policy change, there is also value in discrete acts that disrupt the status quo. Occupying and reclaiming space, even if only temporarily, can give voice to counternarratives and underrepresented publics. Creating report cards for heritage sites and measuring indicators of inclusion in narratives, programming, and operations could activate change across cities and states. Building bridges with K–12 schools and other institutions dedicated to public education can further help to amplify more inclusive conversations in and about local sites. Such cooperation can also help develop civic fluency about heritage and about how place-based narratives shape our understanding of self and community.

Preservation's Engagement in Questions of Inclusion:
A Literature Review

Allison Arlotta
Erica Avrami

The modern American preservation movement has often been characterized as a David-and-Goliath tale: a populist wave of neighborhood
activists mobilizing against rational planning paradigms and greedy real
estate development interests. [1] This origin story promulgates an image
of preservation as an inherently inclusive and socially oriented practice.

In parallel to this on-the-ground advocacy narrative, preservation
theory was shifting in the second half of the twentieth century. While
notions of the "inherent" value of heritage had long underpinned preservation practice, the 1980s saw a move toward understanding heritage as
a social construct. Scholars increasingly recognized that the way people
think about and engage with the past changes over time. [2] Preservation
was also increasingly understood to serve social functions in the present
and to be fundamentally connected to questions of power. [3]

These theoretical shifts manifested in various forms of preservation
policy and practice, especially through greater recognition of the ways
in which different communities and stakeholders ascribe value to heritage. In particular, Australia ICOMOS's Burra Charter, first adopted in
1979 and revised several times since, represented an early application of
this broadened thinking to policy. [4] The notion that different stakeholders
may value a place in myriad, incommensurable, and sometimes incompatible ways has become an established theme of heritage literature. [5]
In practice, greater recognition of vernacular heritage and cultural landscapes
underscores the inextricable links between people and the environment in
which they live. [6] Such approaches challenge the field's focus on material integrity, instead emphasizing the significance of the relationships between people
and place, and of the social and political meaning of these relationships. [7]

Our research initiative, Urban Heritage, Sustainability, and Social
Inclusion, seeks to explore how an evolving understanding of these social
dimensions is playing out in urban preservation policy in the United
States. To do so, this endeavor and this literature review examine the
topic through the lens of social inclusion.

In the social sciences—outside the core of heritage literature—social
inclusion is referenced broadly in discussions of immigration and integration, neighborhood diversity and affordability, economic regeneration,
wellness and mental health, and access to political power. In fact, inclusion
is most frequently defined in the literature by its opposite: the exclusion of
people and groups from participation in economic, social, political, and
cultural life. [8] This exclusion has been extensively explored in cultural
studies, which has established that because cultural identities are varied,
relational, and interconnected, social exclusion exists at the intersection
of multiple marginalities. [9] The recognition of differences in social power
has been central to this discussion.

Within the body of literature focused more directly on heritage, researchers have found that the desire for social inclusion is widely discussed in practice [10] but that the term is used to convey a variety of inexactly defined ideas and infrequently addresses fundamental issues of power. [11] While there is broad agreement that heritage has a role to play in fostering social inclusion, the "how" of this role is unevenly conceptualized. [12] This literature review finds that discussions of how heritage can foster social inclusion generally fall into three broad categories:

- representing diverse narratives and communities through preservation;
- engaging multiple publics in preservation decision-making; and
- promoting inclusive outcomes for communities through preservation.

Just as the concept itself is unevenly defined, social inclusion is not well or explicitly represented in much of the preservation discourse. Thus, the following review is as much about identifying gaps in the research as it is about charting what does exist. Likewise, while this broader research initiative focuses on municipal-level policy, the review investigates the discourse writ large—in the United States and internationally—as well as at varying levels of governance (municipal, national, and global). Similarly, much of the heritage discussion around social inclusion is dealt with in practice-based case studies, so this review also extends beyond the academic and into advocacy-based discourse and gray literature in order to probe the intersection of preservation and social inclusion in different ways.

—— REPRESENTING DIVERSE NARRATIVES

Whose narratives are being represented?
As cities around the world grow and diversify, heritage literature has begun to interrogate prevailing narratives. While this interrogation has some presence in scholarly research, it is more evident in preservation practice. The standard preservation tool of designation or listing has increasingly been challenged in its ability to equitably represent communities. The literature has recognized the underrepresentation of non-Western sites on the World Heritage List [13] and of nonwhite, nonmale historical narratives on the National Register of Historic Places in the United States. [14] Some have noted that the dominance of the Western, white experience in cultural heritage theory also has implications for preservation policy, as regulations of the built environment can reinforce dominant cultures and perpetuate exclusion. [15]

The call for greater narrative diversity is reflected more explicitly in practice through efforts to recognize, designate, and preserve sites related to underrepresented histories. Prominent examples exist at the federal level in the United States, where the National Park Service has directed funding toward the identification of "Civil Rights" sites and the creation of "theme studies" related to the history of certain marginalized groups. [16] The National Park Service's National Women's Landmarks

Project partnered with national history organizations to increase the small percentage of National Historic Landmarks related to the contributions of women. 17 The National Trust for Historic Preservation, the country's largest preservation advocacy organization, has embarked on similar campaigns and recently created the $25 million African American Cultural Heritage Action Fund. Descriptions of similar initiatives at the local and regional levels are prominent in the literature, highlighting examples of communities pushing for their stories to be recognized in broader narratives.

The additive approach of preservation

Public historians have long asserted that we do not all understand the past in the same way and that collective memory is shaped by those with power and resources. 18 Yet the infrastructure that has been built up around preservation policy suggests that objective decision-making is possible and that those decisions can be permanent. 19 Thus, existing cadres of landmarks frequently include sites that ignore, confuse, or minimize the histories of marginalized people. In his book on American memorials, Kenneth Foote notes that this legacy necessitates "altering existing traditions to make enough room for new meanings." 20

Many scholars have examined how established historic places, like historic house museums, battlefields, and designated landmarks, attempt to challenge these legacies by incorporating new stories. 21 The most prominent section of this literature addresses the distortion and silencing of the history of American slavery. But reinterpretation remains an unproven route to representational justice. Case studies of initiatives to excavate, research, and share experiences of slavery at Mount Vernon and Monticello, two sites associated with American founding fathers, have been charged; the initiatives have been met with a mix of enthusiasm, distrust, and rejection from visitors. 22 Analysis of historical markers in North Carolina and Virginia determined that, despite recent additions of more contextualizing markers, these official, sometimes state-sponsored markers still largely ignore or minimize the history of slavery and the contributions of enslaved people. 23 The literature in this area supports Foote's assertion that "once consecrated, sites do not always give way easily to revision" and questions the possibility that traditional preservation can induce a radical shift in prevailing narratives. 24

Considering a subtractive approach

Heritage practice typically reflects an additive approach: more stories, more sites, more designations. Some have challenged this accumulation of heritage and its ability to solve questions of spatial justice and instead have suggested that it bestows the responsibility to care for past biases on future generations. 25 Though many have urged the field to explore the social value of loss, destruction, and alteration, a subtractive approach to heritage has rarely been addressed in preservation literature or in practice. 26

Where it has been raised, the potential for removal has centered primarily on contested monuments and memorials, notably with memorials related to the American Confederacy, Nazi Germany, and South

African apartheid. 27 Despite theoretical shifts in understanding heritage as a construct that serves a social function, nonprofit and professional organizations are still reticent to align themselves with the destruction of landmarks. Recently, national-level organizations have asserted equivocating views, supporting the legitimacy of removal as an option for offensive memorials without taking positions on individual cases. 28 Within scholarly research, memorial intervention has been more readily addressed in the fields of anthropology and geography. These fields have more directly discussed the concepts of spatial justice and symbolic power, recognizing that spatial markers can perpetuate legacies of oppression. 29

Because historical narrative "renews a claim to the truth," understanding whose stories are told is critically important for the heritage field. 30 It is well established in sociology and media studies that social representation—seeing yourself and your experiences in popular and historical narratives—affects individual development. 31 On a collective level, the omission of the contributions of whole groups—people of color, women, immigrants, and LGBTQ people, for example—from national narratives serves to bolster the illusion of white, patriarchal supremacy. Including and valorizing neglected histories in public space is essential for the hard work of justice and reconciliation. 32 These efforts face a difficult challenge, as structural and cultural forces have long excluded many of these groups from both property ownership and political participation on the basis of race, ethnicity, and identity. While this area of research deserves much more attention, some heritage scholars have noted that designation requirements generally rely on strict material integrity and architectural style criteria that fail to compensate for this exclusion. 33

From the perspective of architectural history, Robert Weyeneth describes the physical, built, and lasting examples of American segregation policy, which led to the duplication, division, and manipulation of buildings. 34 While Weyeneth concludes that examples of such distinctive architectural styles (such as duplicate phone booths in Oklahoma or separate entrances in a train station in North Carolina) should be preserved as a visual, public reminder of this de jure segregation, legal scholar Sarah Schindler argues that discriminatory architecture is a form of regulation itself that should be subject to nondiscrimination laws. 35 Though these authors examine different architectural forms, when taken together their two perspectives highlight a tension between the desire to be candid about American history and the need to redress the exclusion these places may perpetuate.

— ENGAGING DIVERSE PUBLICS

Preservation literature has noticeably shifted away from a curatorial perspective, wherein heritage is seen as a "thing" under the purview of "experts," and toward recognizing heritage as a process in which everyone can engage. 36 This shift is linked to urban planning literature on participation and community engagement in the built environment, particularly in the post-1960s, post-urban renewal era, and to the emergence of international heritage instruments like the Burra Charter. 37 The theoretical movements of the twentieth century challenged the long-held, privileged position of heritage "experts" and illuminated the need for preservation decision-making to include a wider range of stakeholders—with more community input, a broader scope of professional disciplines, and a greater diversity of practitioners. However, this literature related to civic participation within the heritage field remains underdeveloped, and trends in practice must be gleaned largely from individual case studies.

Civic participation

While there is a general recognition of the need for more participatory heritage practices, the literature that elucidates how this plays out in the field is extremely limited. The question of who participates is still largely unanswered. A notable exception comes from recent findings that in New York City, interest in preservation tends to come from whiter, older, and wealthier people, who are primarily concerned with physically oriented aesthetic and associative values. [38] There has also been little research on the diversity of heritage practitioners themselves, though this is a critical area of concern. Antoinette Lee, a historian with the National Park Service, was one of the first to argue that the preservation field needs to "look like America." [39] Demographic information on practitioners is scarce, though Keilah Spann notes that people of color accounted for only 10 percent of degrees awarded in historic preservation graduate programs in 2014. [40] In suggesting the unlikelihood "that a place shaped by a select few will fully work to benefit everyone," Justin Moore asserts that the profession needs to reflect the diversity of the country and observes that the problem is not being addressed "at the scale necessary to make meaningful impact." [41] The scarcity of demographic information about those engaging in preservation activities—as concerned citizens, students, volunteers, or practitioners—raises the question of whether an increase in narrative diversity is being conflated with participatory diversity.

The power of heritage to fundamentally contribute to more inclusive, participatory practices, rather than the reverse, is also an underdeveloped area of research. Without making the specific connection to preservation, scholars have begun to get at this potential in literature on oral history and other forms of "memory work." This research has established that oral histories can reveal connections to places where physical evidence cannot, [42] elicit information that subverts dominant narratives, [43] and contextualize tensions between competing values. [44] Leonie Sandercock hits on the dialogical power of heritage in asserting that such memory work is critical to the negotiation of values and identities necessary for creating inclusive cities. [45] This negotiation is central to thinking around "conscious heritage," in which so-called "sites of conscience" act as tools for "critically needed dialogue on contemporary issues" through facilitated reflection. [46] Liz Ševčenko's three urban case studies—the Tenement Museum in New York, Constitution Hall in Johannesburg, and Villa Grimaldi Peace Park in Santiago—provide examples of heritage places that foster participatory dialogue. [47] A "conscious" approach to heritage has thus far been limited to places with active interpretative capacities, like museums or staffed heritage sites, but its potential application to the management of the historic built environment more broadly has not been examined.

Heritage literature more frequently includes case studies that illuminate the mechanics of balancing community engagement and expert assessment in cultural heritage management. An example from the Getty Conservation Institute is Grosse Île and the Irish Memorial National Historic Site in Canada, where the significance of the site as part of a national narrative of "hope and promise" clashed with its stature as a place of profound pain for Irish immigrants. Through public consultation, these multiple narratives emerged, and the management plan changed. [48] This case study highlights how even thorough, well-intentioned expert research can fail to recognize the nuances of a place's significance without meaningful stakeholder participation.

There is also a growing body of literature around the concept of cultural mapping, which is variably and broadly defined. [49] Within preservation literature, the focus has been on practice-based cases that use cultural mapping as a means of eliciting values or community engagement. This is exemplified by the analysis of projects like Missouri Places Stories, which asked residents in St. Louis to make photo stories at meaningful places in their neighborhood. The analysis found that while participants did value many sites officially recognized as "historic," they typically voiced personal, rather than historical, associations with these places in explaining their significance. [50] As a collective, these represent a form of empirical research that has not been richly interconnected or examined robustly in the scholarly literature.

Some municipal governments have engaged in similar initiatives with specific public purposes in mind. The City of Los Angeles embarked on a decade-long effort to survey the entire city. In addition to employing trained field surveyors to assess all five hundred square miles of the city, the project involved extensive community outreach, most notably through an online platform, MyHistoricLA, where anyone could submit a significant place to the survey. While inclusion in the inventory does not come with any of the legal protections of historic designation, SurveyLA was explicitly created to inform land use decisions. [51] In a similar effort, the University of Texas at Austin School of Architecture developed an online tool to help the City of Austin's planning department democratize the preservation process and identify resources that were more reflective of community sentiment. Ultimately, this tool exposed tensions between the material-oriented views of experts and the information that community members wanted to contribute; it also revealed strong mutual distrust between the city and residents of the historically black and Hispanic neighborhood in which the project was piloted. [52]

Perhaps most importantly, the University of Texas team noted that while the data was crowdsourced, "the solutions to how one might preserve a place are not." [53] This point rings true across the literature. There are many innovative efforts to democratize the process of preservation, particularly with the emergence of creative place-making and asset-based planning approaches. But they have been limited largely to the consultation of and engagement with communities to share their stories and identify significant places, while the ultimate power to decide how these stories are used remains in the hands of experts. As Sarah James argues in her examination of Aboriginal participation in Sydney planning processes, it is not enough to solicit community involvement; this involvement must also extend to decision-making. 54 A recent study from the related field of museum conservation found that while public consultation was common, conservators rarely relied on public input when making decisions. 55 This suggests that public participation in the heritage field still generally falls below the level of true "citizen power" described in Sherry Arnstein's seminal model of community participation. 56 While compelling examples may exist in practice, very little has been published on shared decision-making or full citizen control over *how* to preserve.

A related area of research challenges the predominant modes of preservation practice, arguing that the field fails to address the needs of many communities and does not offer a broad enough range of choices on how to preserve. After years of vocal criticism from Native American tribes about the limited definition of heritage in the 1966 National Historic Preservation Act (NHPA), the National Park Service published *Keepers of the Treasures* in 1990. This report affirmed the need for tribal agency in preservation processes and for understanding "preservation as the perpetuation of lifeways as opposed to the protection of artifacts." 57 Incremental policy changes followed, including the creation of traditional cultural properties as a property type on the National Register and the establishment of Tribal Historic Preservation Offices to carry out the responsibilities of State Historic Preservation Offices on tribal land. But as previously mentioned, scholars continue to raise concerns that the field's focus on material integrity, especially in terms of designation criteria at both the local and the national level, inhibits the recognition of significant heritage, especially for marginalized communities.58 Others have called for a broadening of the preservation toolbox beyond the confines of designation, encouraging the search for new policy tools for heritage work.59 Many hope that preservation practitioners will see themselves as facilitators of a process rather than as experts, arguing that the focus should be on the relationships between people and their environments. 60

Two encouraging developments in this arena come from publications by leading global conservation authorities. The Getty Conservation Institute's 2016 report on heritage conflict resolution presented research on the challenges and possibilities of employing consensus-building techniques in heritage management planning. The report acknowledges that because "heritage engages with human feelings and identities," it is rife with the potential for conflict. 61 Echoing calls to define preservation more in terms of facilitation, it argues that conflict management techniques should be within the preservationist's skill set. In a similar vein, the International Center for the Study of the Preservation and Restoration of Cultural Property (ICCROM) published an extensive report on sharing conservation decisions, a compilation of twenty-four essays by heritage professionals on how experts and nonexperts can make decisions about preservation together. 62 The essays are exploratory, however, and only begin to chart how stakeholders can exercise more agency in decisions about their heritage.

Authors from a variety of other disciplines remind us that many of the themes discussed in this review have much longer histories. Suleiman Osman has looked at the history of gentrification, specifically in New York

City, noting that it is far from a new phenomenon. [63] Other historians have sought to shine a light on the spaces of marginalized groups throughout American history, with an emphasis on their agency and contributions to planning, the built environment, and political action. Authors like Angel David Nieves, Leslie Alexander, Marta Gutman, and Andrea Roberts remind us that marginalized communities have always taken place-based collective action in resistance to state-backed oppression. [64] As bell hooks explains, it is precisely because of this ability of place to foster community organizing that the spaces of Black Americans, ethnic minorities, immigrants, and other groups on the margins have been "subject to violation and destruction." [65]

Power and human rights

The preservation field has continued to be pushed toward a greater understanding of the importance of people's agency within the heritage process. The 2005 Faro Convention departed from an earlier focus on guidelines for material conservation and instead focused on people, linking heritage to the "right to culture" enshrined in the UN Declaration of Human Rights. This human-rights approach touches on the importance of individual and community agency in heritage conservation but has limitations in terms of cultural relevance, power relationships, and enforceability. [66] That said, significant connections have been drawn between human rights and indigenous cultural heritage and land rights, access to sacred sites, and the destruction of cultural heritage during war. [67] The importance of agency underpins much of the discussion of social inclusion in preservation, but the assertion of heritage rights has been used to both maintain and challenge the status quo, and it does not solve the aforementioned issue of power imbalances.

To more directly confront the question of equity, some emerging research advocates for developing a social justice framework for heritage work. Melissa Baird suggests that such an approach would be driven by an examination of structural power and would require heritage practitioners to ask questions like the following: "How is heritage mobilized in knowledge claims and identity creation? Are specific discourses or practices privileged in the name of safeguarding heritage? Are certain voices included or silenced?" [68] Andrea Roberts similarly urges the field to contend with issues of power by "challenging preservation regulations that disproportionately exclude sites associated with marginalized communities." [69] She calls on preservationists to listen to those living on the margins, to engage with social activists, and to recognize the interconnections of various social and spatial problems. Because "heritage practitioners unavoidably work with, perpetuate, and have the potential to change [social] inequalities," the question of power is increasingly and necessarily being raised in preservation literature. [70]

— UNDERSTANDING EFFECTS ON COMMUNITIES

Several decades of preservation policy now allow for reflection on and assessment of its outcomes. Beyond evaluating the inclusivity of preserved

231

narratives or preservation practices, an emerging area of literature seeks to understand how communities are affected by preservation decisions. Underpinning this question is a fundamental split in the characterization of the impacts of preservation policy. Some authors see preservation policy as a progressive tool for fostering social inclusion, cultural identity, and civic participation, one that can work in tandem with community development and promote equity. Others see it as a regressive tool that addresses neither social needs for better housing and infrastructure nor the conditions of multicultural societies, ultimately giving social elites control over space. 71 This area of the research is still very much ongoing, but certain threads—and gaps—have emerged, ranging from the role of theory in promulgating exclusionary preservation policies, to empirical studies of community benefits, to preservation's intersection with education and public welfare.

Theory-based critiques

"Critical heritage studies" explores inclusion issues theoretically, finding that Western ideologies have underpinned the creation of international policy and institutions to the exclusion of other ways of knowing. Laurajane Smith calls this phenomenon the "Authorized Heritage Discourse" (AHD) and identifies its roots in European, Enlightenment-era ideas about modernity that were propagated through colonialism and imperialism. AHD is visible in heritage work that relies on "experts" who identify the "usual suspects" as significant, focus on material conservation "for future generations," and advance "Western elite cultural values" as universal values. 72 Researchers have noted that this dominant, self-referential discourse limits who has decision-making authority about heritage, does not easily recognize forms of heritage that are not bound to material, and separates the past from the present in a way that does not allow for active, current engagement. Many argue that the mold set by AHD constrains attempts to recognize new narratives, represent pluralist societies, and broaden participation in heritage processes. 73

Socioeconomics and gentrification

While much empirical research has intended to evaluate the outcomes of preservation policy, it has largely been advocacy driven, seeking to rationalize and support preservation as a way to provide community-wide economic benefits. 74 Early studies sought to rebuff arguments opposing preservation policy as an economic constraint that limits development and hurts property values and to recast it as a positive community program with value that can be measured in monetary terms. 75 As urban contexts change, many cities are increasingly concerned about housing affordability and the displacement of lower-income residents. In this light, preservation has more frequently been viewed as a contributor to rising housing costs and as a regulatory tool that gives outsize control to a small, powerful elite. The field has thus been increasingly compelled to explore preservation's effects on communities, especially in connection to questions of gentrification. The term "gentrification" here describes intense urban demographic changes that may produce some social benefits but are also associated with displacement (direct and indirect) and the loss of heritage, sense of place, and community cohesion.[76] The relationship between preservation policy, particularly designation, and gentrification remains the subject of debate.

While qualitative research has revealed that residents often connect preservation and gentrification in their own experiences, empirical research linking the two is limited and has produced mixed findings.[77] In a recent study of New York City historic districts, Brian McCabe and Ingrid Gould Ellen found that neighborhoods with historic districts see an average increase in socioeconomic status after designation, in comparison to other neighborhoods.[78] In Los Angeles, Karolina Gorska identified changes in economic status, racial composition, or both in 45 percent of the city's neighborhoods with Historic Preservation Overlay Zones when compared with other neighborhoods—but did not directly identify designation as the cause of these changes.[79]

Beyond the specific question of gentrification, some research has addressed preservation's community benefits by looking at the positive characteristics of old and historic neighborhoods. The National Trust's research arm found that older, smaller buildings were more likely to house women- and minority-owned businesses,[80] and Douglas Appler notes that low-income housing in National Register districts tends to be closer to amenities, like libraries and transit, than nondesignated districts.[81] Importantly, these studies do not evaluate the outcomes of preservation policy; rather, they highlight some of the ways older buildings and neighborhoods might contribute positively to cities.

Spatial justice and public access

The focus on gentrification in heritage literature masks a much larger, significant gap in the research. Many decades of discriminatory urban development and housing policies have variously reinforced or introduced intense spatial segregation in American cities, and this segregation has been ossified in the landscape.[82] But there has been little examination of how preservation policy might challenge or, in fact, sustain this history of publicly enforced spatial injustice. For example, the literature has not yet tied monument removal to larger discussions around dismantling the legacies of exclusion that may be maintained through preservation policy and action.

The notion of accessibility in preservation has typically been addressed at the site level and in terms of physical access[83] or access to information.[84] It has rarely been investigated at the municipal or state level or in terms of the public's right to access designated places. Exceptions are the work of legal scholars who have challenged the lack of public access to interior landmarks in New York City[85] and the use of public investment (in the form of historic preservation tax credits) for private property projects.[86] Preservation policy is enacted with the expectation of public benefit; thus, the question of public access to designated properties is an important one that has, so far, been largely unexplored.

Heritage, culture, and community health

The contribution of arts and culture to cities and countries has been widely researched and typically includes heritage. In the United

Kingdom, the Arts and Humanities Research Council undertook a project to understand the impact of the arts and culture on society. Relevant to the question of social inclusion, the council suggests that engagement with culture can provide "'rehearsal-type' situations where we can practice our moral responses." [87] The Urban Institute looks to participation in arts and culture as an indicator of cultural vitality and demonstrates that cultural vitality is characterized differently in different places. [88] These findings are interesting but difficult to instrumentalize for preservation, since heritage work is not specifically addressed within the broad definition of culture. However, this literature can serve as a model for preservation-focused research. [89]

The relationship between heritage and health is another area of developing research, much of which is still considered under the larger umbrella of culture. The Institute of Cultural Capital is researching the contributions of cultural assets to mental health and well-being. [90] Mark Stern and the University of Pennsylvania's Social Impact of the Arts Program looked at this question of well-being in New York City neighborhoods, finding that "cultural assets are part of a neighborhood ecology that promotes wellbeing." [91] In Europe, a couple of case studies show promise for the heritage field's specific contribution to emotional well-being. [92] In the public health arena, the relationship between place and community health is increasingly central. Though some have suggested that historic environments have a role to play in this discussion, little research within a heritage context has addressed questions of health. [93]

Heritage and education

That preserved places impart lessons in the present is such a fundamental tenet of the field that it goes largely unspoken. The literature reflects many claims about the educational value of historic sites and heritage work more broadly, and education and public welfare are the most frequently cited rationales in municipal preservation ordinances. [94] While discrete case studies have examined visitor learning at historic sites, very little research supports these broad educational claims. [95] Kevin Myers and Ian Grosvenor explain that while heritage has the potential to be educational, learning does not happen passively; instead, it requires active participants who have a desire to learn and are compelled to reflect. [96] Because the educational value of historic preservation is so frequently claimed, this is an area of research that sorely requires more attention.

— SOCIAL INCLUSION IN HERITAGE DISCOURSE

The available literature suggests that the need to represent diverse narratives and engage communities in heritage work is increasingly well recognized, even if practice and policy have not yet fully shifted to accommodate these changing perspectives. Much less research has been dedicated to the methods employed to promote inclusive engagement and to probing the outcomes of this engagement and of preservation policy writ large.

This review has identified several underdeveloped areas of research within the preservation discourse. While a large portion of the literature addresses the need for greater diversity in the narratives under preservation's purview, there has been limited exploration of how policy tools might evolve in order to achieve this diversity. For example, there is little discussion about how designation—a primary tool of preservation—may need to change. While there is support for listing more diverse sites, there is little research into how to redress the legacies of imbalance in lists and listing processes. The literature suggests that there is no real dialogue in the United States around quotas, caps, delisting, or other means of furthering equality and/or affirmative action in list representation. Discussions of narrative diversity have also only superficially explored effects on communities. How increased narrative diversity might confront exclusive attitudes at the individual and structural level remains an open question, and one that warrants empirical study in order to ensure the effectiveness of policy.

The literature reveals a push to make preservation practice more participatory, but it has not explored the question of "who participates" and "who decides" beyond individual case studies. A greater understanding of nonpreservationists' agency within the heritage process could come from studying participation at the municipal scale or practices across the field. Jane Henderson and Tanya Nakamoto's study of decision-making in museum conservation offers a useful model for this kind of research. [97] There is a broad need to explore participation in preservation in terms of power and social agency.

The lack of research into inclusive outcomes is one of the biggest gaps in preservation research, particularly as it relates to issues of ossified spatial injustice in urban landscapes. Despite the significant expansion of preservation policy infrastructure across the United States over the last half century, there is a dearth of research on the distributive effects—social, economic, and environmental—of preservation policy in relation to inclusion and equity.

Furthermore, as the effects of climate change continue to intensify, environmental changes will put more pressure on existing social, political, and spatial inequalities. This growing crisis further compels the preservation field to engage with questions of inclusive outcomes in a robust, evidence-based, and sustained way.

This review makes clear that there is an ever-present need for the preservation field to change—in order to remain relevant, to right historic and persistent wrongs, or to contribute to a broader coalition of progressive social movements. A growing discourse in the realm of critical heritage studies explores inequities in the conceptual underpinnings of preservation practice, and many individual projects seek to challenge such inequities with innovative approaches. But the literature is limited in the realm of evidence-based policy reform. A fair amount of heritage research is advocacy driven, seeking to counter the aforementioned critiques and effectively preserve the policy status quo. Less attention has been paid to how governance and institutional structures can adapt in light of new knowledge and emerging needs around these questions of inclusion.

1
Michael Wallace, "Reflections on the History of Historic Preservation," in *Presenting the Past: Essays on History and the Public*, ed. Susan Porter Benson, Stephen Brier, and Roy Rosenzweig (Philadelphia: Temple University Press, 1986), 165–202; Ned Kaufman, "Moving Forward: Futures for a Preservation Movement," in *Giving Preservation a History*, ed. Max Page and Randall Mason (New York: Routledge, 2004), 313–328.

2
David Lowenthal, *The Past Is a Foreign Country* (New York: Cambridge University Press, 1985); Eric Hobsbawm and Terence Ranger, eds., *The Invention of Tradition* (New York: Cambridge University Press, 1983).

3
William D. Lipe, "Value and Meaning in Cultural Resources," in *Approaches to the Archaeological Heritage*, ed. Henry Cleere (New York: Cambridge University Press, 1984), 1–11; Michael Frisch, "American History and the Structures of Collective Memory: A Modest Exercise in Empirical Iconography," *Journal of American History* 75, no. 4 (1989): 1130–1155.

4
Chris Johnston, *What Is Social Value? A Discussion Paper* (Canberra: Australian Government Publishing Service, 1994).

5
Joseph A. Tainter and G. John Lucas, "Epistemology of the Significance Concept," *American Antiquity* 48, no. 4 (1983): 707–719; Johnston, "What Is Social Value?"; Erica Avrami, Randall Mason, and Marta de la Torre, *Values and Heritage Conservation* (Los Angeles: Getty Conservation Institute, 2000); L. Harald Fredheim and Manal Khalaf, "The Significance of Values: Heritage Value Typologies Re-Examined," *International Journal of Heritage Studies* 22, no. 6 (2016): 466–481.

6
Susan Buggey and Nora Mitchell, "Cultural Landscapes: Venues for Community-Based Conservation," in *Cultural Landscapes: Balancing Nature and Heritage in Preservation Practice*, ed. Richard Longstreth (Minneapolis: University of Minnesota Press, 2008), 164–179.

7
Dolores Hayden, "The Power of Place Project," in *Restoring Women's History through Historic Preservation*, ed. Gail Lee Dubrow and Jennifer B. Goodman (Baltimore: Johns Hopkins University Press, 2003), 199–213.

8
Andrew Newman and Fiona McLean, "Heritage Builds Communities: The Application of Heritage Resources to the Problems of Social Exclusion," *International Journal of Heritage Studies* 4, nos. 3–4 (1998): 143–153; John Pendlebury, Tim Townshend, and Rose Gilroy, "The Conservation of English Cultural Built Heritage: A Force for Social Inclusion?," *International Journal of Heritage Studies* 10, no. 1 (2004): 11–31.

9
bell hooks, *Yearning: Race, Gender, and Cultural Politics* (Boston: South End Press, 1990).

10
Nir Mualam and Rachelle Alterman, "Social Dilemmas in Built-Heritage Policy: The Role of Social Considerations in Decisions of Planning Inspectors," *Journal of Housing and the Built Environment* 33, no. 3 (September 2018): 1–19; Erica Avrami, Cherie-Nicole Leo, and Alberto Sanchez Sanchez, "Confronting Exclusion: Redefining the Intended Outcomes of Historic Preservation," *Change Over Time* 8, no. 1 (2018): 102–120.

11
Pendlebury, Townshend, and Gilroy, "Conservation of English Cultural Built Heritage."

12
Newman and McLean, "Heritage Builds Communities."

13
Bruno S. Frey and Lasse Steiner, "World Heritage List: Does It Make Sense?," *International Journal of Cultural Policy* 17, no. 5 (2011): 555–573.

14
Ned Kaufman, *Cultural Heritage Needs Assessment: Phase I* (Washington, DC: National Park Service, 2004), https://www.nps.gov/subjects/tellingall americanstories/upload/PhaseIReport.pdf.

15
Hayden, "Power of Place Project"; Laurajane Smith, *Uses of Heritage* (New York: Routledge, 2006); Avrami, Leo, and Sanchez Sanchez, "Confronting Exclusion."

16
Antoinette J. Lee, "From Historic Architecture to Cultural Heritage: A Journey Through Diversity, Identity, and Community," *Future Anterior* 1, no. 4 (2004): 14–23; Michelle de Guzman Magalong, "Politics of Representation and Participation in Federal Historic Preservation Programs" (PhD diss., University of California, Los Angeles, 2017).

17
Page Putnam Miller, "Women's History Landmark Project: Policy and Research," *Public Historian* 15, no. 4 (1993): 82–88.

18
Michael Kammen, *Mystic Chords of Memory: The Transformation of Tradition in American Culture* (New York: Knopf, 1991); Edward Linenthal and Tom Engelhardt, *History Wars: The Enola Gay and Other Battles for the American Past* (New York: Henry Holt, 1996).

19
Setha M. Low, "Cultural Conservation of Place," in *Conserving Culture: A New Discourse on Culture*, ed. Mary Hufford (Urbana: University of Illinois Press, 1994), 66–77; Alan S. Downer, Alexandra Roberts, Harris Francis, and Klara B. Kelley, "Traditional History and Alternative Conceptions of the Past," in *Conserving Culture*, ed. Hufford, 39–55.

20
Kenneth E. Foote, *Shadowed Ground: America's Landscapes of Violence and Tragedy* (Austin: University of Texas Press, 2003), 28.

21
John A. Herbst, "The Challenge of Interpretation at Historic House Museums," *Pittsburgh History* 73 (Fall 1990): 119–129; Douglas A. Hurt "Reinterpreting the Washita Battlefield National Historic Site," *Geographical Review* 100, no. 3 (2010): 375–393; Timothy E. Baumann, "An Historical Perspective of Civic Engagement and Interpreting Cultural Diversity in Arrow Rock, Missouri," *Historical Archaeology* 45, no. 1 (2018): 114–134.

22
Jonathan Scholnick, Derek Wheeler, and Fraser Neiman, *Mulberry Row Reassessment: The Building I Site* (Charlottesville, VA: Monticello Department of Archaeology Technical Report Series, 2001); Joseph A. Downer, *Hallowed Ground, Sacred Place: The Slave Cemetery at George Washington's Mount Vernon and the Cultural Landscapes of the Enslaved* (Washington, DC: George Washington University, 2011); Gardiner Hallock, "'Build the Negro Houses Near Together': Thomas Jefferson and the Evolution of Mulberry Row's Vernacular Landscape," *Buildings & Landscapes: Journal of the Vernacular Architecture Forum* 24, no. 2 (2018): 22–36.

23
Derek H. Alderman, "'History by the Spoonful' in North Carolina: The Textual Politics of State Highway Historical Markers," *Southeastern Geographer* 52, no. 4 (2014): 355–373; Stephen P. Hanna and E. Fariss Hodder, "Reading the Signs: Using a Qualitative Geographic Information System to Examine the Commemoration of Slavery and Emancipation on Historical Markers in Fredericksburg, Virginia," *Cultural Geographies* 22, no. 3 (2015): 509–529.

24
Foote, *Shadowed Ground*, 295.

25
Clarence Mondale, "Conserving a Problematic Past," in *Conserving Culture*, ed. Hufford, 15–23; Erica Avrami, "Sustainability, Intergenerational Equity, and Pluralism: Can Heritage Conservation Create Alternative Futures," in *Cultural Heritage and the Future*, ed. Cornelius Holtorf and Anders Hogberg (New York: Routledge, forthcoming).

26
David Lowenthal, "Material Preservation and Its Alternatives," *Perspecta* 25 (2019): 66–77; Cornelius Holtorf, "Is the Past a Non-Renewable Resource?," in *Destruction and Conservation of Cultural Property*, ed. Robert Layton, Peter G. Stone, and Julian Thomas (New York: Routledge, 2001), 3–7; Caitlin DeSilvey "Observed Decay: Telling Stories with Mutable Things," *Journal of Material Culture* 11, no.

3 (2006): 318–338; Rodney Harrison, Nadia Bartolini, Caitlin DeSilvey, Cornelius Holtorf, Antony Lyons, Sharon Macdonald, Sarah May, Jennie Morgan, and Sefryn Penrose, "Heritage Futures," *Archaeology International* 19, no. 19 (2016): 68–72.

27
Sarah Beetham, "From Spray Cans to Minivans: Contesting the Legacy of Confederate Soldier Monuments in the Era of 'Black Lives Matter,'" *Public Art Dialogue* 6, no. 1 (2016): 9–33; Sharon Macdonald, *Memorylands: Heritage and Identity in Europe Today* (New York: Routledge, 2013); Daniel Herwitz, "Monument, Ruin, and Redress in South African Heritage," *Germanic Review* 86, no. 4 (2011): 232–248; Sabine Marschall, "Targeting Statues: Monument 'Vandalism' as an Expression of Sociopolitical Protest in South Africa," *African Studies Review* 60, no. 3 (2017): 1–17.

28
National Trust for Historic Preservation, "Statement on Confederate Memorials," June 19, 2017, https:// savingplaces.org/press-center/media-resources/ national-trust-statement-on-confederate-memorials; Dell Upton, "Confederate Monuments and Civic Values in the Wake of Charlottesville," Society of Architectural Historians blog, September 13, 2017, https:// www.sah.org/publications-and-research/sah-blog/ sah-blog/2017/09/13/ confederate-monuments-and-civic-values-in-the-wake-of-charlottesville.

29
Pierre Bourdieu, *Distinction: A Social Critique of the Judgement of Taste* (Cambridge, MA: Harvard University Press, 1984); Paul A. Shackel, *Memory in Black and White: Race, Commemoration, and the Post-Bellum Landscape* (Walnut Creek, CA: AltaMira Press, 2003); Owen J. Dwyer and Derek H. Alderman, "Memorial Landscapes: Analytic Questions and Metaphors," *GeoJournal* 73, no. 3 (2008): 165–178.

30
Michel-Rolph Trouillot, *Silencing the Past: Power and the Production of History* (Boston: Beacon Press, 1995), 6.

31
Gerard Duveen and Barbara Lloyd, eds., *Social Representations and the Development of Knowledge* (New York: Cambridge University Press, 2005); Larry Gross, "Equity and Diversity in Media Representation," *Critical Studies in Media Communication* 18, no. 1 (2001): 114–119.

32
Paul Shackel, "Public Memory and the Search for Power in American Historical Archaeology," *American Anthropologist* 103, no. 1 (2008): 655–670; Ned Kaufman, *Place, Race, and Story: Essays on the Past and Future of Historic Preservation* (New York: Routledge, 2009).

33
Miller, "Women's History Landmark Project"; Lee, "From Historic Architecture to Cultural Heritage"; Stephanie Ryberg-Webster, "Beyond Rust and Rockefeller: Preserving Cleveland's African American Heritage," *Preservation Education and Research* 9 (2017): 7–23; Andrea Roberts, "When Does It Become Social Justice? Thoughts on Intersectional Preservation Practice," National Trust for Historic Preservation Leadership Forum blog, July 20, 2017, https:// forum.savingplaces. org/blogs/special-contributor/2017/07/20/ when-does-it-become-social-justice-thoughts-on-intersectional-preservation-practice.

34
Robert R. Weyeneth, "The Architecture of Racial Segregation: The Challenges of Preserving the Problematical Past," *Public Historian* 27, no. 4 (2005): 11–44.

35
Sarah Schindler, "Architectural Exclusion: Discrimination and Segregation Through Physical Design of the Built Environment," *Yale Law Journal* 124, no. 6 (2015): 1934–2024.

36
Lee, "From Historic Architecture to Cultural Heritage"; Marta de la Torre, Margaret G. H. MacLean, Randall Mason, and David Myers, *Heritage Values in Site Management* (Los Angeles: Getty Conservation Institute, 2005); John Schofield, "Heritage Expertise and the Everyday: Citizens and Authority in the Twenty-First Century,"

in *Who Needs Experts?: Counter-Mapping Cultural Heritage*, ed. John Schofield (Surrey, UK: Ashgate Publishing, 2015), 1–11.

37
Sherry Arnstein, "A Ladder of Citizen Participation," *Journal of the American Institute of Planners* 35, no. 4 (1969): 216; John Friedmann, *Planning in the Public Domain: From Knowledge to Action* (Princeton, NJ: Princeton University Press, 1987).

38
Avrami, Leo, and Sanchez Sanchez, "Confronting Exclusion."

39
Lee, "From Historic Architecture to Cultural Heritage"; Antoinette J. Lee, "Discovering Old Cultures in the New World: The Role of Ethnicity," in *The American Mosaic: Preserving a Nation's Heritage*, ed. Robert E. Stipe and Antoinette J. Lee (Washington, DC: US/ ICOMOS), 179–206.

40
Keilah Spann, "Discussions on Broadening Outreach and Programming," *Forum Journal* 30, no. 4 (2016): 38–46.

41
Justin Garrett Moore, "Making a Difference: Reshaping the Past, Present, and Future toward Greater Equity," *Forum Journal* 31, no. 4 (2018): 21.

42
Jessica Taylor, "'We're on Fire': Oral History and the Preservation, Commemoration, and Rebirth of Mississippi's Civil Rights Sites," *Oral History Review* 42, no. 2 (2015): 231–254; Fionnuala Fagan and Isobel Anderson, "Stories of the City: An Artistic Representation of Sailortown's Oral History," *Oral History Review* 44, no. 1 (2016): 108–116.

43
Mark Riley and David Harvey, "Landscape Archaeology, Heritage and the Community in Devon: An Oral History Approach," *International Journal of Heritage Studies* 11, no. 4 (2005): 269–288.

44
Mwayi Lusaka, "Memory, Oral History and Conservation at Robben Island's Bluestone Quarry," *South African Historical Journal* 69, no. 4 (2017): 583–597.

45
Leonie Sandercock, *Cosmopolis II: Mongrel Cities of the 21st Century* (New York: Continuum, 2003).

46
Liz Ševčenko, "Sites of Conscience: New Approaches to Conflicted Memory," *Museum International* 62, no. 245 (2010): 20.

47
Liz Ševčenko, "Dialogue as a Resource for Heritage Management," in *Consensus Building, Negotiation and Conflict Resolution for Heritage Place Management*, ed. David Myers, Stacie Nicole Smith, and Gail Ostergren (Los Angeles: Getty Conservation Institute, 2016), 161–182.

48
Margaret G. H. MacLean and David Myers, *Grosse Île and the Irish Memorial National Historic Site* (Los Angeles: J. Paul Getty Trust, 2005), 49.

49
Erica Avrami, "Spatializing Values in Heritage Conservation: The Potential of Cultural Mapping," in *Values in Heritage Management*, ed. Erica Avrami, Randall Mason, Susan MacDonald, and David Myers (Los Angeles: J. Paul Getty Trust), 35–49; Alina Álvarez Larrain and Michael K. McCall, "Participatory Mapping and Participatory GIS for Historical and Archaeological Landscape Studies: A Critical Review," *Journal of Archaeological Method and Theory* 26, no. 2 (June 2019); Claudia Guerra, "Cultural Mapping: Engaging Community in Historic Preservation," *Forum Journal* 30, no. 4 (2016): 29–37.

50
Maris Boyd Gillette and Andrew Hurley, "Vision, Voice, and the Community Landscape: The Missouri Place Stories Pilot Project," *Landscape and Urban Planning* 173 (January 2018): 1–8.

51
Ken Bernstein and Janet Hansen, "SurveyLA: Linking Historic Resources Surveys to Local Planning," *Journal of the American Planning Association* 82, no. 2 (2016): 88–91.

52
Jennifer Minner, Michael Holleran, Andrea Roberts, and Joshua Conrad, "Capturing Volunteered

Historical Information," *International Journal of E-Planning Research* 4, no. 1 (2015): 19–41.

53
Minner et al., "Capturing Volunteered Historical Information."

54
Sarah W. James, "Rights to the Diverse City: Challenges to Indigenous Participation in Urban Planning and Heritage Preservation in Sydney, Australia," *Space and Culture* 16, no. 3 (2013): 274–287.

55
Jane Henderson and Tanya Nakamoto, "Dialogue in Conservation Decision-Making," *Studies in Conservation* 61 (April 2016): 67–78.

56
Arnstein, "Ladder of Citizen Participation."

57
Tonia Sing Chi, "Building Reciprocity: A Grounded Theory of Participation in Native American Housing and the Perpetuation of Earthen Architectural Traditions" (master's thesis, Columbia University, 2018), 47; National Park Service, *Keepers of the Treasures: Protecting Historic Properties and Cultural Traditions on Indian Lands* (Washington, DC: US Department of the Interior, 1990).

58
Spann, "Discussions on Broadening Outreach and Programming"; Ryberg-Webster, "Beyond Rust and Rockefeller."

59
Erica Avrami, "Making Historic Preservation Sustainable," *Journal of the American Planning Association* 82, no. 2 (2016): 104–112; James Michael Buckley and Donna Graves, "Tangible Benefits from Intangible Resources: Using Social and Cultural History to Plan Neighborhood Futures," *Journal of the American Planning Association* 82, no. 2 (2016): 152–166.

60
Jamie Kalven, "Looking Forward: The Next Fifty Years of Preservation," *Forum Journal* 30, no. 1 (2016): 16–25; Jeremy C. Wells, "Human Environment Conservation in 2066," in *Bending the Future: 50 Ideas for the Next 50 Years of Historic Preservation in the United States* (Amherst and Boston: University of

Massachusetts Press, 2016), 254–257; World Intellectual Property Organization, *Documenting Traditional Knowledge: A Toolkit* (Geneva: World Intellectual Property Organization, 2017), http://www.wipo.int/edocs/pubdocs/en/wipo_pub_1049.pdf.

61
David Myers, Stacie Nicole Smith, and Gail Ostergren, eds., *Consensus Building, Negotiation and Conflict Resolution for Heritage Place Management* (Los Angeles: Getty Conservation Institute, 2016).

62
Alison Heritage and Jennifer Copithorne, eds., *Sharing Conservation Decisions* (Rome: International Centre for the Study of the Preservation and Restoration of Cultural Property, 2018).

63
Suleiman Osman, "What Time Is Gentrification?," *City and Community* 15, no. 3 (2018): 215–219.

64
Angel David Nieves and Leslie M. Alexander, eds., *"We Shall Independent Be": African American Place Making and the Struggle to Claim Space in the United States* (Boulder: University Press of Colorado, 2008); Marta Gutman, "Race, Place, and Play: Robert Moses and the WPA Swimming Pools," *Journal of the Society of Architectural Historians* 67, no. 4 (2008): 532–561; Andrea R. Roberts, "The Farmers' Improvement Society and the Women's Barnyard Auxiliary of Texas: African American Community Building in the Progressive Era," *Journal of Planning History* 16, no. 3 (2017): 222–245.

65
hooks, *Yearning*, 47.

66
Lynn Meskell, "Human Rights and Heritage Ethics," *Anthropological Quarterly* 83, no. 4 (2010): 839–859; Ian Hodder, "Cultural Heritage Rights: From Ownership and Descent to Justice and Well-Being," *Anthropological Quarterly* 83, no. 4 (2010): 861–882.

67
Helaine Silverman and D. Fairchild Ruggles, "Cultural Heritage and Human Rights," in *Cultural Heritage and Human Rights* (New York: Springer, 2015), 271–312.

68
Melissa F. Baird, "Heritage, Human Rights, and Social Justice," *Heritage & Society* 7, no. 2 (2014): 142.

69
Roberts, "When Does It Become Social Justice?"

70
Robert Johnston and Kimberley Marwood, "Action Heritage: Research, Communities, Social Justice," *International Journal of Heritage Studies* 23, no. 9 (2017): 816; Siân Jones, "Wrestling with the Social Value of Heritage: Problems, Dilemmas and Opportunities," *Journal of Community Archaeology & Heritage* 4, no. 1 (2017): 21–37; Diane M. Rodgers, Lucy Sosa, and Jessica Petersen, "Historic Preservation: A Multilayered Inclusive Approach Honoring Immigrants Past and Present," *Humanity & Society* 42, no. 2 (2018): 193–220.

71
Mualam and Alterman, "Social Dilemmas in Built-Heritage Policy."

72
Smith, *Uses of Heritage*.

73
Smith, *Uses of Heritage*; Dean Sully, *Decolonizing and Conservation: Caring for Maori Meeting Houses Outside New Zealand* (Walnut Creek, CA: Left Coast Press, 2007); Carol Ludwig, "From Bricks and Mortar to Social Heritage: Planning Space for Diversities in the AHD," *International Journal of Heritage Studies* 22, no. 10 (2016): 811–827.

74
Donovan Rypkema, *New York: Profiting Through Preservation* (Albany: Preservation League of New York State, 2000), https://www.placeeconomics.com/wp-content/uploads/2016/08/placeeconomicspub 2001.pdf; Michael Hanson, *First Annual Report on the Economic Impact of the Federal Historic Tax Credit* (Washington, DC: National Park Service, 2010); Donovan Rypkema, Caroline Cheong, and Randall F. Mason, "Measuring Economic Impacts of Historic Preservation," November 2011, https://www.achp.gov/sites/default/files/guidance/2018-06/Economic%20Impacts%20 v5-FINAL.pdf;

ThinkBrooklyn, "The Intersection of Affordable Housing and Historic Districts," March 2016, http://hdc.org/wp-content/uploads/2016/05/Intersection-of-Affordable-Housing-Historic-Districts.pdf.

75
Donovan Rypkema, *The Economics of Rehabilitation* (Washington, DC: National Trust for Historic Preservation, 1991); Rypkema, *New York*; Elizabeth Morton, "Historic Districts Are Good for Your Pocketbook: The Impact of Local Historic Districts on House Prices in South Carolina," South Carolina Department of Archives and History, January 2000, https://dc.statelibrary.sc.gov/bitstream/handle/10827/6889/DAH_Historic_Districts_are_Good_For_Your_Pocketbook_2000-1.pdf?sequence=1&is Allowed=y.

76
Lance Freeman and Frank Braconi, "Gentrification and Displacement New York City in the 1990s," *Journal of the American Planning Association* 70, no. 1 (2004): 39–52; Mindy Fullilove, *Root Shock* (New York: New Village Press, 2016); Malo André Hutson, *The Urban Struggle for Economic, Environmental and Social Justice* (New York: Routledge, 2016).

77
Japonica Brown-Saracino, *A Neighborhood That Never Changes: Gentrification, Preservation, and the Search for Authenticity* (Chicago: University of Chicago Press, 2009); Center for Urban and Regional Affairs, "Beneath the Surface: A Snapshot of CURA's Gentrification Interview Data," 2018, http://gentrification.umn.edu/sites/gentrification.dl.umn.edu/files/general/northeast-2-23-18.pdf.

78
Brian J. McCabe and Ingrid Gould Ellen, "Does Preservation Accelerate Neighborhood Change? Examining the Impact of Historic Preservation in New York City," *Journal of the American Planning Association* 82, no. 2 (2016): 134–146.

79
Karolina Maria Gorska, "Different Shades of Change: Historic Districts in Los Angeles and Their Impact

on Gentrification and Neighborhood Trends" (PhD diss., University of California, Los Angeles, 2015).

80
Preservation Green Lab, *Older, Smaller, Better: Measuring How the Character of Buildings and Blocks Influences Urban Vitality* (Washington, DC: National Trust for Historic Preservation, 2014).

81
Douglas R. Appler, "Affordable Housing in National Register Districts: Recognizing the Advantages of Historic Urban Neighborhoods in Louisville and Covington, Kentucky, USA," *Journal of Urbanism* 9, no. 3 (2015): 237–253.

82
Emily Talen, "Zoning and Diversity in Historical Perspective," *Journal of Planning History* 11, no. 4 (2012): 330–347; Schindler, "Architectural Exclusion"; Richard Rothstein, *The Color of Law* (New York: Liveright Publishing, 2017).

83
David H. Battaglia, "How the ADA Affects Historic Buildings," *Practical Real Estate Lawyer* 9 (July 1993): 1–10; Catherine Kudlick, "The Local History Museum, So Near and Yet So Far," *Public Historian* 27, no. 2 (2005): 75–81.

84
Lisa Kersavage and Daniel Watts, "Digital Tools for Sharing Historic Building Data with the Public," Preservation Leadership Forum 2018, https://forum.savingplaces.org/blogs/special-contributor/2018/01/31/digital-tools-for-sharing-historic-building-data.

85
Nicholas Caros, "Interior Landmark Preservation and Public Access," *Columbia Law Review* 116, no. 7 (November 2016): 1773–1805.

86
David Kohtz, "Improving Tax Incentives for Historic Preservation," *Texas Law Review* 90, no. 4 (2012): 1041–1064.

87
Geoffrey Crossick and Patrycja Kaszynska, "Understanding the Value of Arts & Culture: The AHRC Cultural Value Project," Arts and Humanities Research Council, 2016, 46, https://ahrc.ukri.org/documents/publications/cultural-value-project-final-report.

88
Maria Rosario Jackson, Florence Kabwasa-Green, and Joaquín Herranz, *Cultural Vitality in Communities: Interpretation and Indicators* (Washington, DC: Urban Institute, 2006).

89
Stephanie Ryberg-Webster and Kelly L. Kinahan, "Historic Preservation and Urban Revitalization in the Twenty-First Century," *Journal of Planning Literature* 29, no. 2 (2014): 119–139.

90
Kerry Wilson and Gaye Whelan, *Joining the Dots: The Social Value of Creative Interventions in Mental Health Care* (Liverpool: Institute of Cultural Capital, 2015), http://iccliverpool.ac.uk/wp-content/uploads/2018/05/Joining-the-Dots-Cultural-Assets-and-Social-Value-research-methodology-update-July-2015.pdf.

91
Mark J. Stern, "The Social Wellbeing of New York City's Neighborhoods: The Contribution of Culture and the Arts," https://repository.upenn.edu/cgi/viewcontent.cgi?article=1001&context=siap_culture_nyc.

92
Jenny Isabel McMillan, "Making a Mark on History with the Past in Mind," *Mental Health and Social Inclusion* 17, no. 4 (2013): 195–201; Anette Bengs, Susanne Hägglund, Annika Wiklund-Engblom, and Simon Staffans, "Designing for Suburban Social Inclusion: A Case of Geo-Located Storytelling," *Interaction Design and Architecture(s)* 25, no. 25 (2015): 85–99.

93
Mindy Thompson Fullilove, "Root Shock: The Consequences of African American Dispossession," *Journal of Urban Health* 78, no. 1 (2001): 72–80; Hutson, *Urban Struggle for Economic, Environmental and Social Justice.*

94
Avrami, Leo, and Sanchez Sanchez, "Confronting Exclusion."

95
James Farmer and Doug Knapp, "Interpretation Programs at a Historic Preservation Site: A Mixed Methods Study of Long-Term Impact," *Journal of Mixed Methods Research* 2, no. 4 (October 2008): 340–361; Jonathan Rix, Ticky Lowe, and the Heritage Forum, "Including People with Learning Difficulties in Cultural and Heritage Sites," *International Journal of Heritage Studies* 16 (2010): 207–224; Erin Carlson Mast, "Place, Story, Ritual: An Introduction to the Experience of President Lincoln's Cottage Study and Report," President Lincoln's Cottage, http://www.lincolncottage.org/wp-content/uploads/2018/03/Exec-Summary-and-Visitor-Impact-Study-Report_2018.pdf.

96
Kevin Myers and Ian Grosvenor, "Cultural Learning and Historical Memory: A Research Agenda," *Encounters on Education* 15 (2014): 3–21.

97
Henderson and Nakamoto, "Dialogue in Conservation Decision-Making."

Preservation and Social Inclusion
February 7–8, 2019, New York City

Opening Remarks and Introductions

- Erica Avrami, Graduate School of Architecture, Planning, and Preservation
- Jacqueline Klopp, Center for Sustainable Urban Development – Earth Institute
- Pamela Puchalski, The American Assembly
- Lisa Ackerman, World Monuments Fund

SESSION 1
Taking Stock of Community Effects
Moderator: Erica Avrami

- Ingrid Gould Ellen – *How Can Historic Preservation Be More Inclusive?*
- Brent Leggs and Michael Powe – *Cultural Preservation and Neighborhood Change in Historically African American Neighborhoods*
- Mark J. Stern – *Institutional Networks and the New Geography of Exclusion*

SESSION 2
Shifting Policy Toward Inclusion
Moderator: Jacqueline Klopp

- Lisa Kersavage – *Preservation in a Diverse City: Recent Initiatives of the NYC Landmarks Preservation Commission*
- Janet Hansen – *Heritage Surveys and Historic Contexts: Pathways to Social Inclusion in Urban Preservation*
- Donna Graves – *Notes from the Field: San Francisco's Efforts to Increase Equity Through Preserving Heritage*
- Claudia Guerra – *Finding the Soul of Communities*

SESSION 3
Challenging and Rewriting Narratives
Moderator: Erica Avrami

- Andrea Roberts – *Bootstraps, Old Wives' Tales, and Good Masters: Implications of Disremembered Black Agency in Texas' Public History*
- Andrew Dolkart – *Preserving LGBT Places: The New York City LGBT Historic Sites Project*
- Fallon Samuels Aidoo – *Black Power in Preserving the "Accommodations" of Privately Owned Public Space*

PUBLIC SESSION
Toward Spatial Justice
Moderator: Erica Avrami

Exploring questions of heritage, inclusion, and community power
in preservation policy and practice

- Brent Leggs, National Trust for Historic Preservation
- Maria Rosario Jackson, Arizona State University
- Emma Osore, BlackSpace

FRIDAY, FEBRUARY 8

SESSION 4
Preservation as a Tool for Community Development
Moderator: Pamela Puchalski

- Vicki Weiner – *Historic Preservation and Community Development: Past and Future Synergies*
- Ciere Boatright – *Pullman Revitalization, Historic Preservation, and Community Engagement*
- Caroline Cheong – *Preserving Community: Community Land Trusts and Historic Preservation*
- Maria Rosario Jackson – *Toward Equitable Communities: Historic Preservation in Community Development*

SESSION 5
Redefining Community Agency in Preservation Practice
Moderator: Erica Avrami

- Michelle Magalong – *Building a More Inclusive, Diverse, and Relevant Historic Preservation Movement from the Ground Up: Case Study of Asian and Pacific Islander Americans in Historic Preservation*
- Emma Osore – *BlackSpaces : Brownsville // Heritage Conservation for Practitioners*
- Stephanie Ryberg-Webster – *The Path to Inclusive Preservation: Lessons from Cleveland's Buckeye and Lee-Harvard Neighborhoods*

Breakout discussions

Concluding discussion and recommendations

FALLON SAMUELS AIDOO is Jean Boebel Chair of Historic Preservation at the University of New Orleans, where she teaches urban design, planning, and preservation. For fifteen years, she has investigated built environments endangered by chronic neglect and acute risks. Specializing in adaptation plans and policies, Aidoo advises housing, transit, and preservation advocacies; architecture, engineering, construction, and place-making firms; public agencies; and community organizations. Her research on postdisaster adaptation currently concerns disinvestment in postwar constructions, which disproportionately house minority families and businesses. Aidoo holds a PhD in urban planning, an MS in architectural history, and undergraduate degrees in architecture and civil engineering.

ALLISON ARLOTTA is a research specialist at Robert A. M. Stern Architects. She is a graduate of Columbia University's MS in Historic Preservation Program, where she wrote her award-winning master's thesis on the reciprocal relationship and areas of potential collaboration between historic preservation and waste management. She also serves on the board of Build Reuse, a national nonprofit that advocates for community development through the reuse of building materials.

ERICA AVRAMI is the James Marston Fitch Assistant Professor of Historic Preservation at the Columbia University Graduate School of Architecture, Planning, and Preservation, and an affiliate with the Earth Institute–Center for Sustainable Urban Development. Her research focuses on the intersection of heritage and sustainability planning, the role of preservation in urban policy, and societal values and spatial justice issues in heritage decision-making. She was formerly the director of research and education for World Monuments Fund and a project specialist at the Getty Conservation Institute. Avrami earned her BA in architecture and MS in historic preservation, both at Columbia, and her PhD in planning and public policy at Rutgers University. She was a trustee and secretary of US/ICOMOS from 2003 to 2010 and currently serves on the editorial advisory board of the journals *Change Over Time* and *Future Anterior*.

CIERE BOATRIGHT is the vice president of real estate and inclusion for Chicago Neighborhoods Initiative, a nonprofit community and economic development organization. Since joining CNI in 2013, Boatright has managed the planning and development of new projects, including Pullman Park, the 180-acre retail center. In addition to planning and development, Boatright has been instrumental in leading CNI's community engagement process. By forging positive relationships with community groups, elected leaders, and community members, she fostered widespread support for Artspace, an innovative new work/live space now under construction; the new Whole Foods distribution center in Pullman; a new Mariano's in Bronzeville; and the Pullman Community Center, the largest year-round, indoor athletic complex of its kind in the region.

SANGITA CHARI is the first relevancy, diversity, and inclusion program manager for the National Park Service. In this role, she oversees efforts to implement the agency's national diversity and inclusion strategies, which include building a more safe and inclusive internal culture, increasing capacity to design and conduct inclusive programming and engagement strategies, and working with external partners to increase diversity throughout the natural and cultural resource field. Chari started in the NPS as the grants coordinator for the National NAGPRA Program from 2008 to 2012. Prior to coming to the NPS, she spent over fifteen years working in museums and nonprofits as a funder, program manager, technical assistance provider, grant writer, and community organizer. Chari holds a BA in international relations and anthropology from American University and an MA in cultural anthropology from the University of Florida. She is the coeditor of *Accomplishing NAGPRA: Perspectives on the Intent, Impact, and Future of the Native American Graves Protection and Repatriation Act*, published in 2013.

CAROLINE S. CHEONG is an assistant professor in the University of Central Florida's History Department. Her research spans historic preservation and economic development, focusing on the relationship between urban heritage conservation, urban regeneration, and poverty reduction, with a particular focus on the Global South. She earned her PhD from the University of Pennsylvania in city and regional planning, her MS in historic preservation from the University of Pennsylvania, and her BS in anthropology from the University of Chicago. She was a US/ICOMOS international exchange intern in Al Houson, Jordan, and a graduate intern at the Getty Conservation Institute, where she evaluated the challenges and opportunities facing historic cities. Previously, Cheong was the director of research for Heritage Strategies International and PlaceEconomics, through which she published numerous research reports and professional publications focusing on the economic impacts of

historic preservation with preservation economist Donovan Rypkema.

SARA DELGADILLO CRUZ has a master's degree in heritage conservation from the University of Southern California. She is the data coordinator for Los Angeles's historic resource inventory system, HistoricPlacesLA. In her role with the City of Los Angeles, Delgadillo Cruz works in partnership with the Getty Conservation Institute's Arches project team on planned improvements to HistoricPlacesLA and the Arches heritage inventory platform. Delgadillo Cruz also has experience conducting research on sites associated with underrepresented communities in the National Park Service's Pacific West Region, and she serves on the executive committee of Latinos in Heritage Conservation, the leading organization for the preservation of Latino places, stories, and cultural heritage in the United States.

ANDREW S. DOLKART is a professor of historic preservation at the Columbia University Graduate School of Architecture, Planning, and Preservation. He is a preservationist and historian specializing in the architecture and development of New York City, with particular interest in the common yet overlooked building types that line the city's streets. He is the author of several award-winning books, including *Morningside Heights: A History of Its Architecture and Development*, which received the Association of American Publishers' award for best scholarly book in architecture and urban design; *Biography of a Tenement House in New York City: An Architectural History of 97 Orchard Street*; and *The Row House Reborn: Architecture and Neighborhoods in New York City, 1908–1929*, which won the Society of Architectural Historians' prestigious Antoinette Forrester Downing Award in 2012. He is also a cofounder of the award-winning NYC LGBT Historic Sites Project (www.nyclgbtsites.org).

JENNA DUBLIN is a PhD candidate in urban planning at Columbia University. Her research examines how and why community-based groups utilize historic district designation as a means to affect neighborhood trends of socioeconomic change and gentrification. Currently, she is a research manager at the National Trust for Historic Preservation Department of Research and Development, and she has been a Columbia University research assistant to Lance Freeman and a teaching fellow of urban economics and cost-benefit analysis over the past three years. In 2016 Dublin participated in the US/ICOMOS international exchange program; she lived in Delhi, India, and contributed to the heritage-based infrastructure upgrading plan for the city of Amritsar, in northwestern Punjab. Dublin graduated with dual master's degrees in urban planning and historic preservation from the University of Maryland, and she has a BFA from the Cooper Union School of Art.

INGRID GOULD ELLEN is the Paulette Goddard Professor of Urban Policy and Planning at NYU Wagner and a faculty director at the NYU Furman Center. Ellen is the author of *Sharing America's Neighborhoods: The Prospects for Stable Racial Integration* (Harvard University Press, 2000) and co-editor of *The Dream Revisited: Contemporary Debates about Housing, Segregation and Opportunity* (Columbia University Press, 2019). She has also written numerous journal articles and book chapters related to housing policy, community development, and school and neighborhood segregation. Ellen has held visiting positions at the Department of Urban Studies and Planning at MIT, the US Department of Housing and Urban Development, the Urban Institute, and the Brookings Institution. She attended Harvard University, where she received a bachelor's degree in applied mathematics, an MPP, and a PhD in public policy.

DONNA GRAVES is an independent historian/urban planner based in Berkeley, California. Her work on projects that emphasize social equity and sense of place began with tenure as executive director of the Power of Place, which received national acclaim for its groundbreaking work interpreting the history of downtown Los Angeles through urban design, historic preservation, and public art. Graves has been instrumental in establishing and developing California's Rosie the Riveter World War II Home Front National Historical Park, and she directed Preserving California's Japantowns, a statewide effort to identify and document what remains of the many pre-World War II communities destroyed by federal policy. She recently coauthored a citywide study of LGBTQ historic places in San Francisco and a chapter for the National Park Service's theme study on LGBTQ America (2016). Graves holds an MA in urban planning from UCLA and an MA in American civilization from Brown University. Recognitions for her work include awards from the Vernacular Architecture Forum, the National Park Service, the California Governor's Office, and a Loeb Fellowship at Harvard University's Graduate School of Design.

CLAUDIA GUERRA is San Antonio's first cultural historian, a position in the Office of Historic Preservation created in 2013. As cultural historian, Guerra engages the San Antonio community in identifying places of cultural significance. This includes working with a multicultural and multigenerational citizenry. She is dedicated to fostering the next generation of heritage stewards as well as including voices of those who may feel disenfranchised from historic preservation. As cultural historian, Guerra has instituted the collection of oral histories and conducted cultural mapping to engage community members in identifying places that matter to them. Her goal is to expand understanding of heritage and to develop holistic policies that perpetuate tangible and intangible resources by using principles from international perspectives on living heritage. Previously she worked for the Center for Cultural Sustainability at the University of Texas at San Antonio; her research focused on the connection between spirit of place and spirit of people. She earned her MA in consciousness at Goddard College.

JANET HANSEN has more than twenty-five years of experience in urban preservation planning, working in both the public and private sectors. She has expertise in developing, implementing, and using heritage surveys to inform preservation policy and practice in local government environments. Hansen now works as an independent preservation consultant. In her previous position as the deputy manager of the City of Los Angeles Office of Historic Resources, she managed the recently completed SurveyLA project, the largest citywide heritage resources survey undertaken in an American city to date. Hansen serves as an advisor for other municipalities planning citywide surveys and regularly lectures on the topic at conferences and universities nationally. She has published numerous papers on aspects of SurveyLA and is collaborating with the Getty Conservation Institute on a forthcoming technical book on heritage surveys and inventories. Hansen holds a master's degree in historic preservation from the University of California, Riverside. She is also a governor-appointed commissioner to the California State Historical Resources Commission.

MARIA ROSARIO JACKSON's expertise is in comprehensive community revitalization, systems change, the dynamics of race and ethnicity, and the roles of arts and culture in communities. She is Institute Professor at Arizona State University in the Herberger Institute for Design and the Arts and the Watts College of Public Service and Community Solutions. Jackson is a senior advisor to the Kresge Foundation and has consulted with national and regional foundations and government agencies on strategic planning and research. In 2013 President Obama appointed Jackson to the National Council on the Arts. She is on the boards of the Smithsonian Center for Folklife and Cultural Heritage, LA Commons, the Alliance for California Traditional Arts, and the Music Center of Los Angeles County. She also currently cochairs the Los Angeles County Cultural Equity and Inclusion Initiative. Jackson advises a number of national and regional projects and initiatives focusing on arts organizations and changing demographics, arts and community development and health, and initiatives focused on equitable community planning and development and equitable evaluation. Previously, for almost twenty years, Jackson was at the Urban Institute in Washington, DC. There she was a senior research associate in the Metropolitan Housing and Communities Policy Center and founding director of the Culture, Creativity, and Communities Program.

LISA KERSAVAGE is the executive director of the City of New York's Landmarks Preservation Commission, the largest municipal preservation agency in the nation. She previously served as director of special projects and strategic planning. Prior to joining the Landmarks Preservation Commission, she was the project manager of Changing Course, an ambitious design competition to reimagine a more sustainable Lower

Mississippi River Delta, bringing teams together from around the world to create innovative visions for one of America's greatest natural resources. She was responsible for the planning, development, and implementation of the project, in collaboration with staff from the Environmental Defense Fund and Van Alen Institute. Prior to that she was the senior director of preservation and sustainability at the Municipal Art Society of New York. She has held positions as a public policy consultant to the William Penn Foundation in Philadelphia, executive director of the James Marston Fitch Charitable Foundation, and executive director of Friends of the Upper East Side Historic Districts. Kersavage received her MS in historic preservation, with an urban planning focus, from Columbia University and her BA in art and architectural history from Penn State University.

JACQUELINE M. KLOPP is currently an associate research scholar at the Center for Sustainable Urban Development at Columbia University, a Volvo Research and Education Foundations Center of Excellence in Future Urban Transport. She taught for many years at the School of International and Public Affairs and now teaches in the Sustainable Development Program at Columbia University. Her research focuses on the intersection of sustainable transport, land use, accountability, data, and technology. Klopp is the author of numerous academic and popular articles on land and the politics of infrastructure with a focus on Africa, and she is increasingly exploring the potential of new technologies to impact transportation for the twenty-first century. She is also a founder of Digital Matatus, a consortium that mapped out and created open data for bus routes in Nairobi, Kenya, a project that is part of a global movement to create open data for improved planning.

BRENT LEGGS is the executive director of the African American Cultural Heritage Action Fund, a $25,000,000 fund-raising and preservation campaign of the National Trust for Historic Preservation. A Harvard University Loeb Fellow and author of *Preserving African American Historic Places*, he led efforts to create the Birmingham Civil Rights National Monument in Alabama, which President Barack Obama designated in January 2017. Other campaign successes include preserving iconic spaces like Villa Lewaro, the estate of Madam C. J. Walker, in Irvington, New York; Joe Frazier's gym, in Philadelphia; Hinchliffe Stadium, in Paterson, New Jersey; A. G. Gaston Motel, in Birmingham; Nina Simone's birthplace, in Tryon, North Carolina; and more. Leggs is also an assistant clinical professor at the University of Maryland's Graduate Program in Historic Preservation and the recipient of the 2018 Robert G. Stanton National Preservation Award.

MICHELLE G. MAGALONG is a Presidential Postdoctoral Fellow at the School of Architecture, Planning, and Preservation at the University of Maryland. Her doctorate in urban planning at the University of California, Los Angeles, focused on the process and development of the National Park Service Asian American Pacific Islander Heritage Initiative and Theme Study. She received her BA in ethnic studies and urban studies and planning at the University of California, San Diego, and her MA in urban planning at UCLA. Magalong serves as president of Asian and Pacific Islander Americans in Historic Preservation (APIAHiP), a national volunteer-run, nonprofit organization. Her research and professional experience focus on community engagement, historic preservation, and social justice.

BRIAN J. MCCABE is an associate professor of sociology at Georgetown University and an affiliated faculty member in the McCourt School of Public Policy. His research addresses a range of topics related to cities and social inequality, including affordable housing, homeownership, historic preservation, and campaign finance. McCabe's first book, *No Place Like Home: Wealth, Community and the Politics of Homeownership*, was published in 2016. He is currently working on a new book manuscript about the voucher lotteries used by housing authorities to administer the housing choice voucher program. McCabe completed his MSc in urban geography at the London School of Economics and his PhD in sociology at New York University.

EMMA OSORE is a systems thinker with expertise in equity, access, and participatory design. She cofounded BlackSpace, a collective of young, Black residents, changemakers, systems thinkers, learners, leaders, and lovers, and directed the BlackSpaces: Brownsville work. BlackSpace works to nurture and support Black people in fields of influence that shape our social and spatial environments, to promote and protect Black communities through collaborations that strengthen Black assets, and to bridge gaps between policy, people, and place to realize equity and justice. BlackSpace moves away from perfunctory forms of engagement and toward planning that recognizes, affirms, and amplifies Black agency. Osore is also a national program manager at Americans for the Arts, building the first program portfolio and team advancing equity in arts leadership. Prior to Americans for the Arts, she worked for the City of Beverly Hills building solutions for citywide challenges ranging from strategic planning to risk management and wrote an award-winning capstone on optimizing the city's percent-for-art program. Prior to graduate school, she led community partnerships as founding chief of staff at a reconstituted Washington, DC, public high school, founded a citywide teen garden enterprise, prevented recidivism of youth in the county juvenile justice system, and developed strategies for school leader selection and evaluation. Osore holds a bachelor's degree in urban and regional studies from Cornell University and a master's degree in public administration from Baruch College, where she was a National Urban Fellow.

MICHAEL POWE is the director of research for the National Trust for Historic Preservation's Research and Policy Lab. In this position, he has spearheaded the National Trust's recent Older, Smaller, Better and Atlas of ReUrbanism projects, and he played a leading role in the Partnership for Building Reuse with the Urban Land Institute. Powe holds master's and doctoral degrees in urban and regional planning and in planning, policy, and design from the University of California, Irvine.

PAMELA PUCHALSKI is executive director of the American Assembly, a nonpartisan policy institute based at Columbia University. In addition to the overall administration and strategic direction of the institute, Puchalski oversees the middle neighborhoods project and a new initiative to establish a global institute on innovation districts. Prior to joining the American Assembly, Puchalski led a civic consultancy advancing forward-looking models for inclusive growth, city-to-city learning, and collaboration. Working in the United States and internationally, she has designed and implemented initiatives for urban resilience, neighborhood revitalization, economic development, and competitiveness. Her work helps cities and communities persevere and prosper in the face of a growing list of threats linked to climate change, economic instability, and inequality.

Puchalski was part of the founding team for the Rockefeller Foundation's 100 Resilient Cities, where she led the effort to develop resilience strategies through community-based approaches and public-private-civic partnerships. She launched the Global Cities Initiative at Brookings Institution to help American metro regions pivot their economies toward increased engagement in world markets. Puchalski has written for numerous publications and was assistant editor of *The Endless City*, cited as best innovation and design book by *Business Week*. She was also a producer for the documentary film *Urbanized*. In addition to an MS in urban planning from Columbia University, she has degrees in economics and literature (Phi Beta Kappa) from the University of Maryland.

ANDREA ROBERTS is assistant professor of urban planning, faculty fellow with the Center for Heritage Conservation, and associate director of the Center for Housing and Urban Development at Texas A&M University. Roberts is also the founder of the Texas Freedom Colonies Project, a research and social justice initiative documenting historic African American settlements, place-making history, and descendant communities' grassroots preservation practice. Her scholarly publications engage the relationship between social justice, intersectionality, and historic preservation; rural Black women's place-making; and grassroots preservation practice. She aims to diversify planning history and practice and amplify descendant communities' concerns in policy arenas. Currently, she is writing a book about freedom colony preservationists and developing an interactive map of freedom colonies. Before joining Texas A&M, Roberts was an Emerging Scholar Fellow at the School of Architecture, University of Texas at Austin, where she also earned a PhD in community and regional planning.

Roberts holds an MA in government administration from the University of Pennsylvania and a BA in political science from Vassar College.

STEPHANIE RYBERG-WEBSTER is an associate professor in the Department of Urban Studies at Cleveland State University's Levin College of Urban Affairs, where she also directs the Master of Urban Planning and Development Program. Her work addresses the intersections of historic preservation and urban development. Ryberg-Webster's current work explores the 1970s-era history of historic preservation within the context of Cleveland's escalating urban decline. She has published research on preservation and community development, African American heritage, historic rehabilitation tax credits, and preservation amid urban decline. Ryberg-Webster is also the coeditor (with J. Rosie Tighe) of *Legacy Cities: Continuity and Change amid Decline and Revival*. She holds a PhD in city and regional planning from the University of Pennsylvania, a master of historic preservation from the University of Maryland, and a bachelor of urban planning from the University of Cincinnati.

MARK J. STERN is a professor of social policy and history at the University of Pennsylvania. A historian by training, his scholarship covers US social history, poverty and social welfare policy, and the impact of the arts and culture on urban neighborhoods. He has authored or coauthored seven books and monographs, including *One Nation Divisible: What America Was and What It Is Becoming* (with Michael B. Katz), which examines the history of social inequality during the twentieth century, and *Engaging Social Welfare: An Introduction to Policy Analysis*. Stern is cofounder and principal investigator of the Social Impact of the Arts Project (SIAP), a research group at Penn's School of Social Policy

& Practice. SIAP's report, *The Wellbeing of New York City's Neighborhoods: The Contribution of Culture and the Arts*, was released in 2017.

GERARD TORRATS-ESPINOSA is an assistant professor of sociology at Columbia University and a fellow at the Data Science Institute. His research draws from the literatures on urban sociology, stratification, and criminology, and it focuses on understanding how the spatial organization of the American stratification system creates and reproduces inequalities. His current research agenda investigates how the neighborhood context, particularly the experience of community violence, determines the life chances of children; how social capital and social organization emerge and evolve in spatial contexts; and how place and geography structure educational and economic opportunity in America and elsewhere. His work has been published in numerous academic journals, including the *American Sociological Review, Housing Policy Debate, and the Proceedings of the National Academy of Sciences.* Torrats-Espinosa holds a PhD in sociology from New York University and a master's in public policy from Harvard University.

VICKI WEINER is the academic coordinator of the MS in Historic Preservation Program and an adjunct associate professor at Pratt Institute. She has served as the director of two nonprofit historic preservation organizations in New York City, was the first Kress Fellow for Historic Preservation at the Municipal Art Society, and has provided historic preservation policy consulting services to dozens of community organizations and government agencies. She is the author and coauthor of numerous research reports, briefing papers, and articles on preserving community culture in low-income neighborhoods,

and she is a recipient of the James Marston Fitch Mid-Career Fellowship. Weiner recently stepped down as the deputy director of Pratt Center for Community Development, where since 2011 she was responsible for overseeing the center's planning and policy projects and leading all aspects of organizational management. Her work at the center included projects that explore connections between preserving culturally important places and creating more equitable communities, and heritage conservation studies in such places as Fulton Street Mall, in Downtown Brooklyn; the East Village, in Manhattan; and Cypress Hills/East New York, in Brooklyn. Weiner has a BA from Drew University and a MSc in historic preservation from Columbia University.

This is the second book resulting from the research initiative Urban Heritage, Sustainability, and Social Inclusion, co-sponsored by the Columbia Graduate School of Architecture, Planning, and Preservation; Center for Sustainable Urban Development–Earth Institute; and The American Assembly. The initiative is generously funded by the New York Community Trust. Through a series of symposia and related publications, this research explores how the next generation of preservation policy can become more inclusive and environmentally sustainable.

A two-day symposium in February 2019 convened twenty-three scholars and practitioners in New York City to ask how the preservation enterprise can represent more diverse narratives, engage multiple publics in decision-making, and better serve communities writ large. This dialogue served as a platform for the exchange of ideas and the development of lines of inquiry. Over the spring and summer, the chapters herein developed through interviews and participant-authored texts.

A debt of gratitude is owed to Allison Arlotta, who served as a research associate for the project, and to graduate research assistants Shreya Ghoshal, Scott Goodwin, and Jenna Dublin. Jesse Connuck, our managing editor from Columbia Books on Architecture and the City, once again ushered this volume from concept to completion with patience and professionalism. Jacqueline Klopp of the Center for Sustainable Urban Development–Earth Institute continued to provide invaluable guidance in the development of this initiative.

Special thanks go to the New York Community Trust (NYCT), in particular to the vice president for philanthropic initiatives, Kerry McCarthy. Shifting preservation policy to better address the challenges on the horizon requires the time and space to think creatively and collaboratively, which has only been made possible through the vision and financial support of the NYCT. As an institution equally committed to the future of the heritage field, World Monuments Fund (WMF) generously provided the venue for the symposium and we thank all the WMF staff who provided logistical support over the two-day event. We likewise remain grateful to the continued investment of the Graduate School of Architecture, Planning, and Preservation and Dean Amale Andraos.

The symposium participants and volume authors deserve special recognition for their contributions. The subject matter of this publication led us into complex terrain, and those who participated showed tremendous openness and generosity of spirit. Their critical insights allowed for a dialogue that was at once sensitive and candid, reflective and provocative. Their commitment to questions of inclusion within their own preservation-oriented work will undoubtedly help build a better future.

Columbia Books on
Architecture and the City
An imprint of the Graduate
School of Architecture,
Planning, and Preservation

Columbia University
1172 Amsterdam Ave
407 Avery Hall
New York, NY 10027
arch.columbia.edu/books

Distributed by
Columbia University Press
cup.columbia.edu

Preservation and Social Inclusion
Edited by Erica Avrami

Graphic Designer
Common Name

Copyeditor
Erica Olsen

Printing
KOPA, Lithuania

978-1-941332-60-3

Director of Publications
James Graham

Assistant Director
Isabelle Kirkham-Lewitt

Managing Editor
Jesse Connuck

Associate Editor
Joanna Kloppenburg

Library of Congress Control Number
2020931367